Eleanor Roosevelt, An Eager Spirit

The Letters of Dorothy Dow
1933–1945

Eleanor Roosevelt in Florida, March 1941.
Courtesy: Dorothy Dow Butturff.

ELEANOR ROOSEVELT,

AN EAGER SPIRIT

The Letters of Dorothy Dow
1933 - 1945

Edited by
Ruth K. McClure

W. W. NORTON & COMPANY
NEW YORK
LONDON

Copyright © 1984 by Ruth K. McClure and Dorothy Dow Butturff

Published simultaneously in Canada by Stoddart, a subsidiary of
General Publishing Co. Ltd, Don Mills, Ontario.
Printed in the United States of America.

The text of this book is composed in Caledonia, with display type
set in Caslon 471. Composition and manufacturing by
The Maple-Vail Book Manufacturing Group
Book design by Holly McNeely

First Edition

Library of Congress Cataloging in Publication Data

Butturff, Dorothy Dow, 1904–
    Eleanor Roosevelt, an eager spirit.

    1. Roosevelt, Eleanor, 1884–1962. 2. Butturff,
Dorothy Dow, 1904–   3. Presidents—United States—
Wives—Correspondence. 4. Presidents—United States—
Staff—Correspondence. I. McClure, Ruth K., 1916–
II. Title.
E807.1.R48B88   1984   973.917′092′4   84–6105

ISBN 0-393-01879-2

W. W. Norton & Company, Inc., 500 Fifth Avenue, New York, N. Y. 10110
W. W. Norton & Company Ltd., 37 Great Russell Street, London WC1B 3NU

1 2 3 4 5 6 7 8 9 0

In memory of
Frances Dow Spencer
who first collected these letters
and made this book possible

CONTENTS

ILLUSTRATIONS

PREFACE

Without the efforts of Frances Dow Spencer, Dorothy Dow's sister, this book would not exist. Mrs. Spencer kept all of her sister's letters and in 1948 decided to type up the most interesting parts of them to ensure their preservation for the family's enjoyment. To her delight, she found that her mother and Robert Butturff, Dorothy Dow's husband, had also kept the letters written to them. These were added to the collection, and after weeks of work, Mrs. Spencer presented the family with loose-leaf copies of what soon became known as "the book." It contained most of the letters, or parts of letters, written by Dorothy Dow to her family between 1933 and 1945. Eventually, several copies of "the book" and some, but not all, of the original letters came into Mrs. Butturff's possession and had been packed away for years when I first saw them.

Dorothy Dow Butturff and I became acquainted by chance. Early in 1983, while I was writing an article about Malvina Thompson, Eleanor Roosevelt's longtime secretary, my research led me to Miss Thompson's niece, Eleanor Zartman, who referred me to Mrs. Butturff for information about the system used in the White House for handling Mrs. Roosevelt's mail. To answer my questions, Mrs. Butturff sent me a copy of "the book." I soon realized that it contained a fascinating contemporary account of Eleanor Roosevelt's activities at Val-Kill, written from an unusual viewpoint. Two friends who also read "the book," Emily Wright, Park Ranger-Historian at the Eleanor Roosevelt National Historic Site, and Dr. Maurine Beasley, reinforced my belief that these letters deserved publication. Fortunately, Mr. George P. Brockway, chairman of W. W. Norton & Company, concurred.

Mrs. Butturff felt unable to undertake the task of editing the letters herself and asked me to do it. She then turned over to me all of the original letters that had survived. Among them were a number of letters not included in "the book." On the other hand, "the book" contained many letters for which no originals now exist. I have, therefore, collated the original letters with the typed versions where possible, used the typed versions where no original letters were to be found, and used the letters themselves where they were not included in "the book." The editing has been largely a matter of excising family matters, dating undated letters, writing clarifying footnotes, and setting the stage in the introduction and transitional passages. I have also prepared an appendix for the purpose of identifying persons mentioned in the letters.

One of the final, and most pleasant, tasks of any author or editor is to voice appreciation to all who have helped along the way. People are amazingly willing to share information. Hudson Valley neighbors, members of the Roosevelt family, librarians, especially at the Franklin D. Roosevelt Library, and friends have answered many questions, provided photographs, granted permissions, and encouraged this project in countless ways. Dorothy Dow Butturff herself has been unfailingly helpful. She joins me in acknowledging, with much gratitude, the assistance of:

Mr. and Mrs. Roy Johannessen and Mr. and Mrs. Clifford Smith, of Hyde Park, N.Y., and Miss Deborah Dows, of Rhinebeck, N.Y.;

Franklin D. Roosevelt, Jr., the literary executor of Eleanor Roosevelt's estate, Mrs. John Roosevelt, Joan Roosevelt Schoonmaker, and Nina Roosevelt Gibson;

Dr. William R. Emerson, Director of the Franklin D. Roosevelt

Library, and his staff, especially Shelly Eyckoff, Sherrill Griffin, Robert Parks, Mark Renovitch, and Dr. Frances Seeber;

The reference librarians at the Adriance Memorial Library, Poughkeepsie, N.Y., the Hyde Park Free Library, the New York Public Library, and the Vassar College Library, especially Nancy MacKechnie;

George Wise, Historian for the General Electric Company;

Dr. Maurine H. Beasley, Emily L. Wright, and Eleanor Lund Zartman;

And my husband, Walter McClure, Jr., who has listened with patience and sympathy to the problems of an editor.

RUTH K. McCLURE

Eleanor Roosevelt, An Eager Spirit

The Letters of Dorothy Dow
1933–1945

INTRODUCTION

Dorothy Dow's letters, like those of the great letter writers of the past, tell more than a single story. Of first importance, of course, is what she has to say about Eleanor Roosevelt, and she says it from an unusual point of view. Most books about Mrs. Roosevelt have been written either by members of her family or by close friends—individuals emotionally entangled with her—or by people who never knew her at all. But from her position in the White House Social Bureau and, during summers at Hyde Park, from her post as assistant to Malvina Thompson Scheider—from the halfway station of the secretary who is neither servant nor social equal—Dorothy looked on, regarding the First Lady with admiration and interest and sometimes with concern but never with any feeling of involvement. She appraised Mrs. Roosevelt and her circle with cleareyed detachment and wrote her long letters home with no thought except her desire to share her experiences with her family. And because she saw "Mrs. R." informally every day at Val-Kill, she came more and more to think of her as a private person, so that she was occasionally surprised when events nudged her to remember that Eleanor Roosevelt was also very much a public figure.

At the same time, almost incidentally, Dorothy Dow's letters remind older readers and inform younger ones how it was to live in the depression years of the 1930s and the war years of the 1940s. More than almost anything else, except diaries, good letters weave the fabric of another time, for they convey, sometimes directly, sometimes by inference, not only the minutiae of daily living—what people wore and ate, where they went and what they did, and what it all cost—but, more importantly, how they thought and what they believed. This is the stuff of social history. It is also, for those who lived through those years, the stuff of memory.

And, finally, the letters tell the story of Dorothy Dow herself, a story of a young woman who came to Washington from Wisconsin seeking adventure and found it in ways she could never have imagined, who married happily but endured for years the anxiety of watching the struggles of her cerebral palsied daughter, and who observed at close range the powerful, the wealthy, and the celebrated, often with amazement but never with envy. For after the summer of 1938 at Val-Kill Dorothy was no longer just a clerical worker in a White House office. As assistant to Mrs. Roosevelt's private secretary, she became, it seemed, all things to all people—a swimming coach for Roosevelt grandchildren and for Mrs. Roosevelt as well; a driver taking Val-Kill visitors hither and thither; an assistant hostess at countless picnics; a dance partner at summer parties; someone to fill in at dinners lest there be thirteen at table; a buffer between celebrities and a too avid public; a patient listener for those who needed a friendly ear. She was, Mrs. Scheider once said, "The Fitter-inner." But, despite any surface appearance, she was not really one of the Roosevelt circle. She did not want to be.

Dorothy Dow's letters to her mother and sister in Wisconsin, and to her husband in Washington while she was in Hyde Park, were not written for publication. Indeed, had she thought of such a thing, they would undoubtedly have been shorter, more formal, more self-conscious. As it was, her breezy letters home, colloquial in style and often slangy, reflected without inhibition her reactions to happenings around her in the world of Eleanor Roosevelt.

When Dorothy first entered that world in 1933 as a secretary, she had already pursued a very different career: she had been a physical education teacher in her native Wisconsin. She was born on March 1, 1904, in La Crosse, the daughter of staunch Republicans, Edward Everett and Amie Tappan Dow. Her father, a graduate of the New England Conservatory of Music, was the proprietor of a music store and, in addition, installed and tuned large organs. He was an accomplished musician as well, playing the piano, cello, and tuba; Dorothy's mother was a singer, and Dorothy and her older sister, Frances, inherited their parents' talent and often played piano duets. Alike in their love of music, the sisters differed greatly in personality. Frances was the quiet one; Dorothy loved sports, action, and excitement. Although by no means a "flaming youth"—she was too much a small town girl for that—Dorothy was a true child of the twenties.

After graduation at the age of eighteen from La Crosse State Normal School (now a branch of the University of Wisconsin), where she majored in physical education, Dorothy began teaching in 1922 in Wauwatosa, a suburb of Milwaukee, at a salary of $1,300 a year. She remained there until 1925. From 1926 to 1928 she taught in Ashland, Wisconsin. In both communities she directed the physical education program for girls in high school and junior high school and supervised physical education in the elementary schools. During the summers she did graduate work at the La Crosse Normal School.

Dorothy's parents never tried to restrain her bent for adventure. During the summer after her graduation from Normal School, she and another young woman paddled a canoe down the Mississippi by themselves. They traveled one hundred and fifty miles in a week and returned home extensively sunburned but without further mishap. So her family thought it quite natural when Dorothy became restless at the end of the 1927–1928 school year and decided to prepare herself for a different occupation by studying typing and shorthand at the La Crosse Vocational School. Six months later she took and passed a civil service examination, and in 1930, eager for change and new experiences, she left La Crosse for Washington to work in the Oil and Gas Division of the General Land Office, Department of the Interior, at a salary of $1,440 per annum. Her parents and her sister may have felt doubtful about the wisdom of her decision to accept this position, but if so, they said nothing and wished her well. As it turned out,

Dorothy had insured herself against the joblessness, poverty, hardship, fear, and despair that were already settling over the country like an endless, impenetrable fog.

The Wall Street crash had occurred in October 1929, only a few months before Dorothy set off for Washington, and the assets of a million or more investors had vanished overnight. With this enormous loss of capital, the Great Depression had begun. People stopped buying; stores stopped ordering; manufacturers stopped producing, and more and more workers lost their jobs. Both state and federal governments floundered helplessly, unable to hold back the tobogganing economy or to alleviate the mounting misery. Anyone who still had a job crossed his fingers, worked harder for longer hours, and took a cut in pay lest he be the next one laid off.

But people with civil service jobs could think themselves lucky and safe, although the budgetary restraints placed on all departments of the government forbade hope of promotion or substantial raises in pay. Nevertheless, Dorothy Dow's salary at the Department of the Interior—increased after a year or so to $1,620 per annum—was considerably larger than the amounts many women received for their secretarial skills. Thousands of secretaries were employed five-and-a-half or six days a week for eighteen to twenty dollars and fourteen dollars a week was not uncommon. With prices so cheap for almost everything, Dorothy's thirty dollars a week could provide a comfortable standard of living, especially for a single woman. However, when her supervisor offered her an opportunity to transfer to the White House Social Bureau in 1933, Dorothy felt a dual attraction: not only might she find new and interesting work there, but also such a position might lead to a higher income, and, in fact, it did. Shortly after she moved to the Social Bureau, her salary was increased to $1,800 a year.

At that time the Social Bureau, officially titled the Office of Social Correspondence, was tucked away behind a door marked "Private" on the first floor of the White House. Two men directed the work of the dozen or so persons employed there. Ralph Magee oversaw the handling of mail addressed to the First Lady, the maintenance of correspondence files, and the disposition of gifts. William Rockwell supervised the issuance of invitations to receptions and dinners, the preparation of place cards, and the care of records relating to entertainments. Both men had held their positions for years, but the forms used for standard replies to letters had been around even longer— some dated back to the time of President Cleveland.

When the Roosevelts moved into the White House in March 1933, Mrs. Roosevelt did not know that such an office existed. She and her secretary, Mrs. Scheider, tried to deal with all correspondence themselves, but almost at once were overwhelmed by the enormous inpouring of mail. Everyone in the country, it seemed, needed a friend in Washington, and everyone considered the President's wife that friend, naïvely attributing to her the power to solve every problem that letters could present. Fortunately, Edith Benham Helm, who had served Mrs. Wilson as Social Secretary, soon put the two women straight, and when she agreed to take on the duties of Social Secretary once more, reorganization followed with Mrs. Helm directing all social activities, aided by Mr. Rockwell and his group, while Mrs. Scheider supervised the work of Mr. Magee and his subordinates.

A whole new system for handling the mail quickly evolved. Letters from family and friends went directly to Mrs. Roosevelt. Requests for contributions to church bazaars received in reply the traditional engraving of the White House with its equally traditional engraved message from the president and First Lady. Letters asking for information were forwarded to the government agency best able to supply it. Letters asking for contributions, speeches, messages to organizations or publications, and the like, were referred to Mrs. Scheider for instructions. Guidelines for answers took the place of stilted forms. And the letters never stopped coming. During the first year of the Roosevelt regime, three hundred thousand pieces of mail addressed to Mrs. Roosevelt arrived at the White House. As Dorothy noted in her letters home, some were advisory, some were argumentative, some were funny, and many were sad.

In the summer, of course, there were no social activities at the White House, and the mail grew a little lighter, but work never completely ceased for Mrs. Scheider. This led Mrs. Roosevelt in the summer of 1933 to institute the practice of taking women from the Social

Bureau to Hyde Park from time to time so that "Tommy," as nearly everyone called Mrs. Scheider, would have some assistance. Each woman stayed two to six weeks and received, in addition to her usual salary, a per diem to cover the cost of room and board at Nelly Johannessen's Val-Kill Tea Room, located conveniently near Mrs. Roosevelt's cottage, which was not really a cottage at all. The rambling building had formerly housed the Val-Kill Furniture Shop, a project organized by Mrs. Roosevelt and her friends, Nancy Cook and Marion Dickerman, to provide employment and training for local young men. When manufacturing ceased, the building was converted into apartments for Mrs. Roosevelt and Mrs. Scheider, with many extra bedrooms for guests.

Dorothy went to Hyde Park for the first time in the summer of 1938 and found it much more exciting than working in the White House. Thereafter she spent a part of the summers of 1939, 1940, and 1941 in Hyde Park and returned in 1945 for a longer period of time to help with the flood of letters of condolence that inundated the Val-Kill cottage after the President's sudden death in April. By that time Dorothy was far less exuberant and far more sophisticated than she had been during her first year in the White House.

1933

Varieties of working experience
are good for us all.

ELEANOR ROOSEVELT, *My Days*

DEAR MOM,

I have a new job. I've been transferred to the White House, and today was my first day. However, I'll start at the beginning. Friday morning Mr. Obenchain, the head man of the Land Office, called me upstairs and asked me if I would be interested in being detailed to the White House. The Interior Department has one detail, and the girl who has been over there is getting married and quitting, so they had to send somebody else. Mr. Obenchain said that they demanded someone very competent, someone who could catch hold of things fast. He also said that the girl who had been over there was drawing $2100 a year.

I didn't know what to say. I liked my job where I was very much and told him so. However, he said that he would be perfectly frank and tell me that he had been wanting to push me up and just couldn't do it, that his hands were tied, and that he couldn't do anything for three or four years more the way the appropriations were running. But if I went to the White House, I would stand much more of a chance. Gosh—I didn't know what to do. I really liked my job at the Land Office and didn't know what I would be getting into. I had heard stories of how they worked overtime, on Saturday afternoons, and Sundays. I figured, though, that he must have been trying to give me a break, and if I didn't take it, I probably would never have another chance. Anyhow, I was really getting sort of bored with being at the same place all of the time and was hankering to find new fields to conquer. So I said I would take it. All of the girls were green with envy; it seems that several of them had been trying to get the detail. I hadn't even thought about it, so it hit me like a thunderbolt.

I go over at the same salary and have no assurance whatever that I will get a raise. But I'm only detailed; that is, I can have the job over there as long as there is a job and as long as I want it. If I don't like it or don't get the raise, Mr. Obenchain said they would revoke the detail and bring me back. So I figured I couldn't be out very much no matter what I did, and it would be a change.

I was nervous as a cat all weekend; I didn't know what to expect. Went down Saturday afternoon and bought two dresses so I would feel respectable anyhow. Today was the day. Went over this morning with fear and trembling. Went in the Executive Office building and asked for Mr. Webster, the man to whom I was told to report. He came up and took me down to the offices. I had expected some very nice offices to work in, but they are lousy. The plaster is all falling off, and there isn't room for an extra flea—they are so crowded. My spirits started to fall right then. However, I sat there for a while, and Mr. Webster came and said he was taking me over to the Social Bureau. I didn't know where that was, but I followed him. We went up and through the West Wing of the White House, and he showed me the President's swimming pool, which surely is keen. I said I wished he would invite everyone to take a swim sometime, and Mr. Webster said that maybe he would. Then we went into the White House proper, through the kitchens, and to the lower floor where sightseers are allowed to go. We finally came to the office where I'm stationed. It is an office, called the Social Bureau, which handles just Mrs. Roosevelt's correspondence and, when the social season starts, takes care of the invitations and lists for the receptions and dinners. Mrs. Roosevelt gets about 600 to 700 letters a day, and, believe me, it is some job taking care of them all. There are six girls and six men in the office on that work besides Mrs. Roosevelt's own secretary who is upstairs.

I sat around for a while and finally the man in charge came up and said that I could start by indexing letters. He brought a mammoth pile of them, and all I had to do was to take the name, file number, and date off of them and put them on file cards. Surely was a hard job! It made me laugh as they were so insistent upon getting someone who was very capable, etc. Any child could do that work.

I think I'll get very little dictation—probably once in a while I'll get to go upstairs and take dictation from Mrs. Scheider, Mrs. Roosevelt's secretary. Most all of Mrs. Roosevelt's correspondence is opened in our office, and a number is put on which indicates the kind of answer that should be written, so at best, I'll just be writing what practically amounts to form letters—if I ever get off indexing. I don't see how I could possibly get a raise on this job—the work is *so* simple—but I'm going to do my darndest because it is my only chance and, believe me, if I can get $2100 a year for whatever kind of job it is, I'm going to get it. I never would stand a chance in the Land Office, although the work I was doing was very responsible and took me three years to absorb it all. But such is the inconsistency of the Government! I wouldn't be a bit surprised if they did give me $2000 for this job, and it isn't worth $200 a year as far as brains go.

It is going to be an interesting place to work at least. One of the girls just came back from Hyde Park where she had been taken while the Roosevelts were up there. She was there two weeks and had tea with the Roosevelts and also was invited to a clambake at the Morgenthaus, who are very good friends of the President. We are right in the White House proper in a place marked private on the first floor. The White House is open from 11:00 to 2:00 for sightseers, and when they see anyone come out of a room marked private, they all stare at you as though you were something out of a museum.

It is going to seem more or less like a perpetual vacation here, I'm afraid. I've always worked so hard at the Land Office and been held down so rigidly to time—a half-hour for lunch, etc.—that I'm going to have a hard time getting used to the leniency allowed here. This noon I asked the girls how long we had for lunch, and they said, "Oh, take as much time as you want; we never get back in less than an hour." We can go any time we feel like it and come back at any time. I left about 12:00, came home for lunch, and got back about 1:15. The girls were sitting on a davenport in the hall, so I sat, too. Nobody seemed to be in a hurry to get to work.

A screen had been put up at the end of the hall, and we were told that the President was due to arrive back from his vacation. They shooed all the visitors out, and the guard called to us and asked if we wanted to see the President. We said, "Sure," so he told us to go into the dispensary and dentist's office and ask Dr. Fox if we could stay in the room, as they brought the President right through there. We went in, but no Dr. Fox. We didn't dare stay as we weren't supposed to be in there, so came back to the guard and told him he would have to find some other place. He called a Mr. Reeves, who turned out to be the head florist, and told him to try to think of some place where we could see the President. He tried every room where it would be possible to see, but with no success. Finally we went out in the East Wing, and the guard let us out into the private gardens. And there we waited and waited, but no President. It was about 2:00 then, so we decided that maybe we had better go in and get to work. Went inside and just got nicely seated when a man came in and said it was announced that the President had just left the Navy Yard. So out we went into the garden again. He came this time, and we stood next to the house where the car stopped. They had his wheelchair out waiting for him. They wheel him all over—to and from the office, and from the car to the house. Think he can't do much by himself. One of the big huskies he has with him took hold of his ankles and pulled him from the seat of the car so that his feet were resting on the running board. Then another one lifted him up and sat him in the wheelchair. It was very neatly and quickly done, but he seems to be quite helpless. I'll bet he has gained thirty pounds since he was elected. He is getting terribly fat, at least according to his pictures taken during the campaign. He certainly is a huge man. I don't see how he ever gets into the swimming pool. His dog was there to meet him and was so glad to see him that he jumped all over the car. Mr. Astor and Mr. Morgenthau were with him, and also Ike Hoover and the chief detective, and the press men came up in back of him. It was way after 2:00 by the time we went back to work.

I think we don't have to put in any overtime on this job—at least, not until the social season starts. The girls who were here last year said they all had invitations to one of the White House receptions. Hope they come across this year. One of the men in the room was printing place cards for the dinner tonight. It is the most beautiful printing I ever saw; it was written on a white card with the White House insignia on the top. I asked him to make me one, and he said he would. Then, there was a great to-do about the proper places to seat people; a chart was drawn of the table and different colored slips to represent the people were placed around it. I think that if we get chummy with the guards, we will have a chance sometime to see the dining room when the tables are set for a big dinner party.

Some of the letters written to Mrs. Roosevelt are surely crazy. One of them said, "I hope this letter will be answered by you personally and not by some little 2 by 4 clerk." Did we get a laugh out of that! There are hundreds asking for secondhand clothes, money, autographs, invitations to the White House, and everything else under the sun. There are wedding invitations, invitations to speak—just everything.

Well, anyhow, the work itself amounts to nothing—will get terribly monotonous, I imagine—but it will be an experience to be around the place. The girls say that Mrs. Roosevelt often comes down to the office and that both she and the President are seen quite often. So, whether I get the raise or not, I think I'll stay here for a few months and see how things work out. After working as hard as I have been for so long, it will give me a good rest to have an easy job for a while and won't hurt me a bit. In fact, I think it will be good for me. It might lead to something, too. I don't know if I'm to stay in the Social Bureau all of the time or whether it is only for a little while and then go over to the Executive Offices. I would rather stay where I am as it is in the White House proper, and there will be more to see, and the office is nicer.

Went up to Thurmont, Maryland, yesterday and had a swell chicken dinner at the Firemen's carnival for 35¢ and then saw the parade. It is a little town in the mountains. Didn't bother to go to the parade here. Isn't that the perversity of human nature? Here we go up to some little town to see their Labor Day parade, and people come for miles and miles to see the grand spectacle of Washington's parade. I'm sick of parades here, though, and enjoyed the one yesterday immensely.

I only hope I don't regret this move too much.

[*Week of September 11, 1933*]

DEAR MOM,

I certainly had no idea that my new job would cause such a turmoil among the home folks. I'm glad you think that you have reason to be proud of me. I can't see that it is anything so wonderful; it doesn't mean a thing except that I got a break and was sent and took it only because I might have a chance at more salary than I would where I was. I might be disappointed in that, too. It is hard to tell where a person stands with this new economy business.

I shall have to disillusion you, though, as you don't understand government routine as I do. My job isn't nearly so glamorous as it sounds. I suppose that at a distance of 1200 miles, working in the White House seems quite something; however, to me it is just another government job. The work is very monotonous except for an occasional break. All I do is answer one darned letter after another. There seems to be just millions of them. Have to read them through and then write some sort of something that doesn't amount to a row of pins. As far as the work itself is concerned, I would much rather have my job in the Land Office. I'm afraid I shall lose my ability in shorthand because I don't use it enough to keep in practice. Occasionally I go up to the second floor, the Roosevelts' living quarters, and take dictation from Mrs. Scheider, Mrs. Roosevelt's personal secretary, or from Mrs. Dall when she is here. The rest of the time I stay down on the first floor and answer letter after letter after letter.

However, the job does seem to have its compensations at times. For instance, last Friday I was writing letters and Mr. Rockwell, the

President Roosevelt addressing a group on the White House lawn, September 8, 1933. Dorothy Dow is at the right in the group of three women seated directly in front of the speaker. Mrs. Roosevelt is seated second from the left in the front row on the platform. Courtesy: Franklin D. Roosevelt Library. Credit: Underwood & Underwood.

head of the Social Bureau, came up to me and asked if I could take the President's speech. I didn't know what he was talking about, but I said, "Sure." He said, "Get your book and come on." I tore out of there and onto the White House lawn. There they had a platform built and people were assembled. It seemed that the President was to address the people representing the Community Chests from all over the country. He was to make an extemporaneous speech, and the only record would be what they had from the stenographers.

There were two girls from the Executive Offices and I from the Social Bureau. They sat us up on the platform first, right where the President was to talk and in back of him. I knew we couldn't hear well enough there, so I asked Colonel Starling if we could sit down in front. He sent a man tearing after chairs, and we finally were seated. They went to bring a table so we could write on it, but we didn't get it before the President started talking, so we had to do the best we could on our laps. It was very awkward, but we pitched in. We were right in the boiling hot sun, and the temperature was over 90 that day. Between the excitement of taking the speech verbatim and the hot sun, I was simply wringing wet.

The President's back looked just as though someone had taken a bucket of water and doused him with it. He came on the arm of his young son Franklin, and with Mrs. Roosevelt, and was introduced by the Secretary of War. Then he started, and maybe you think it wasn't hard work trying to get it down word for word! They finally brought us a table but put it so far away that we couldn't reach it, and he didn't stop long enough so that we could move up. We just had to keep scribbling away to beat all. Finally he said something funny, and when the people laughed, it gave us a little breathing spell. I tried to move my chair up, but it seemed to be stuck in the ground, and I could get only far enough to put my book and my wrist on the table. That was awful, but I didn't have time to change, so kept right on. He talked a half-hour, and by the end of that time, I was a complete wreck. When Mrs. Roosevelt came out, and everyone was standing while the President walked to his place, she saw the three of us down there with our notebooks and gave us a broad grin.

After the speech was over we had to tear back in and begin to transcribe it, as the press men were waiting for it. I would just finish a page when Mr. Rockwell would grab it out of the machine and chase over to Secretary Early with it. It was rather nerve-wracking as I had a hard time reading some of my notes and had to stop to figure them out the best way possible. I started about 11:00 and finished the transcription at 12:45. As I went out for lunch, I went through the Executive Offices to see how the other two were getting along. They were not finished—one of the girls couldn't read her notes at all, so she was doing the typing, and the other one was trying to figure out her notes. So I think I didn't do so bad.

That was a very unusual event, because usually the President has his speeches all prepared and ready for the press before he delivers them. I was anxious to see the paper that night to see whether they had left it the way I had it. There were very few changes, so I think it must have been pretty good. The picture I'm enclosing was in the next morning's paper, so I thought I would send it to you. You can see the setting of the thing; glad it didn't show the perspiration running off me. Boy, was I *hot!*

However, since then I have done nothing but answer letters and more letters. Mrs. Roosevelt is away so there is very little dictation. I imagine I won't take dictation once in a coon's age, as it is divided among the six of us, and there is very little to start with. I'll never take it from Mrs. Roosevelt. She isn't nearly so bad looking as her pictures make her out to be. I was really quite surprised. Of course, she is no beauty, but she isn't quite so bad as one would expect.

Charlie, the handy man around the house, took me out in the kitchen one afternoon and showed me around. Surely is quite some place—and so clean. We went in the iceboxes and rummaged around, and he gave me a piece of ice as refreshment. All of the staff are colored. Charlie said that previously there were French and Swedish girls in the kitchen, but when the Roosevelts came in, they dismissed the whole crew and brought their colored help down with them from New York.

Today another girl and I were taken on a personally conducted tour of the first floor. It is open to sightseers if they have passes from their Congressman. I had been through there a long time ago but decided I might as well go again. The guard knew we worked in Rockwell's office, so he let us in. He asked us if we had ever been in the parlors, and we said, "No." So he took us in the Green, Red, and Blue Rooms, the State Dining Room, and the Roosevelts' private dining room, and explained all the furnishings to us. People can pass on the outside of these rooms and look in the doors but can't get the full effect of the beauty of the rooms until they get inside. Then we went out on the porch and sat while he talked. He has been there since the beginning of Cleveland's administration. He said that Rockwell would let us up sometime when the tables are all set for a big State Dinner so we could see them. I'll bet they are pretty.

During the hot weather, at 3:00 every afternoon, one of the liveried butlers comes in the office with a big silver tea service and cocktail cups and serves iced tea or lemonade. The silver is beautiful, all marked with the "President's House." The florist puts a fresh bouquet of flowers in the office every morning, and the girls take turns taking them home at night. My turn was tonight, so I have a dozen beautiful Ophelia roses. We also get passes to the shows occasionally. They send some every week, and they are distributed so that everybody gets them sometime.

Oh, the place has its compensations all right in spite of the monotony of the work. If we want to get off, all we have to do is to mention this fact to Mr. Rockwell, and he says to go ahead. Some different from the rest of the government bureaus where one has to put in a card for ten minutes leave and have it charged against his precious 15 days annual! Usually, I take 1½ or 2 hours for lunch, and nobody seems to care particularly what time one arrives or leaves. No one takes advantage of the liberal allowances, however, so things run very smoothly. I haven't had to work overtime as yet, but, believe me, we work while we are there—just sit at those typewriters, read all those letters, and devise answers. Some of the letters are so pitiful—people are so terribly down and out—it kind of preys on one's sympathies. Won't have time to write letters at work any more—that is, my own personal letters.

Don't mistake me about the President. I hope you haven't spread it around that he is hopelessly crippled. He can walk all right with support, but they ride him around in a chair most of the time because it is easier for him and everyone else. He never appears before the public in it. I won't be able to give you much gore on the family. In the first place, we aren't close enough to get much, and, in the second place, we are sworn to absolute secrecy; if any family matters do come through the Bureau, they are not to be told. And that means definitely. The Secret Service is too active to fool with it. There was a mistake of some kind made in our place one day, and they got the whole Secret Service force out, and such a time! I don't particularly care about working in a place like that, but it is a new experience anyhow. Don't know what we will have to do when the social season starts. They get in four script writers to do all the invitations, and Mr. Rockwell takes care of sending them out. I can't imagine what we will do, but no doubt will find out soon enough.

You asked about the Government's paying for Mrs. Roosevelt's secretary. The Government allows $3500 for her secretary to take care of official matters. I suppose Mrs. Roosevelt pays her extra for private work. Every letter we get that is written in response to one of her articles in the *Woman's Home Companion*, or anything else, we don't answer but send right up to Mrs. Roosevelt, and she takes care of it. If she wants a stenographer, or Mrs. Dall wants one, she keeps track of the time spent and pays that amount into the White House fund. It is all very complicated. Mrs. Dall has her own private secretary with her now, so we don't have to do any of her work.

[*ca. September 29–October 4, 1933*]

DEAR MOM,

Haven't anything much to write about as nothing different or exciting has happened. The Roosevelts have been away all of the time. Right now the only ones staying at the White House are James Roosevelt's little girl and her nurse, while ma and pa are enjoying a jaunt in Europe. Pretty soft for them, says I. She is a darling youngster, about 2 years old; we see her quite often.*

Had a nice trip around the White House the other day. The head electrician, "Doc," took another girl and me upstairs. We went in the Lincoln study on the second floor. It is a very interesting room. He was going to take us into the President's and Mrs. Roosevelt's rooms, but the new head usher, Raymond Muir, came up and told him he hadn't better. It wouldn't have hurt anything, but I suppose he feels

---

*This was Sara Delano Roosevelt, oldest child of James Roosevelt and his first wife, Betsey Cusing; she was born in 1932.

sort of responsible as he has just been promoted to the job since Ike
Hoover died.* He is surely a good-looking guy, 36 years old, but
married.

Then we went up on the third floor where some guest rooms and
the servants' quarters are. He showed us the room the Roosevelt boys
always use when they come down. Surely isn't anything at all, just a
very plain, ordinary affair. He also showed us a typical servant's room,
which was about the same as the room the Roosevelt boys use. Of
course, if a guest is really somebody, they put him on the second
floor; but the overflow use the rooms on the third floor. We went out
into the solarium, which is enclosed with violet ray glass. It is nothing
at all—furnished in wicker and cretonne furniture—and the baby had
her toys strewn all over. Mrs. Coolidge had it built because she was
subject to so many colds, and she used to lie up there. Mrs. Hoover
used it as an office for her secretary, and now it is used as a sort of
sun porch for the family. We walked around the roof, and the view
down over the south grounds and the rose gardens is certainly gorgeous.

Outside of that trip, haven't done anything out of the ordinary at
all. It is a nice job though. I like it better and better all of the time.
Everyone is *so* pleasant, and we have so much freedom. The guards
around the place are all big six-footers, most of them good looking,
and they surely keep us on our toes. Kidding is their favorite pastime.

Some of the letters we get are so funny; for instance, an Italian in
New York wrote to Mrs. Roosevelt and complained because the relief
agencies wouldn't help him. He said that just because he didn't have
children, he couldn't get any help at all, and he wanted Mrs. Roosevelt please to send him enough money so he could send to Italy and
bring his children over here so he could get relief from the charities.
That's reasoning for you!

Another one had her letter enclosed in an envelope inside of the
mailing envelope. On the back of the flap of the inner envelope, when
I pulled it out to read it, this greeted me: "Everybody but Mrs. Roose-

---

*Irwin H. ("Ike") Hoover died on September 14, 1933; Raymond D. Muir was
appointed Chief Usher to succeed him on September 16.

velt keep out of this. It is nobody else's business." I got a laugh out
of that. There are always many good laughs throughout the day over
some of the letters. One of them said her father was a veteran of the
Spinach-American War. There surely are lots of dumb people in this
world.

Am surprised that you saw me in the newsreel. I knew they were
taking movies, but I never thought I'd be in it. Could you see the
perspiration dripping off my back? Gosh, was I hot!

Have been trotting people through the White House quite a bit. I
never realized how many people come to Washington who know me,
or know someone I know who refers them to me to be shown through
the White House. Gets kind of tiresome, but I suppose I shall have
to continue as long as I work here.

About 5:00 the other evening, while we were working, we heard
the worst noise out in the hall. There was to be a reception that night,
and I thought that maybe the band had arrived early and were tuning
up. We looked out and here was Sistie with a drum parading down
the hall with Buzzie in back of her blowing on a horn that sounded
like a kazoo. They kept time very well, but poor Buzzie had a tough
time keeping up. They went down to the kitchen, then paraded way
back through the hall, down to the East Wing, and then all the way
back again. It was the funniest looking sight I ever saw, but nothing
seemed to fuss them; they were having a parade and that was that.
They are really cute youngsters. I don't know what has happened to
Mr. Dall; I think they are separated, but I don't know a thing about
it. He has been down here only about twice since March. Something
must be wrong. Mrs. Dall is taking care of Mrs. Roosevelt's correspondence from her *Woman's Home Companion* articles.

It is Saturday afternoon and I'm supposed to be off, but Mrs. Scheider wants to clean up some work, so I got stuck on the job.

[ca. October 13, 1933]

DEAR FRAN,

Last week Marie Dressler was a house guest at the White House.
We girls were dying to see her but thought we wouldn't get the chance.

35

However, the morning after she came, the head usher was showing her around, and he brought her down to the lower floor to take her out to the garden. The messenger stuck his head in the office and said that if we wanted to see Marie, it was a good chance while she was downstairs. So we flocked out with pencils and cards and met her when she came in. We asked her if she would give us her autograph, and she said, "Why, I'd love to." So she stood there and signed away, and then she said, "My, I really feel like quite somebody doing this." She talked, and we talked to her, for about 10 minutes. She certainly was darling—just exactly what one would expect her to be. She said they had called her from London the night before for an interview by telephone as to what was happening at the White House while she was there. She said, "I couldn't say anything funny; all I did was gabble and stutter and try not to say what I felt like saying." We surely enjoyed meeting her, and I shall add her autograph to a collection of things from the White House which, unconsciously, I seem to be making.

The other morning Mrs. Scheider called the office to say that Mrs. Roosevelt was coming down to thank us for the birthday card that the Social Bureau had sent her on her birthday. It was about 11:30, and we didn't expect her until afternoon when the visiting hours were over. All of us were working like the devil when she came in, and nobody saw her. She stood right by my desk, which is nearest the door, and then I looked up. I didn't know what to do or say. I didn't want to holler at the rest of them, and they didn't see her until she started thanking us for the card, which she said was lovely and which she appreciated a great deal.

The men finally struggled to their feet, but we girls just sat there like so many dead stumps. She finished her speech and went out, and nobody had said a word; we didn't even stand up! Well, as a social call, it surely was a complete flop! Everyone was so astonished that he couldn't seem to get himself together until after she had gone. She really is very nice; I have been pleasantly surprised. She doesn't like formality of any kind and is very gracious. She isn't nearly so bad looking as her pictures; she is tall and carries herself well. I had to pass her the other afternoon when I went out, and she smiled and spoke and wasn't at all what I had expected a President's wife to be. Of course, she doesn't know me from a hole in the wall; I think she knows I'm in the Social Bureau and that's about all.

[*November 17, 1933*]

DEAR FRAN,

Saw a very pretty sight last night. The first of the State functions—the Cabinet dinner—was on. We were allowed to go upstairs about 7:30 and see the tables all set and the decorations, etc., in the East Room where the musicale was to be later in the evening. It was really a sight worth seeing, too. There were to be 50 for dinner and the table was *beautiful*. It was laid, of course, with beautiful white linen and service plates at the places. They have a wide gold band on the outside, a narrower black band next to it, and the center is white with the gold White House insignia in the middle. The knives, forks, and spoons are gold instead of silver and have mother-of-pearl handles. The goblets were of the most sparkling cut glass. There was smilax laid on the table in the middle and huge bouquets of lavender pom-pom chrysanthemums down each side. There were solid gold fruit vases with carved figures on them, holding huge bunches of grapes; gold nut cups—I can hardly describe it. There were huge candelabra at each end, and the big crystal chandelier was lit above.

The East Room was banked with palms and ferns and big yellow chrysanthemums, and the little platform for the musicians was sur-rounded by ferns. They have a gold Steinway piano, and that was in the center with the big harp on one side. They have two huge crystal chandeliers in the room, which were lit and reflected all the lights. I wish I could describe things better—but, anyhow, it really was a sight. I was wishing I could hide somewhere and watch the people because I imagine, with all the pretty dresses and glittering jewels on the women, it would be worth seeing.

December 24, 1933

DEAR MOM,

I'm so thrilled! This morning Mrs. Roosevelt sent all of us beautiful poinsettia plants—one for everybody in the White House. This afternoon Mrs. Scheider, her secretary, sent the Social Bureau a big box of Sherry's chocolates with a nice note about perfect cooperation, etc.

And the crowning event was this afternoon. The President received all of the office help. We were so excited. We went over to the lobby of the Executive Office, lined up, and went into his office. He was standing by a window with Mrs. Dall; a man announced our names, and the President shook hands with each of us and wished us a very merry Christmas, and then Mrs. Dall did the same. He had a present for everybody. It is a copy of the President's book, *Looking Forward*, and on the flyleaf was the autograph, "To Dorothy Dow, with a Merry Christmas from Franklin D. Roosevelt—1933." He did that for everyone, and each one was wrapped. Talk about thrilled! Everybody was almost breathless.

We all gathered out in the lobby afterward and were so pleased. Imagine what a job that must have been for a man as busy as he is to write in all those books. There must have been well over a hundred. This is the first time any President has ever done anything like that, and even the old veterans of the White House were pleased to death.

And the President! He *is* the *nicest* looking man I have ever seen and just radiates personality, charm, and friendliness. He stood up there and smiled and joked and was in no hurry at all to pass anyone on. I didn't know what to say, so I just said, "Merry Christmas, Mr. President," and he shook hands with me and wished me a very pleasant holiday, and then Mrs. Dall did the same. Miss LeHand, the President's secretary, gave me the book. Mr. Louis McHenry Howe, one of the President's secretaries and an old friend, jumped into line, and the President said, "Get out of there, Howe; I suppose you're after a book." He was just joking with everyone. Secretary Early was perched on his desk swinging his feet. Well, we all had a grand and glorious time.

Forgive all of this raving, but I was so thrilled over it all—and especially over the book—that I had to tell someone. I never was a staunch Roosevelt supporter, but after this, and really seeing him, I can understand just why the people love him so. Mrs. Dall is charming, too; in fact, the whole family are as friendly as though they might be just neighbors.

1934

My own life has been
crowded with activity
and, best of all,
with people.

ELEANOR ROOSEVELT, *You Learn by Living*

February 2, 1934

DEAR MOM,

On the President's birthday he had us all over to his office. We
went about 4:30, and he was sitting at his desk, smoking the inevita-
ble cigarette. Right by one of the doors was a mammoth birthday
cake. He said that it weighed 250 pounds and came from California.
He had the big, fat, colored cook and Gus, his bodyguard, there with
huge knives cutting it. It was made in four layers and would cover
the top of a card table, at least.

We passed around, shook hands with the President, wished him a
happy birthday, and then passed by the cake. They cut each one a
piece and wrapped it up in oiled paper and gave it to us. While we
were passing around the office, the President was joking with everyone and kidding Gus. The cake was difficult to cut, and poor Gus was
working like a trooper. The President said, "This is the most work
Gus has had in a year," and then Gus dived in hand and foot, with
the President yelling over to him, "What's the matter, Gus? Speed
up a little; you're holding everyone up." He joked all of the time, and
everyone was laughing and having fun.

I think it was the President's own idea, and I know he enjoyed it immensely. The cake was marvelous. At first I thought I would send it home, but then I decided to eat it myself, with the help of four others. It was a fruit cake, and each piece weighed about a pound, I do believe. It was just filled with rum and whole pieces of fruit and was the most delicious stuff I have ever eaten. They gave each one part of the decorations, too, so that he could keep it. I have sort of a scroll with gold and silver leaves on it.

Mrs. Roosevelt entertained at a luncheon for all of the movie stars who were here for the Birthday Ball and afterward brought them over to the office to view the dimes. Franklin, Jr., and his wife, Ethel Dupont, came with them, and we all gave them our votes. They far outshone the movie actors in looks and everything else. They are the best looking people one ever saw. Jean Hersholt, Eleanor Powell, Errol Flynn, Lili Damita, Annabella, Mitzi Green, Bruce Cabot, Ralph Bellamy, Andrea Leeds, and some others were here. I go to the movies so seldom that they didn't mean much to me, but I did recognize Eleanor Powell without help, and she was very pleasant. She talked to us all and was just a nice good-looking girl—not nearly so artificial as the others, who were so made up. They certainly didn't amount to much. The men were blah. As I said, Franklin, Jr., is so much better looking that the contrast was pathetic. All of the men are quite short, and the girls are tiny. They were very nice, though, gave autographs to the autograph hounds, shook hands and talked to anyone who spoke to them. They all looked rather scared: I think they didn't know what they were getting into.

So far, approximately $123,000 has been counted in the "March of Dimes," and there are many mail bags which haven't even been opened and literally thousands of letters, which have been sorted and slit but not opened further. It has really been something! I heard one of the men say he wouldn't be surprised if it hit $200,000. Last year the net proceeds were $90,000, so that is a big increase. You never saw so many dimes in your life.

And last night was the reception! And did we all get a thrill! I spent about three hours dressing and didn't look too bad if I must say so. We took a cab, got out at the East Entrance, and went into the cloak room to take off our coats. Of course, it had to snow yesterday—the only snow we have had this year—and it made it rather bad getting a taxi. We dropped in the office and let Mr. Rockwell look us over, and then lined up by twos and went up to the East Room. The Cabinet members and high society came in the front door and lined up out in the lobby and hall. There were many people ahead of us.

We stood right by a door that led out to the hall. We were looking out, and there was Will Rogers right in the middle of the room talking to a group of women. He was dressed in a plain business suit with a wrinkled old collar, and his hair looked as though it had never been combed—just as it does in the movies. One of the ushers, Mr. Crim, came over when he saw us, and we told him to go and tell Will to turn around so we could see him. He said, "Do you want to meet him?" And, of course, we did. So he told us to go back and come into the outer hall, and he would let us through. And were we glad, because we would have spent half the evening waiting to get through the line to be received.

So there we stood—right out with those who were somebody! Will Rogers was occupied all of the time and always had someone around him. We didn't have nerve enough to go up and tell him we wanted to shake hands, although the usher said we should. Soon Mr. Crim came back and asked if we wanted to go down the receiving line. We said, "Yes," although we had met the President and Mrs. Roosevelt innumerable times. So he let us through the private way that is reserved for the elite and put us right at the head of the line. Then they put General Johnson, head of the NRA, and his wife and $6,000 secretary right in front of us and shoved us through. They received in the Blue Room in front of a bank of palms and ferns. Mrs. Roosevelt had a beautiful, delicate pink satin dress on. The President was flanked by his aides. One of them took my name, told the President, and he shook hands and said, "Good evening, Miss Dow."

We went straight through to the State Dining Room then and stopped for refreshments. In back of a long table were about a dozen butlers who were serving punch (delicious), and along the edge of the table were plates of cakes, others of dainty party cookies, and big dishes of candy and nuts. We just helped ourselves.

There was an enormous crowd, so we just wandered around to see if we could recognize anyone. It surely was grand knowing the White House force. We were standing by one of the guards we know very well, and he leaned over and said, "There is Alice Roosevelt right behind you." We turned, and sure enough, there was Mrs. Longworth. She had on huge gold earrings, hollow and sort of shell-like, that hung to her shoulders. We heard her tell Mr. Morgenthau that she kept a cigarette in one and a sandwich in the other. We saw a great deal of her during the evening. I couldn't help but stare at her and think that she had grown up in the White House and had been married there.* Then we saw General Hines, the head of the Veterans' Bureau, the Public Printer, Mr. and Mrs. Black—he is the head of the Federal Reserve Board, Mr. Ickes, the Secretary of the Interior, Mrs. Dern and Betsy Dern, the wife and debutante daughter of the Secretary of War—and, gosh, I can't think of all the rest.

Our main object was to shake hands with Will Rogers. I was standing right in front of him once, and a naval aide came up to shake hands with him. Then Will started in and said, "When I saw all these Army and Navy people here, I went right up to the President and said, 'I belong here; I have my discharge papers right in my pocket,' and the President said, 'Maybe so, but you're not going to get a pension.'" And at that, as I was the closest to him, he came down on my arm with a slap that almost knocked me over, it surprised me so.

Well, we roamed around and talked to those we knew; Mrs. Scheider and Mrs. Helm, the social secretary, were grand to us. At 10:30 we were right in the front row of the lane they made when the President and Mrs. Roosevelt were to leave—just accidentally, but there we were. The President left, but Mrs. Roosevelt stayed to mingle with the crowd and was around all evening. The Marine Orchestra

---

*Alice Roosevelt, daughter of President Theodore Roosevelt, lived in the White House from 1901 until her marriage at age 22 to Nicholas Longworth on February 17, 1906. She wore her long, gold, Hindu earrings, a heavy gold necklace, a gold watch-bracelet and side combs, with a blue velvet dress, as a deliberately defiant statement of her feelings about President Roosevelt's having taken the country off the gold standard by signing the Gold Reserve Act on January 30, 1934. The *New York Herald Tribune* of February 2, 1934, recognized her motive with the headline, "Mrs. Longworth Takes Gold Into the White House."

came and started music for dancing in the East Room. And it was a pretty sight: the beautiful dresses, the full dress of the men, the red coats of the orchestra, and the gorgeous room with its huge chandeliers, flowers, ferns, palms, etc.

We stood and watched, and then Mrs. Helm came up and wanted to know if we were enjoying ourselves. She said she would take us around and try to point out celebrities to us. It was rather late at that time, however, and many of them had gone home, but we did see Mrs. Cummings and Mrs. Roper. Then Mrs. Helm went to bring Frances Perkins over to us and introduced us to her. She is wonderful—one would think she might have been wanting to meet us all evening, she was so cordial. She stayed and talked a while.

Then we saw Will Rogers with his wife and daughter—the one who entered the movies under the name of Mary Howard. They were getting ready to go. Will slapped one of the Naval aides on the shoulder and said, "Well, I'll see you in Nicaragua,"* and, of course, that got a laugh out of everyone. He had on a brown overcoat and an old slouch hat, but ma and the kid were dressed fit to kill.

One of the boys in the file room came up and asked me to dance, so we danced until "Home, Sweet Home." I was the only girl in our crowd who had the chance, and I was glad as I just like to know that I did dance in the East Room. Then it was time to go home, but we didn't want to go. However, it was being done, so we went to get our things, and then the fun started—trying to get a cab. People were lined along the steps of the East Entrance, and it looked hopeless. However, one of the guards we know came to our rescue; he said, "Follow me," and he got us right through, went out in the street, got a cab, and put us in.

It really was grand and worth all the effort it took to get there. Everyone was so nice: there wasn't one of the White House staff, from the doorman to the ushers, who didn't come around and want to know if we were enjoying ourselves. They all just seemed to be

---

*Since 1926 Nicaragua had been torn by insurrections and civil war, during which the United States had sent in the Marines to keep order and had also played peacemaker. The Marines were withdrawn in 1933.

trying to show us a good time: Mrs. Scheider, who stayed with us quite a bit; Mr. Crim, who let us in with the important people and got us through; and Mrs. Helm, who pointed out people to us. The housekeeper, custodian, and all of the guards always made a way for us. We felt like guests of honor, absolutely.

Well, I think this finishes my social life. I forgot to say that the Marine Band played all of the time, and at 9:30, when the President and Mrs. Roosevelt came, there was a flourish of trumpets, and the color guard took their places by the door of the receiving room; then the "Hail to the Chief," and they took their places. It was thrilling!

However, we were all struck by the way the President looked—just dead tired—completely exhausted. I really think that is a terrible thing to inflict on him—to make him stand there and shake hands all evening with a lot of goops. He did look so all in, and so did Mrs. Roosevelt. There was such a marked contrast to the times he has us over in his office and can sit at his desk and smoke and joke with people and have everything very informal. I'm sure that is always his own idea, and he thoroughly enjoys himself. But he didn't look as if he were having a very good time last night. That really must be quite an ordeal for him. When he left the line and walked to the elevator, I thought it was really remarkable how well he walked. He leans heavily on his aide, but exept for that, his limp is very unnoticeable. It must be an effort for him as they wheel him around all of the time, and he would walk, I know, if it weren't such an exertion.

Easter Monday
[April 2], 1934

DEAR FRAN,

Today is "Easter egg rolling" day at the White House, and what a jam there is! We have attempted to get some work out, but it is rather useless. There are mobs of people streaming right by our windows, the band is playing, children screaming and crying because they are lost—and it is just hopeless. I decided for the last half-hour I was going to write personal letters and even give up the pretense of working.

I can't get much sense out of this egg rolling. Children accompanied by their parents bring their Easter baskets and eggs and come and spend the day on the south lawn of the White House. They play games, eat their picnic lunch, and just hang around. The Marine Band provides the music, and there are big imitation animals that perform all over the lawn. Mrs. Roosevelt has been out three times today to greet people. She is the best person I ever saw. We were outside when she came down the last time, and she isn't satisfied just to stay in a sheltered place and wave at the people; she pushes her way right into the crowd and shakes hands with all she can. It is terribly hot out today, but that doesn't seem to make a bit of difference to her. She is certainly the most socially minded person I have ever seen. I am sure that if I told you what her program has been for today, you would be exhausted just thinking about it.

We are plenty busy here at work. Have thousands of letters that are not yet answered, but we keep plugging along and have a very kind and considerate boss who doesn't worry, so we aren't pushed.

[*1934*]

DEAR MOM,

I had a very nice compliment yesterday. Mr. Magee, the head of the stenographers here in the office, was over at the Executive Office— in Secretary Early's office—talking to the head of all the press men. He brought up the subject himself to Mr. Magee, and it was about the President's speech that I took in shorthand quite a while ago. He told Mr. Magee that it was the finest piece of work, outside of a professional reporter's, he had ever seen, and that out of the three, it was the only one that was accepted, that the punctuation was excellent, and that I really had put life into it. He told Mr. Magee to be sure that I didn't get away from here.

Mr. Magee came right over and told me, for which I was very appreciative. A little good news once in a while surely does wonders toward cheering up a person. Mr. Magee seemed to think that it was quite a compliment, coming from him, plus the fact that, after so many months, he had brought up the subject himself. Believe me, it made me feel darned good. Personally, I didn't think I had done such a hot job on it. It seemed to take me an awfully long time to transcribe it, but I did have a complete speech when I finished. I noticed that the other girls had left blank spaces where they had missed out. I set out the salutation separately, put dashes in where he repeated himself, paragraphed it, and I think that is what they liked. I really didn't think much about how I was doing it—just wrote it as I would write anything. I was going to let my shorthand drop as I don't get enough of it around here to keep in practice, but after this, I'm going to practice it at least one night a week. Mr. Magee said that no doubt every time the occasion arose, I would get the job, and as I like to do it, I think I had better be prepared. One loses speed so fast.

[ca. May 24, 1934]

DEAR FRAN,

I have been to two very nice parties—one a garden party here at the White House, and the other a garden party at the home of the Secretary of War and Mrs. Dern. Mrs. Roosevelt's secretary gave us the invitations and provided a table for us to play cards. We had a grand time. We enjoyed the party here at the White House the most, as the Marine Band played all of the time, and the grounds were so pretty that it was a pleasure just to wander around them.

There is the lousiest looking bunch of men in town that I have ever seen.* They are delegates for unemployment insurance or old age pensions or something—just a bunch of tramps, colored and white— and they are enough to scare a person to death. This town does draw the wildest assortment of people. One man stopped me this noon, when I came through the State, War, and Navy Building, and said, "Pardon me, Miss, could you tell me what kind of an institution this is?" I felt like telling him it was a Federal workhouse but didn't. They approached the office here en masse just as I left; it was quite a for-

---

*These were, undoubtedly, some of the 650 ragged veterans of World War I who assembled in Washington between May 11 and May 24, 1934, to march in support of their plea for immediate payment of the veterans' bonus.

midable looking outfit, but I think they turned back with no trouble, as all of the policemen were lined up on the steps. I was almost afraid to go out for lunch.

Now to answer your question: of course, all of the girls get invited to the parties I do. Why should they single me out? They issue separate invitations to each of us—one reception and one garden party. That is the most anyone, no matter how important, ever gets invited to, except the Cabinet members and their wives.

December 1, 1934

DEAR FRAN,

We have moved into our new offices here at the White House. They enlarged the Executive Office, and we are all installed at present in places where we can see and breathe at the same time, which is more than we could ever say before. So—as sort of a housewarming last evening—the Roosevelts entertained the whole office staff at tea. I thought it was mighty nice of them.

We went into the President's office and shook hands with him and Mrs. Roosevelt and then went into the Cabinet Room where they had the big table spread with beautiful linen. There was an immense bouquet of roses in the center and elaborate silver tea services at both ends. Miss LeHand and Miss Tully poured, and there were plates of dainty sandwiches, cookies, and cakes, and dishes of chocolates, bonbons, and salted nuts on the tables. After the President and Mrs. R. were through receiving, they both came in, and the President sat at the table and more than enjoyed his lunch. Mrs. R. mingled with everyone, and a good time was had by all.

I can say one thing: regardless of what anyone thinks of the administration's policies, he would have a hard time in finding any finer people than the Roosevelts personally. The President could have had his tea served to him in his office, and no one would have thought anything of it. But, no sir! Not him! He had to be in with the rest of the bunch and seemed to enjoy himself as much as anyone else.

[*December 9, 1934*]

DEAR FRAN,

I wish you could have been with me at the Gridiron Widows' party at the White House last night. It was really something and a big thrill. Saw many notables, but the chief one was Fannie Hurst, the writer. I would give anything if you could have seen her as you like exotic persons. I never have seen a more fascinating get-up in my life. I have been wanting to see her as her stationery has always intrigued me; it has her name in red across the top, and she signs her name in red ink—most individualistic.

Anyhow, she always dresses out of the ordinary, and she surely was out of the ordinary at that party. They say she is about 50, but she looks 25—has a grand figure, coal black hair, which was parted in the middle and skinned right straight back with a knot in her neck. Over her head she had a very gossamer black veil, which hung down to her shoulders and which was dotted with gold spangles. The makeup on her face was a sort of gray, with scarlet lips and eyes very much shadowed, etc. It was just right under that veil, and I didn't want to take my eyes away from her. She had on a skintight, white satin dress— sort of mandarin style with a high neck and long tight sleeves. It hung to the floor, and around her waist was a white silk cord, hanging to the hemline. Then, beginning right under her chin, there were yards and yards of white beads wound around from her neck to her shoulders and then falling in a yokelike effect to her waist. Around each arm she also had these white beads wound up to her elbows. Well, believe me, she was a sight. I've read about exotic people but previously had never seen one in the flesh.

They gave a lot of funny skits in the East Room, which was fixed up as a theater. Mrs. Roosevelt took part in some. A lot of them were take-offs on the New Deal, etc. After that, when we were all seated at the tables that had been placed throughout the parlors and State Dining Room, Mrs. Roosevelt called on various persons—notables— for little speeches, and there were surely some good ones.

Fannie Hurst was the best, though. She started out by saying she had been warned that she might have to talk, so she had been thinking about what to say and had decided that she was like a friend of hers, who said everything she wanted to do was either illegal, immoral, or fattening! She really was rare. Others called on were big shots in the newspaper field, Mrs. Nathan Straus, Mrs. Gene Tunney, Lady Lindsay, the wife of the Ambassador from Great Britain, several Senators and Congresswomen, and Mrs. Morgenthau. I stood by Frances Perkins during all of this, and she talked to me the whole time; she is a grand person to meet. I sat by and ate with Miss Helen Ferris, who is the Editor of the Junior Literary Guild and, to my surprise, had lived six years in La Crosse and had gone to high school there for one year! We got along swell. It was a grand party, and I feel quite privileged to have been allowed to go to it.

[*Late December, 1934*]

DEAR MOM,

The White House treated us royally as usual. Mrs. Helm, the social secretary, gave each of us two beautiful handkerchiefs and gave the three girls who do her work a $5.00 bill apiece. Then Mrs. Scheider called Miss Orndorff and me over to her office—we are the only ones who do her work—and she gave me a darling pair of bookends. They are bright red poodle dogs and look too pretty for words on our mantel. She gave Miss Orndorff driving gloves with fur cuffs. Mrs. Helm sent over 5 pounds of candy for everyone and a couple of boxes of cigars for the men. Mrs. Scheider also sent over 5 pounds of candy and a couple of cartons of cigarettes. The boys brought us each a poinsettia plant.

At 12 o'clock the President received us in his office. We lined up, and he and Mrs. Roosevelt stood by the door and shook hands with us all; then Mrs. Dall gave us our presents from the President. It was his other book, *On Our Way*, autographed like the one he gave us last year. The two make a nice pair to have, I think. Mrs. Roosevelt gave us big fruit cakes, and we all felt that we certainly were very well remembered. Sistie and Buzzie were also in line and looked so cute. They stood there by their mother—so straight they almost fell over backward. They didn't shake hands but seemed to think they were quite somebody. The two Irish setters, Jack and Jill, were lying in the middle of the office, and it made quite a nice, homey picture.

1936

I always have a sense that public occasions
of any kind are not times during
which you live, they are
just times which you live through.

ELEANOR ROOSEVELT, *My Days*

[*January, 1936*]

DEAR MOM,

I went to the Gridiron Widows' party, and for some reason, it was more fun than usual this year. It is a good party. The outstanding person there, in my estimation, was Dorothy Thompson. I had never seen her before, and she certainly is a grand person. I couldn't take my eyes off her all evening. Fannie Hurst was there in one of her outlandish get-ups, as usual. She surely is a sight. She wore a black sheathlike dress this year, with fringe hanging from her shoulders almost to the hem. She had the usual gray makeup under a shoulder-length black veil, which was spotted with brilliants and hung in front of her face. One honestly thinks he is seeing things when he sees her! And he is! I don't think anybody else in the world dresses as she does.

We were invited to the Judicial Reception but didn't go. The receptions get rather boring, and we've been to so many that we don't care about them any more.

(Opposite) Dorothy Dow, taken in 1936. Courtesy: Dorothy Dow Butturff.

1938

Nothing you learn, however wide of the mark
it may appear at the time,
however trivial, is ever wasted.

ELEANOR ROOSEVELT, *You Learn by Living*

By 1938, when Dorothy Dow made her first visit to Mrs. Roosevelt's cottage at Hyde Park, she was no longer Miss Dow, for she had married Robert R. Butturff, a government employee, on October 20, 1934. But she continued to be known professionally as Miss Dow because most people found her married name difficult whereas "Miss Dow just rolls off anyone's tongue."

And change was on the way for Malvina Thompson Scheider, Mrs. Roosevelt's private secretary, too. In March she had quietly filed for divorce from her husband, Frank Scheider, from whom she had been separated since leaving New York to accompany Mrs. Roosevelt to Washington in 1933. The divorce was granted in September 1938, and the Court allowed her to resume use of her maiden name.

"Tommy" was much in need of Dorothy's help that summer, for she had undergone an emergency appendectomy on June 7 and was still recuperating when Dorothy arrived at Val-Kill.

Hyde Park, New York
July 6, 1938

DEAR MOM,

I feel as though I have been transported to another world. This is the most gorgeous place, and they are the most wonderful people!

And they call it a job! I think I shall have one hell of a good vacation and that is all, because the work I did today probably took all of an hour.

To begin with, I landed in Poughkeepsie and was met by Schaffer, the White House chauffeur, in a 12-cylinder Pierce Arrow with the President's seal on the door. Ahem! I certainly felt like Lady Astor herself, ensconced in the back seat and being chauffeured out to the President's estate. He let me off at Nelly Johannessen's where I am staying. It is just a house by the side of the road, but a most attractive place inside. It is all furnished with Val-Kill furniture and is simply ideal as far as I am concerned. I have a nice, big room with twin beds, and it is furnished so prettily. Nelly is a Swedish woman and a *wonderful* cook. I'll bet I gain about 20 pounds while I am here. She is full of fun and a fascinating person to talk to. She has a five-year-old grandson staying with her, and he provides the entertainment and amusement.

Molly was still here last night but left early this morning. She took me up to the cottage last night after dinner; it is about 7/10 of a mile along a country lane. As far as one can see, the land belongs to the President, and everywhere he has planted thousands of pine trees, which smell like the north woods. There are at least seven or eight houses on the land; the occupants are sort of tenant farmers who pay rent to the President and get their living out of their places and work around the Big House (old lady Roosevelt's place) and the cottage.

Mrs. Scheider met us at the cottage, and she looks grand and seemingly feels fine. One wouldn't even know she had been operated on or been sick. What they call the cottage is where Mrs. Roosevelt stays, except when the President is here; then she stays at the Big House, which is about two miles away. They call it a cottage? It isn't my idea of such a thing! There is an apartment there for Mrs. Scheider—a big living room, two bedrooms, two baths, a kitchen, and a grand porch. Then, in the front Mrs. Roosevelt has her apartment, consisting of a big living room and a living porch, and upstairs I think she has about six bedrooms and as many baths—didn't go up there.

Next door is a house which belongs to a friend of Mrs. R., Miss Cook. It is perfectly beautiful. She is quite a horticulturist and has a

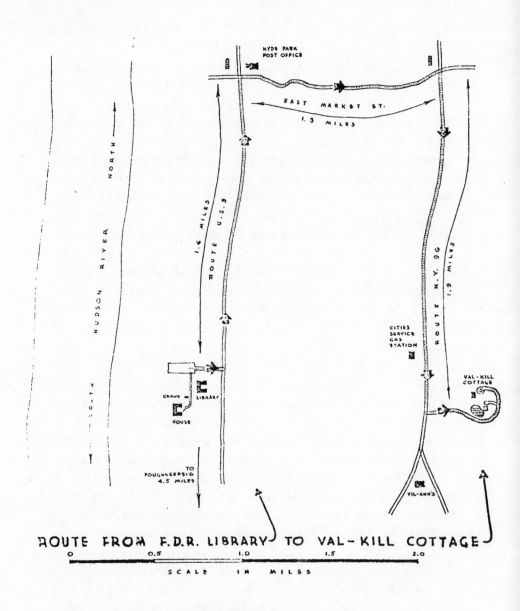

ROUTE FROM F.D.R. LIBRARY TO VAL-KILL COTTAGE

SCALE IN MILES

Courtesy: Franklin D. Roosevelt Library.

marvelous garden, also a cutting garden, herb garden, an enclosed
patio with a fountain, etc. etc. Out in the yard is a grand swimming
pool and an archery field, a net for deck tennis, quoits, and a huge
outdoor fireplace, all surrounded on two sides by what looks like a

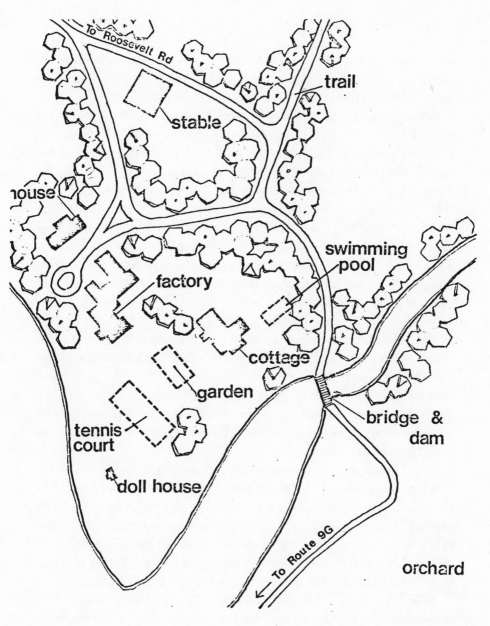

To Roosevelt Rd

trail

stable

house

swimming
pool

factory

cottage

garden

bridge &
dam

tennis
court

doll house

To Route 9G

orchard

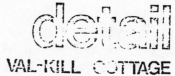

detail

VAL-KILL COTTAGE

small lake but is really just a drained swamp. It adds so much to the picturesqueness of the place. We talked to Mrs. Scheider until about ten o'clock and then came back to Nelly's and went to bed.

Got up about 7:30 this morning and Schaffer took Molly to the train. I started out about 9:00—after a delicious breakfast—to walk to the cottage when along came Mrs. R. and Earl Miller, one of her guests, down to get me. They took me up to the cottage. We sat around Mrs. Scheider's apartment and talked and talked, and when the mail came in, I did a little something on it, with Mrs. R. flying in and out. About the most I did was answer the 'phone and take messages, send a few telegrams, call up the plumber and tell him to get a man out here in a hurry to repair the swimming pool, and in between lounged in a comfortable chair or stretched out on the porch in the sun and unlaxed and read the papers. Oh, me—it's a tough life! At noon Mrs. R. asked me to have lunch with her, Miss Cook, Earl Miller, and Mrs. Scheider. We went out on her porch and had a nice lunch of Welsh rarebit on toast, tomato salad, hot biscuits, iced tea, cut-up peaches, and sugar cookies. There are three colored servants who take care of the place. After lunch went back with Mrs. Scheider and lopped around some more and did a little more 'phone answering, etc., and all of the time Mrs. R. was having a fit because we didn't come out of doors.

Finally I got on my swimming suit and went in swimming with her and Earl, and then Mrs. Morgenthau, the wife of the Secretary of the Treasury, came; she is a grand person. We all went over to the archery field, and Earl gave us lessons. I'm rotten—terrible—but it was fun. Right now my arm feels like soup. I haven't had any exercise for so long that I don't know how to take it any more, but it certainly feels swell to be moving around instead of just sitting in an office.

After the archery, Mrs. R. got some cherries and plums, and we consumed those; then I came back to Nelly's, and it is now about 6:30. Mrs. Scheider apologized for having me work an hour overtime! She says she wants me to take her car whenever I want it, to feel perfectly at home, to ask Schaffer to do anything for me that I want him to do, or to call him to take me into Poughkeepsie if I should want to go, to go swimming whenever I want to, and to look as sloppy as I choose. They all wear the very plainest of clothes—backless dresses, shorts, ankle socks, no powder or makeup, hair any old way—which suits me to a T as I never did like to stay dressed up.

Mrs. Roosevelt is the grandest person. I never feel at all that she is the President's wife; she seems just like everyone else and is like everyone else. She was so concerned today for fear I wouldn't get outside as much as I could and do the things I wanted to do. And while I didn't particularly care about having lunch with them all, I couldn't have felt more at home if I had been eating in our own kitchen. I am afraid I am going to be absolutely spoiled to return to normal living again. And to beat all, I am up here on detail, and the Government pays me $5.00 a day for sustenance over and above my salary. I feel like a criminal taking it besides all of my traveling expenses, but plenty of other people chisel all they can, and if the Government is willing, I guess I shouldn't holler.

Mrs. Scheider wants Bob to come up for a few days, and I surely hope he will. She said that we could take her car at any time and do the surrounding countryside—Bear Mountain Park, West Point, Connecticut, or any place we might want to go. He would love it, and I want him to see the layout of the place. It makes me fairly dizzy to see how much one family can possess and how much comfort and luxury a little cash will bring.

It would take a young fortune to run the cottage alone. There is a big farm and also the Big House, where the old lady stays. It is one of those old, huge, almost medieval palaces right on the Hudson. I haven't seen it as yet, but Mrs. R. said that she would take me over someday. She hates the place, I think, and never stays there unless she has to. The President is building himself a "cottage," for a retreat, on one of his hills; that will make about 25 houses on his acreage. Tough—eh, what? It must be nice to be rich, but next to being rich, it is nice to have the privilege to taste the things the rich enjoy, and

(*Overleaf*) Val-Kill in summer. The stone cottage, occupied by Nancy Cook, adjoins the swimming pool. Mrs. Roosevelt's cottage (the converted factory building) is behind the stone cottage. Courtesy: Miss Deborah Dows and Mrs. John Roosevelt. Credit: Drawing by Olin Dows.

Olin Dows © 1949.

I can do it without the least bit of envy. All I have to do is to think how much it costs to maintain, and I'm very happy with our five rooms and forty-foot lot.

Later:

Just had dinner—and what a meal! We had broiled steak, potatoes, carrots, string beans, tomatoes, pickles, tomato juice cocktail, wonderful homemade ice cream, devil's food cake, and coffee. And cooked as only Swedes can cook.

Saturday Sistie and Buzzie Dall are coming up here, and they are giving a picnic for Shirley Temple, who is also coming. I think that ought to be interesting as I saw Shirley at the White House, and she really is a little honey. Outside of that, I don't know of anything very exciting that is to happen. The President is away on his western tour, so he won't be here at all.

All in all, this isn't a bad place. There are hundreds of new books here of every kind, so I'll have plenty of reading material, and read is probably all I will do in the evening. But it suits me. Mrs. Scheider said something today about my staying until the middle of August, which is lots longer than I expected, but I guess I can stand it, and Bob is so big hearted that he wouldn't holler about my being away, I know. I just wonder what condition the house will be in when I get back, but I'm not going to worry about it. In fact, one couldn't worry about much of anything up here—it is so quiet and peaceful.

[*July 7, 1938*]

DEAR FRAN,

Boy! I'm so stiff I can hardly move. This strenuous exercise is rather tough for an old lady who hasn't even walked to the store for about two years. But it surely is fun and feels grand to be really active again and do the things I used to like to do so much. Mrs. Roosevelt is such a vital, energetic person that she thinks everyone must be also, and, believe me, she surely keeps us, and all who happen to be her house guests, on the go in the afternoons.

I read last night until 11:00 and then I think I must have died until about 7:30 this morning. Whew! Did I sleep! This country air surely does things to a person.

Got to work about 9:30 and really did a little something all morning. Mrs. R. gave me quite a few letters, and I had several telegrams to 'phone in and many instructions to give to Schaffer. It is all quite hectic for me, though, as I sit at Mrs. Scheider's desk—which is always in the most godawful mess for no rhyme or reason—and Mrs. R. comes running in and says do this or do that, and I never can find a pencil. This morning I had to keep two telegrams in my head after she had left and dig around for a pencil; I almost died! Then, Mrs. Scheider starts to talk just when I am in the midst of a letter or something, or Mabel, one of the servants, comes in to ask me something; anyhow, it is quite different working in this atmosphere than at the regular office, but I like it. The room is so lovely and filled with fresh flowers.

The president of Arnold Constable's in New York sent Mrs. Scheider a huge box this morning, and I had more fun unpacking it. It was just loaded with huge oranges, plums, peaches, pint boxes of immense black cherries, dried apricots, fresh dates, a jar of fresh caviar (Ugh! It stunk!), and some crackers to serve it on. I found a beautiful, big, fruit bowl and fixed everything very nice and then plowed in and chewed on it—mostly the cherries—the rest of the day.

I came back to Nelly's for lunch and got back to the cottage about 2:00. Except for a few odd things, there was no more work. I had to receive a lady who had come by appointment to see Mrs. Roosevelt. I got her comfortably seated, with cigarettes, etc., in Mrs. R.'s apartment, where she waited for Mrs. R., who had disappeared someplace.

After that appointment was over, Mrs. R. came in and drove Mrs. Scheider and me outside. She simply will not hear of our staying inside after 3:00. Mrs. Scheider asked her who she thought she was— Mrs. Hitler or Mrs. Mussolini! I put on my swimming suit, went out to try to locate my cap—with no success—and came back in, thinking I had left it in Mrs. Scheider's bathroom. Mrs. R. jumped on me right away and wanted to know if I were coming in so soon. I said, "No, I am just in search of my cap," so she told me to go down to the bathhouse, help myself, and stay out and get some sun. Mrs. Morgenthau, Mrs. Fayerweather, a personal friend, her son, and another man, Donald Stephens, were here, and we all went swimming; Mrs. R. joined us later.

Then I took the canoe and went by myself all the way up a little stream; it was so pretty, and it seemed so good to be paddling a canoe again. I think I must have gone about a mile when I rounded a curve and heard a great splashing of water and flapping of wings, and came onto a flock of wild ducks, the cutest little things. But they all flew away with a great commotion when they heard me, so I turned around and came back.

Got back to the pool and Mrs. R. asked me to play deck tennis. The court is alongside the pool. The court and net are just like tennis, and the rules are the same, but it is played with inflated rubber rings about 8″ across and hollow. The idea is to serve, just as in tennis, but one throws the rings across the net, and they must be caught with just one hand and tossed back. It is really fast. Mrs. R. and I took on Mrs. Morgenthau and Mrs. Stephens, and we beat the hell out of them. I had never played the game before, but Mrs. R. thought I was very good, and I surely was better than they were, thanks to my training in Physical Education and the years I spent on a tennis court.

It is such a joy to know how to do things when they are expected of one. They like the way I swim, too, and I wouldn't be at all surprised if I would be wheedled into giving swimming lessons before I get out of this place. Mrs. R. swims, but Mrs. Scheider doesn't, and she asked me if I thought I could teach her. Miss Cook was interested in learning, too. However, I'm not going to volunteer unless someone really wants me to teach her, as it is hard work, and I would rather play around by myself.

It was 5:30 when all that was over. I was simply exhausted and had blisters on both big toes from my swimming shoes and skidding over the grass in deck tennis. Mrs. R. tried to get me to try the archery again, but I flatly refused. I had had plenty, and I'll bet that tomorrow I'll be as stiff as cement. But, gee, I feel good; outdoor exercise surely is a real bracer, and I feel better than I have in years.

Came back to Nelly's, a good half-mile walk, and had a delicious dinner. Will spend the rest of the evening reading; there are so many

Nelly Johannessen and her Val-Kill Tea Room where Dorothy Dow
boarded during summers at Hyde Park, N. Y. Courtesy: Mr. and Mrs. Roy
Johannessen.

books I want to read while I'm here that I don't object at all to these
rather lonesome evenings. I get my letters written, have a bath, and
read until I can't keep my eyes open. Maybe I'll tire of this before
the month is out, but I doubt it. It is a real change, just what I have
been craving for months, and everyone is so nice to me. I am treated
just as though I were one of them. Luckily, I know enough to keep

my place and don't try to barge in anyplace or ask any favors, and I think that all helps.

I can't get over Mrs. Roosevelt. I have always thought she was a wonderful person, but seeing her up here and being more closely connected with her only emphasizes that feeling. Not only that, but when the tenant farmers and Nelly talk to me about her, they say they simply worship her. Nelly was telling me that one day last summer she had a terrible cold and was so sick she couldn't get out of bed. Mrs. R. heard about it, came down, rushed in with camphor, rubbed her chest, and fixed her all up. Then, Nelly said, she left, but Nelly felt so rotten she didn't say anything to her. Pretty soon Mrs. R. came back with her sleeves rolled up and obviously had been working; she had gone into the kitchen, washed all the dishes, and cleaned up the whole place. Nelly's sons had prepared their own breakfast and had left everything in a mess. Mrs. R. knew that Nelly would be worrying about the looks of the place as she is such an immaculate housekeeper, so she just went out there, cleaned up everything slick as a whistle, told Nelly to stay in bed and not to get up for anything as the house was clean and there was nothing to worry about. It isn't every woman who would do a thing like that, and I think Nelly was just mortified to tears to think that Mrs. R. did it. She just can't get over it. Nelly used to be Mrs. R.'s cook before Mrs. R. started her with weaving in this little place.

[*July 9, 1938*]

DEAR MOM,

Oh, boy, what a day! I'm completely exhausted. Today was the day the picnic was held for Shirley Temple, and it was a huge success. She is, without a doubt, the sweetest little girl I ever saw. It was necessary to just stop and think if you wanted to remember her as being different from any other child you might know. Took work home last night and did it here in my room until about ten o'clock. There was a lot of it, and I thought I would get it out of the way before this morning, as I had an idea it would be rather hectic—and it was.

In the first place, Mrs. Scheider wasn't feeling well, so she was in bed, and the 'phone rang continuously. I think every movie company, news company, the AP, and New York papers called up to see if they would be allowed to be at the picnic to take pictures and to get a story. Mrs. R. had said that the answer to all of them was distinctly "No," and if you ever had any experience in trying to tell a newspaper man "No," you know what I was up against. They are the most persistent people. The Fox Movie-Tone men were the only ones allowed in. I had to make a list of the cars and give it to the State Trooper at the entrance to the grounds, and he was to allow only those cars in. One newspaper guy called me and said that he was at the gate and the Trooper wouldn't let him in. I explained that no reporters were allowed, etc., but he kept on—that he had come all the way from New York, etc., and finally I got sore and told him the answer definitely was "No," and hung up.

Then, too, this morning Mrs. Scheider said that the guests would probably be coming through her place, and would I please try to straighten up the joint a little and get the mail and junk out of sight, at least. That was all I needed; the lack of system she uses gets on my nerves. So, with a free hand, I lit in: collected mail from every table in the place and chucked it in a desk drawer; went over her desk and threw away all I could; got a dust rag and shined it up; then got Pearl, the servant, and she and I went over the room and threw out some dead flowers, moved old boxes, and folded up folding tables, and Pearl gave it a good cleaning.

When Mrs. Scheider finally got up and came out, she almost fell over. I thought she would probably kill me, but she seemed pleased— just wanted to be sure I hadn't thrown away anything important, which I was sure I hadn't. Mrs. R. came in and said, "My, but you look neat and clean in here." Mrs. Scheider said, "Well, with no mail, I guess we don't have any work." But I showed her what I had chucked in a drawer, so that gets done tomorrow, Sunday. Every day here is just like every other day. At least, I got the desk in some sort of order, so when the 'phone rings, I can find a pencil and pad to take the message.

Sistie and Buzzie Dall gave the picnic for Shirley, of course, and they were so excited about meeting her. When she first came, the Fox Movie-Tone man was there to take some movies of her and Mrs. Roosevelt. They were the only ones allowed, and they were only allowed because she works for the company, and they couldn't very well keep them out. Then, when the Fox man got ready to take pictures, he wanted to take Sis and Buz, and, as that was not to be permitted, I had to head him off. Boy! The taste of being Mrs. R.'s secretary that I am getting is going to be plenty for me; Mrs. Scheider can have the job and is perfectly welcome to it. It was fun to watch how naturally Shirley did everything she was told to do. Quite a few of the invited guests had cameras—like a goop, I didn't think about taking one—and took a lot of pictures of the group. However, I think I can get some prints from some of the negatives that were taken.

Sistie and Buz wanted to take Shirley swimming, but Mrs. Temple said she couldn't go on account of her hair. Mrs. Roosevelt said that maybe they could just pin it all up, and she could keep her head out of the water, but Mrs. Temple said that she had better not go in. So, Shirley went inside and put on a little playsuit, and her mother wrapped her hair all up in a bandanna, and then we all adjourned to the picnic grounds.

There were, besides the Temples, Mrs. R., Earl Miller, Sis and Buz, Mr. Bye, who is Mrs. R.'s literary agent, Mrs. Bye, and her sister, brother-in-law, and niece, who is about 6 years old. There is a huge outdoor fireplace, and Mrs. R. superintended the broiling of pork and lamb chops over the open fire, and were they good! The servants had set a buffet table with cold ham, kedgeree (fish, rice, and hard-boiled eggs), potato chips, rolls, and ice cream (made by Nelly), doughnuts, little cakes, milk, iced tea, coffee, cigarettes, and cigars.

It was interesting to watch Shirley pick out her lunch. Evidently, she has to watch what she eats so she won't get too fat—she is right

(Opposite) Shirley Temple and others at a Val-Kill picnic, July 9, 1938. Left to right in the front row are "Sistie" Dall, Shirley Temple, and "Buzzie" Dall. In the rear are an unidentified New York State Trooper and Mr. Temple. Courtesy: Mr. and Mrs. Clifford Smith.

chunky even now—and she wouldn't take a roll or potato chips. When it came time for the ice cream and cake, she took a cake and then went to ask her mother if she could have another one. Sistie fell over a stump and spilled milk all over herself and all over the table, so we had to help her get out of that mess. Mrs. R. asked me if I would help her at the table to be sure everyone was served, so I presided over the chops.

After lunch the fun began. Shirley made herself right at home, and of all the uproar! There were five kids altogether, and they chased around; Shirley got out her police badge, and of all the hollering and hooting you ever heard! Then, they all tried archery—with no success—and finally they got one of the State Troopers, who had escorted the Temple car, to play with them. Shirley made him get into the boat. Then the little devils turned the boat loose. Luckily, there were oars in it, but every time the Trooper would get in toward shore, they would kick him out again. He was a grand guy, played along with them, and had them about crazy running along the shore trying to keep him from landing.

I talked quite a while with Mr. and Mrs. Temple and also with Mr. Mulchahy, Shirley's publicity man from the Fox Studio. It was all very interesting. Mr. Mulchahy was telling me many of the experiences they have had on this trip. He said that Shirley has no idea how important she is, and I believe it. Once in a while she asks her mother why people always stare at her so, but her mother is extremely good with her, and Shirley is entirely unspoiled. He said that they have received 20 threats of kidnapping, and that protecting the child was a man-sized job, although they try to do it in such a way that she doesn't realize that she is being protected. Mr. Temple is very nice. They certainly are grand people to be the parents of such a child.

Mrs. Temple certainly doesn't let the child get away with anything. The kids were cutting up and running around, and Shirley got kind of smarty—no more than any of the others—but her mother said, "Shirley, now you stop that right away; I can't stand that smarty business," and, believe me, she straightened right out. Mrs. Temple seemed to be rather nervous most of the time when Shirley was out of sight, which was only natural because of the lake surrounding the place, etc., but she just turned her loose, and when I was talking to her, she said she hadn't seen Shirley really enjoy herself for a long time as she was then.

We were sitting over by the pool talking, and we suddenly realized that there wasn't a child around. Mrs. Temple said she wished they would come back, so I said I would go to look for them. I found them playing back of the garage and told Shirley that her mother wanted her to go back to the pool. She said, "Oh, dear, these grownups always interfere." But she came along with me and talked a blue streak all of the way over.

I hadn't seen Sis and Buz since they moved to Seattle, and they certainly have turned out to be nice children. Sis is going to be a little beauty; she has the nicest features. Little Buz is a honey—he is the sweetest child. He is 8 now, and Sis is 11. One thing I notice about all these "children of the rich," they do have nice manners when introduced to anyone or when they are spoken to. They always reply so nicely and have quite a bit of poise. But turn them loose, and you wouldn't know them from any other kids.

I also had a good talk with Mr. Bye, who is one of the biggest literary agents in NYC and is a man whom I have wanted to meet for some time. So, I was particularly glad of that opportunity. His wife is charming.

All in all, we had a grand party. Earl was going to take the kids over to the Big House to say hello to old Mrs. Roosevelt; he got them all in the car, and then Sis and Buz decided they wanted a sasparilla. Shirley yelled out of the car window, "Mom, can I have a sasparilla?" Her mother said, "You have never had one; how do you know you will like it?" She said, "Well, Buz says it's just like Coke," so they all got their drinks.

Anyhow, it was all so perfectly natural that it was necessary to pinch myself to realize that here was poor, lowly me on the President's estate, cavorting with the First Lady, the President's grandchildren, and a $10,000,000 movie star. It didn't seem possible, as they all seemed so common and everyday. Of course, nothing could be stilted with Mrs. Roosevelt around. She is simply the *grandest* person I have ever known. I just admire her more and more. You would have died to see her broiling chops with her swimming suit on, engineering all the food, shoving the servants aside, and running around to see that everyone was waited on.

Well, I guess this is about enough—and besides, Nelly says my supper is ready.

[*July 14, 1938*]

DEAR MOM,

Things haven't been very exciting here since the Shirley Temple picnic, and I have been working rather hard. I find it quite difficult, as one must work in a turmoil all of the time. There are millions of interruptions: Mrs. Roosevelt comes in in the morning with a few letters to dictate, some telegrams to 'phone, orders to give the yard boy and help, and instructions for Nelly, who makes all of the ice cream and rolls and, in a pinch, helps to serve. I just start to do my letters and carry out instructions when Mrs. R. is apt to dash in again, ready to do her daily column, "My Day." She dictates that as I type, and it made me rather nervous at first, because she talks so low that it is very hard to understand her. However, I can do it with ease now.

Then, before I get that copied, with her corrections and changes, she is likely to have more instructions, or Mrs. Scheider wants me to do something, or the mailman comes, and I have to get the mail ready to go out and sign for all the registered mail; then Mrs. Scheider will start talking to me, and in the meantime, the 'phone rings and rings, with Western Union messages or some of the family, and I have to hunt up Mrs. R. and get her to the 'phone. Or it is someone calling Mrs. Scheider; all in all, it keeps me on the jump—plenty. However, it is interesting, and I think it is a real privilege to work so close to Mrs. R., as no one can realize what a big and fine person she is without close contact. I have never seen anyone like her.

The names of the places around here are still strange to me, and I find it rather difficult, when Mrs. R. tells me to call the Rhinebeck Exchange and order a cake to be sent down to Zeff's by bus, to know whom to call, what is Zeff's, and on what bus. The swimming pool filter goes on the fritz periodically, and I have to call a man about that. I have a note on the desk now from Bill, the yard boy, to order ten bales of hay and ten bushels of oats, but I haven't found out yet from whom or where to have it delivered. No one can imagine the myriad details of carrying on a job like this without being in it.

I mailed out checks yesterday in payment of some of Mrs. R.'s bills, and they fairly staggered me; for instance, the 'phone bill for the month was $123. Just a small item. The plumbing bill was $300; the light bill, $35, and the gas bill, $10. These people use Western Union and long distance telephone just as we would use a three-cent letter and local calls. It seems to mean nothing to them: Mrs. R. tells me to call New York, or to call the usher at the White House for this or that. And, then, the other day her brother was trying to get a transatlantic call through to London. It makes me dizzy thinking of the expense, but it doesn't worry them, so I don't worry either. I just go ahead and do as I'm told.

Yesterday noon Miss Cook, who, by the way, has a wonderful police dog, Dean, who comes into the cottage every morning for a drink of coffee, had a picnic. We had it on the swimming pool grounds, and it was very nice—not very picnicky, as we sat at a table and the food was served in silver or handmade pewter dishes. However, she had a charcoal grill, and we broiled lamb chops. Sistie and I did this and got them nicely charred. There were Mrs. J. R. Roosevelt, the President's half-brother's widow, Mrs. Roosevelt, Sis and Buz, Mrs. Scheider, Miss Cook, and little Ann Smith, the four-year-old daughter of Miss Cook's maid. She is a cunning youngster but dawdled along with her food until it got on our nerves. Finally, Mrs. R. went over, knelt down beside her, and fed the whole dinner to her—just stuffed in one mouthful after another until poor Ann was almost floundered. Sis and Buz are nice kids and surely are full of life. In the afternoon they all drove over to Tivoli to visit some relative and, thank heavens, I had the afternoon to myself.

I lit in tooth and nail and finished up all the odds and ends that I necessarily had had to put aside because of more pressing things. I worked like a sucker until almost five o'clock; then, when at last everything was done, I put on my swimming suit and had a grand swim all by myself. I took the canoe and went for a boat ride, came back, swam some more, and was just going in when they returned. Sis and Buz came out and asked me if I would please stay so they could go in. I said, "Sure," of course, so played around with them for a while.

Today was quiet, outside of a rather hectic one as far as work was concerned. Didn't do anything out of the ordinary. Didn't feel very peppy this afternoon and decided I wouldn't go swimming, but Buz came in about 3:30 and begged me to go in, so I played lifeguard, as I knew Mrs. R. had somebody in seeing her and couldn't take them. I have been teaching Sistie to stand on her hands in the water, and she is finally getting it swell. She is a most persistent somebody when she once starts something.

Later on Mrs. R., Earl Miller, and Henry Osthagen (Mrs. Scheider's friend) came in; Earl and I played a game of deck tennis and swam some more. Then Miss Cook brought out some homemade ice cream and raspberries, and Mrs. R. brought out a big plate of fruit, and we sat around and talked until after 6:00. I am so darned sick of homemade ice cream I could scream. Ice cream has never been one of my long suits, and this is so rich it fairly makes me sick. I take as little as I possibly can, but I feel as though I never want to see the stuff again as long as I live.

There is a big picnic next Tuesday for Hall Roosevelt, Mrs. Roosevelt's brother, and she has ordered—for 35 people—10 quarts of peach ice cream from Nelly! Makes me ill to think of it. Also, for once in my life, I am getting enough of those big, black cherries: on every available table there are plates of them, and I never go by a plate without grabbing one; I think I have just about reached the saturation point. They are huge ones and certainly are delicious, but enough is enough.

I certainly like living in the country, but I have decided that it is foolish to try it without a lot of money. The expenses are terrible— especially with the swimming pool. And the things that make it so nice are the comfortable house, plenty of servants, cars on order, the pool, money for all kinds of entertaining, and all the conveniences one could ask for, all of which cost many hundreds of dollars. I have decided that enjoyable country life is only for the rich, but I don't see why, if anyone could afford it, he would willingly live in the city.

I think I know definitely now that I won't be home this year. If I spend six weeks up here, I won't really need a vacation, and it is hardly fair to be away from the office so long and make it impossible for some of the others to leave who might want to go away. Have finally gotten around to reading *The Citadel* by A. J. Cronin, and it is a swell book. You ought to get it.

[*July 20, 1938*]

DEAR FRAN,

We had quite a party last night; it was Hall Roosevelt's birthday.* He is Mrs. Roosevelt's brother, and she gave it for him. I didn't particularly look forward to the occasion, as I knew everyone would be strange, but Mrs. R. invited me, so, of course, I went. Hall is the biggest moose you ever saw. He must be 6'4", at least, and weighs about 300 pounds. He has a laugh that, I think, could be heard in Poughkeepsie, six miles away, and it is so contagious that I just about go into hysterics every time he lets loose. He is 47 and filled with the zest of living. This was his party, and, believe me, he had fun!

The guests arrived about 4:00 p.m.—five couples and one bachelor. We all went swimming; then Hall mixed some martinis, and we sat around the pool and drank them and slapped mosquitoes. I sort of hung around Mrs. Scheider, as I knew she wasn't any too keen about getting chummy with the gang either. So, I thought that if I stayed close to her, it wouldn't be too awful. We were supposed to have a picnic supper, but it had rained all morning and looked as though it might pour any minute, so the tables were set on the porches. All afternoon there were two butlers and four maids getting things ready. They had a huge ashcan full of beer on ice, gingerale, soda, and every kind of hard liquor imaginable. Hall drinks like a fish; I don't see how he can possibly stow away so much and still keep his balance. He had had a good start before he ever arrived and kept on drinking after he got here. For a man as huge as he is, he gets around like a young kid; he is light on his feet and particularly agile.

* It was a belated celebration. Hall Roosevelt was born on June 28, 1891.

He had great fun in swimming, pushing everyone in, etc. About 7:30 we went in to supper. Mrs. R. put Mrs. Scheider at a table on her porch and me at another table on Mrs. R.'s porch. I was terribly distressed, as I felt sort of out of place, but by the time supper was served, the men had had enough to drink to be more than congenial. I had half of one martini and called it quits. I certainly am no drinker. I don't like it and just refuse all that are pushed at me. At my table were a lady from Detroit, who had flown here for the party, a retired Army General, a vice-president of General Electric, the bachelor, and a Federal Judge, Judge Biggs, from Wilmington. We had great fun, although I sat next to the Judge and fairly had to keep one elbow in his ribs to keep him from getting *too* confidential.

We had fried chicken, baked ham, homemade rolls, potato chips, salad, fresh homemade peach ice cream, and cakes, and anything one might want to drink. I had coffee but could have had a good, second-hand drunk from the Judge's breath! Mr. Allen, the G. E. man, was a scream, and we all had a good time. Mrs. R. joined us for the ice cream and announced that this was a double occasion as she had just talked to Franklin, Jr., in Philadelphia, and had a new grandson; so everyone drank a toast to the new Roosevelt.

After dinner we all gathered in the dining room and sang "Happy Birthday" to Hall while he cut his birthday cake. Mingo, the butler, gave everyone a birthday candle which, according to the Roosevelt custom, was held until the cake was cut; then everybody wished a wish for Hall and blew out his candle. Sis and Buz had been allowed to stay, and they were surely having fun. Buz is such a darling and such a little gentleman; he helped pass the birthday cake and run errands and got such a kick out of everything.

Hall had brought up from New York a six-piece orchestra, Irving Conn's, and a girl who sang with them. They were grand, and the girl was very good; she circulated around as she sang with the orchestra. She started to sing to Buz once when he was staring at her wide-mouthed, and he blushed about ten different colors and just tore out of the room.

We pushed all of the furniture back and danced. I had the first dance with Judge Biggs—good dancer—and we hit it off fine as he wasn't entirely drunk yet. Then, the next dance I had with Hall, who, incidentally, is a marvelous dancer—so light on his feet. He is so huge that there was nothing to do but just go along with him. However, he was simply dripping with perspiration and had already changed his shirt once. But he continued to drip and to drink.

He had brought with him a Russian lady, who had been up once before. I guess she is crazy about him, but he hasn't a serious thought in his head. Anyhow, she is very nice—nothing cheap or flashy about her—and she and I had a long talk during intermission. She talks brokenly, has lots of style, and is quite fascinating. She was driven out of Russia, spent a good many years in China, and is now living in New York. Her name is Zena Raset.

The orchestra retired to the porch for drinks, and after that, they went out on the lawn and played, and it was simply beautiful; it was such a perfect setting. The girl would sing from way off in the distance, and, for once, the party quieted down and just listened. Then they came in, and the old songs started; everyone bellowed as loudly as possible "Carry Me Back to Old Virginny," etc. Then Mrs. R. got up a Virginia Reel, and of all the crazy, wild performances, that was the worst! And, horrors! I had Hall for a partner. When we had to swing our partners and do the reel, he simply took me right off my feet, and by the time I reached the end of the line, I was so dizzy that I didn't know what I was doing.

Mrs. R. finally rescued me, but by that time everyone was laughing so hard there was nothing to do but call the whole thing off and just collapse. The party broke up about 11:30 as they all had to get back to New York. Mrs. R. drove me home—nothing like being chauffeured by the First Lady—but I was surely glad that I didn't have to ride with Hall. I felt sorry for poor Mme. Raset, as she hadn't, with us, had a drink all evening, and I know she didn't particularly like the idea of Hall's driving to New York, but there was nothing to do about it. I can't think of anything worse than having to drive with him last night. But he really did enjoy his birthday party. One can't help but like the guy—he has the typical Roosevelt charm when one meets him and is so full of fun. He really is perfectly wonderful to Mrs. R. and will give up anything to be with her—take her to the theater, or have dinner with her; he danced with her every chance he had last night in preference to anyone else.

We had quite a different group today for a picnic luncheon—about 25 youth leaders from all over the U.S. I didn't even go out, as I had a lot of work to do and didn't feel like talking to a lot of punks. Mrs. Scheider went out for about 10 minutes but sneaked away as soon as possible. I worked hard all day—Mrs. R. gave me her column and lots of letters, and Mrs. Scheider gave me a lot, so I didn't get through until almost 6:00. Then, as Mrs. R. was still at the Youth Meeting, and the deadline for the column is 7:00, I took Mrs. Scheider's car, drove into Poughkeepsie, and filed it at the Western Union office. Didn't even get my swim in today, but it wasn't a very nice day anyhow, so I didn't care.

Don't read this to anyone, as it wouldn't be too good. I know you won't be shocked at the idea of such a party at the Roosevelts', but there are plenty of people who would be willing to spread it around, and I wouldn't, for the world, bring criticism upon them. It was a good party, and I know you have been on plenty of "good parties" and won't hold it against the Roosevelts. One must be careful in a position of this kind about what one tells, so be discreet.

I think there isn't anything exciting scheduled to come off from now on, so life probably will run more or less in routine. Sis and Buz leave the last of this week.

[*July 25, 1938*]

DEAR MOM,

What a day! I don't know just what I'm supposed to be around here—General Flunky, I guess. I have had to make three trips into Poughkeepsie today. It was a fatal day when Mrs. R. learned that I could drive a car as she thinks it is perfectly swell and keeps me at it most of the time. However, I am glad to do it as it is hard for people who come on the train to get here, and it is necessary for someone to meet them and take them back. There were three people who came this morning, and Mrs. R. herself went in to get them, but before she left, she asked me if I would take them back. So, of course, I said, "Sure."

Mrs. R. was talking to one, Mrs. Scheider had another on Mrs. R.'s porch, when the third showed up; she had driven herself, so no one had to meet her. Mrs. R. asked me to entertain her until she could get to her, so I took the lady into Mrs. Scheider's room. She was Miss Marguerite Wilson, who classes herself as a Cotton Authority—has been in the cotton industry all of her life and is now working toward establishing a cotton research laboratory. She was quite interesting and told me lots about the cotton industry I hadn't even suspected. Such as: one out of every 10 persons depend upon cotton for a living, and that it was the biggest industry in the U.S. even including automobiles, etc. I had her about 15 minutes; then Mrs. R. came in and dictated a couple of letters for me to give Miss Collins, to whom she had been talking. Then, I had to put in a 'phone call for her, and, finally, take her into Poughkeepsie to Vassar College. She was very interesting, about my age, I imagine, and very, very English. I could hardly understand her.

Anyhow, I had no more idea than a rabbit where Vassar was, but Henry gave me some directions, so we started in. Fortunately, she had about an hour to kill; I did get off the way once, and we rode out into the country about three miles before we decided that we were on the wrong road. But we got quite chummy, and we both enjoyed the trip. She is the International Secretary of the Youth Congress, with headquarters in Geneva, Switzerland, and is here to make arrangements for the American Youth Congress, which is to be held at Vassar in August.* Quite a job for a person of her age, I should think, and she said the responsibility rather got her down at times. This was her first visit to the States, and she was so pleased with her reception and couldn't get over Mrs. R. herself meeting them at the train this morning. She was comparing the difference in attitude of the high-ups here and in England and couldn't get over the spirit here.

*This was the Second World Youth Congress that met at Vassarr College August 16–24, 1938. It was attended by more than 700 young people from fifty-four countries and also by Mrs. Roosevelt. Germany and Italy, however, were not represented.

Well, we finally found Vassar; I let her off, then stopped for my lunch, and went back in time to get Mrs. Woodward, the Director of Women's Work in the Works Progress Administration, who had to be taken to the train. And I had never driven to the station! But, armed with directions, and with only about 20 minutes to make the train, we started off. Luckily, I found the darned station, and she had five minutes to spare. I just about had kittens, though, all the way in for fear that I wouldn't find the way and that she would miss the train, but we got there O.K.

Got back about two o'clock, and Buz came in and was on my neck to go swimming. Yesterday when I was out touring around the countryside to see things by myself—it was Sunday—Mrs. Scheider said Buz had come in to get me and was mortally crestfallen when he found out I wasn't there. She called me, but I had gone, and Buz just kept after her to find out if I was coming, why wasn't I there, would she please call again to see if I wouldn't come up and go swimming with him, etc. But I didn't get back until after 5:00 and had had a nice jaunt by myself, and it was a little cool for swimming anyhow. So, today he was just beaming when I said I would go in. Mrs. R. has absolute confidence in me and won't let Sis and Buz go in unless I go with them. And I do have lots of fun with the kids. I have taught them several tricks and have been trying to give Buz more confidence, which he is gaining rapidly. They think it is perfectly swell to have someone play with them in the pool.

Mrs. R. finally came in swimming and also some other guests, and we had a gay time. Henry's two girls, one 12 and one 18, are here until Thursday with Mrs. Scheider, so I had them on my hands, too. Took the younger one canoeing and have promised to play Ping-Pong with the older one tomorrow morning. I asked Mrs. Scheider just what I was supposed to be up here—the poor woman had to do the column herself today—and she suggested that next summer I apply for the job of Recreational Director of Val-Kill Cottage. It certainly is queer how things one has learned become useful at the most unexpected times. When I quit teaching, I thought I was through with Physical Education for good, but everything I learned comes back readily and has been such a big help up here, especially to Mrs. R., who knows that she can trust the kids with me and that I can keep them amused and out of danger. MORAL—learn how to do everything possible as you never know where or when it might be useful!

Tonight Mrs. R.—all dressed up in evening clothes—came running in with 70¢ and said she had completely forgotten to pay a man for some sweet corn she had bought that morning, and would I mind running in to give it to him, as she had promised to send it in right after lunch. So I had to find that duck and give him his 70¢. Thank heavens, Henry took the column in and filed it. If I had had to make one more trip, I think I would have rebelled. It is only about 6 miles, but that is far enough.

This chauffeuring business is O.K. if I only knew the city, but it is a perfectly strange place to me and is a town of about 60,000, so it is not too small. And I get panic-stricken when I have to take these people here and there when I don't know where I'm going myself. However, I say "Yes" every time Mrs. R. asks me to do anything, and I always make out somehow. I feel now that I could find almost anyplace as I have learned the names of a few streets, and that helps.

Many thanks for offering to send the swimming suit, but I have a perfectly good wool one. And just between you and me, I wouldn't want to take a chance on wearing that rubber one in the pool more than once. The rubber rots in the suits, and after one season they are liable to split from top to bottom with no provocation. And I wouldn't want that to happen.

The rumor you heard about Franklin, Jr., and Ethel getting a divorce is a lot of hooey. Walter Winchell started that little morsel, and he also took it back over the radio and reneged on every word he had said. I don't see what possesses people to start such stories when there is no basis for them. The night Franklin called his mother to tell her about the baby, he told her that it was "simply beautiful." Mrs. R., when she came in to tell all of us, was laughing and said she "couldn't imagine that it was very beautiful," but she was glad that Franklin thought so, anyhow.

Poor Bob—I'm afraid he is getting rather lonesome: his letters are getting that lonesomey touch—and I do feel rather guilty about being away for so long. But I figure it will do him good to have the house on his hands for a while. I think he has found it difficult to keep the place even halfway respectable looking and to remember to send off the laundry and such things. I suppose I'll find everything in a turmoil when I get back, but I'm not worrying about it.

Must get to my sewing. Mrs. Scheider gave me a couple of dresses of hers—just wash dresses—but they are swell for up here, so I have been taking in the sides, shortening them, and will finish wearing them out for her. I'm not proud!

August 7, 1938

DEAR FRAN,

I haven't written to you simply because I haven't had anything very special to write about. Nothing so spectacular as the Shirley Temple picnic or Hall's birthday party has occurred. The things that seemed quite outstanding to me when I first came here have turned into ordinary routine happenings now.

I am going to stop in New York on my way home and try to get a new fur coat. Mrs. Scheider is going to give me a letter to Mr. Ritter, and I understand that the guy almost grovels in the dust to be of service and to satisfy anyone working in the White House. Gee, but people are silly! But if that is the way he feels about it, I don't see why I should be backward about accepting a good rake-off on anything I select.

Sis and Buz went home last week, and I certainly do miss them. They were the grandest little sports I ever have known, and it was a real pleasure to be with them. Mrs. R. told Mrs. Scheider that she wants me to go to the Val-Kill Forge and pick out something I want as a gift from her. I would rather be shot than do it, as I feel that she has given me all and more than I deserve. But Mrs. Scheider said that I must, because if I don't, she will send me something anyhow, and it might be something I wouldn't want. Of course, Mrs. R. has had me for luncheons, picnics, evening entertainments, etc., but I suppose those things don't count with her.

We went over to the Big House and went through it the other day.

That is the real family homestead and what you saw in the movies. It is definitely of another era; there are hundreds of almost priceless paintings and other things in it. In the living room is a Dresden china chandelier that is gorgeous; they have never converted it and still use candles as was originally intended. The President's library is the most fascinating place; it is huge and lined with books from floor to ceiling. One could spend days in there and never see all the things: ship models, ship pictures, figures of all kinds, and just hundreds of things which have been given him and which he has collected. It really is a sight!

The setting of the house is perfect; it is approached from a driveway—about a mile long—with huge overhanging trees on each side, and the velvety lawns and beautiful gardens and the view from the back over the Hudson toward the Catskill Mountains is like a dream. It seems hard to imagine one family being able to pay for all that the Roosevelts have. There are large stables, and, in addition, the President owns 2,000 acres in this one spot. There certainly are mammoth country estates in this neck of the woods. But as far as I am concerned, he is welcome to the whole business. Gosh, what a responsibility! I couldn't even afford to live one month at the cottage. Lord, what bills! The plumbing bills alone at the cottage average about $300 a month. The light bills run about $35 a month, the gas about $10, etc. 'Phone bill is almost $100 a month what with the telegrams they send charged to it.

I have heard a lot of inside stuff since I've been here, not only as far as the Roosevelts are concerned but also about other prominent people. I wouldn't repeat it to anyone; in fact, I think I won't even tell Bob but a little of what I've heard, because if any of it ever got out, I would have a guilty conscience. It is nothing bad, just little personal, intimate details that not everyone knows.

I'm afraid I'm going to find it rather difficult to get back to the office routine again, but I'm getting anxious to go home. It certainly has been a wonderful six weeks up here, but enough is enough! The other girl who works for Mrs. Scheider is coming up when I leave but will only be here for about three weeks. I surely got the plum this summer!

President Roosevelt's home at Hyde Park, N. Y., 1934.

Courtesy: Franklin D. Roosevelt Library.

[*August 8, 1938*]

DEAR MOM,

I have no idea when I last wrote to you—whether it was a week or two weeks ago or what. I have simply lost all track of time up here; the days zip by a mile a minute, and I'll be leaving for home a week from tomorrow—August 16. I'll be awfully glad to see Bob again and the house, but I certainly have had a marvellous time up here and feel as though I've been on a grand vacation, even though I have worked quite hard.

That swimming pool has been such a joy, and today, for the first time, I got up nerve to do any diving. I was just plain scared as I hadn't done it for years. But toady I summoned my nerve up and was soon back with the handstands, jackknives, etc., and loved it. I've even been teaching Mrs. R. tricks! Mrs. Scheider told her friend Henry that she would like to keep me up here all summer, and Henry said, "Don't be so damn selfish," meaning that he thought it was mean to take me away from Bob for so long. However, he has gotten along real well—he talks about cleaning the house all the time, cleaning and scrubbing out the icebox, scrubbing and waxing the linoleum, etc., so the place will probably be in good condition. Anyhow, I'll soon get it that way if I haven't forgotten how to work. Six weeks without a bit of housework or cooking will make it hard to get into the swing of things again. And yes, the kittens have arrived—6 of them—I said *SIX!* That fool cat!

Yes, being able to do more than write shorthand and pound a typewriter has been a decided asset up here. Mrs. R. gets me to do all of her shopping for her and meet people at the train and take them back. I'm getting quite good at that, now that I know where the station is. She came in this morning with scads of instructions: had to order 30 hot dogs, a hind quarter of lamb, and 14 slices of calves liver from the butcher; call Nelly and ask her to make 3 dozen cookies and enough ice cream for 20 people and get it ready by one o'clock; call the veterinarian and ask him why the hell he didn't get up here yesterday as he had said he would—and then she asked me if I would go into Poughkeepsie and do the shopping, as it would take Bill so long. I said "Sure," so she gave me a check for $50.00 to cash at the bank, and I bought $13.27 worth of groceries and some other stuff at the department store and hardware store and had a swell time spending somebody else's money. I thought of you in the grocery store—what fun you would have not caring what the bill came to and just picking out the very best of everything.

It took me a little over an hour, and Mrs. R. almost dropped dead when I got back because I had done it so rapidly. She had 14 members of the Youth Congress group here for a picnic lunch on her porch, so, of course, we went, too. She almost always does most of the serving, although the butler passes the plates and food, but she usually assigns one thing to me. Today it was to serve the macaroni and cheese and also the ice cream. We had hot dogs broiled over a charcoal fire in her fireplace, macaroni and cheese, tomato salad, ice cream, oatmeal cookies, and iced tea—very good.

After they left, she came in, and I did her column for her, and then Mrs. Scheider and I went into Poughkeepsie and filed it. When we came back, I went swimming. So, you see, I don't do an awful lot of real stenographic work, but I do manage to keep busy.

Now to answer your question: Mrs. R. always calls me Dorothy unless she gets particularly businesslike; then it is Miss Dow. I don't even attempt my married name, as it is hard for people to get, and Miss Dow just rolls off anyone's tongue. So, it is a matter of convenience for everyone concerned. Mrs. Scheider calls me by my first name, of course.

Today Mrs. Roosevelt gave me a little pewter plate and matchbox from The Forge* on her place; she said it was a little remembrance of the children. She thought that I was so nice to them, and she left them with me quite often. Mrs. Scheider had told me that she insisted on giving me something. I would have given anything if she hadn't,

---

*The Forge was a part of Val-Kill Industries, which Mrs. Roosevelt, Nancy Cook, and Marion Dickerman established in 1926 to train young men, especially local farmers, in cabinet-making. Later the crafts of pewter-making and weaving were added. Operations were discontinued in 1936, and the factory building that had housed the enterprise was converted into apartments for Mrs. Roosevelt and her secretary, Malvina Thompson Scheider. The building used by the Forge was remodeled in 1941 for use as a recreation area.

but what can one do? I certainly miss Sis and Buz since they left, as I had a perfect circus with those kids. Mrs. Scheider also gave me a present—a lovely bud vase in the pewter. Gosh, all these presents get me down. Somehow I don't like people to give me things when I think they have no cause for doing so.

Last week Mrs. Scheider's baby niece and the baby's parents* were here for the week, so I had her to watch in the pool. She is 2½ now and really is a little honey. At first, Eleanor was scared even to get her feet wet, but by the end of the week, she just about had me goofy, as she would jump right into my arms, and if I weren't looking, it would have been just too bad. This week we have no company— about the first week since I've been here.

Incidentally, Mrs. Scheider is going to give me a letter to Ritter in New York City, who is a high-class furrier, and who just about breaks his neck for White House customers and gives them a good rake-off if they go to him with a letter. My raccoon is 13 years old and very shabby, so we decided that I must get a new one this winter. So, on my way home, I'm going to lay over in New York and go up to Ritter's and see if I can't find something. With the rake-off he gives, I should be able to get a very nice coat for $150. I know I wouldn't get gypped. Mrs. R. and Mrs. Scheider buy from him, and I have seen lovely coats that come from there.

Well, if I didn't write last week, you will have to admit I've made up for it with this lengthy epistle. It must take you half the night to read one of my letters. Anyhow, you can thank your lucky stars they aren't written in longhand!

August 19, 1938

DEAR MOM,

Well, I'm back at the office again, and my six weeks' sojourn at Hyde Park is over. Believe me, it was grand and is something I shall

---

*The baby niece was Eleanor Lund (named for Mrs. Roosevelt); her parents were Charles and Muriel Thompson Lund, sister of Malvina Thompson Scheider.

never forget. Everyone was so wonderful to me, and with the pool and the Steinway grand piano, I was all set for a good time even if I had been there alone. I know Mrs. Scheider hated to see me go; she told me that she would like to keep me there all summer, but out of pity for Bob, she wouldn't even suggest that I stay longer. Then, too, I was anxious to get back; after all, there is no place like home.

The Sunday before I left Mrs. Roosevelt asked me to stay for supper and play for them afterward. I would rather have been shot than do it, as I don't touch a piano from one year to the next. However, every time I had a chance up there I had taken a crack at the Steinway and really enjoyed it. Needless to say, all I could play was junk, as I don't remember anything that is worthwhile or that I had memorized. However, they all seemed to enjoy it immensely. Then, Mrs. R. said that, seeing it was Sunday night, she thought we all ought to sing some hymns—that it would be good for everyone's soul. So, she sat down on the bench on one side, and Mrs. Scheider sat on the other, and we really hit it off and had a lot of fun.

I am enclosing some clippings of Mrs. R.'s column, "My Day," wherein she mentions me. Thought you might be interested in seeing them. I taught her a lot along the swimming and diving lines; she was so grateful and was such a wonderful pupil that we got along just fine. I think it was certainly nice of her to mention me in her column; hundreds of people beg her to do it for them, or about things they happen to be doing, and she won't, so I really was quite honored. The columns are syndicated in 56 papers throughout the U.S., so you may have seen them, but I'm sending them to you in case you didn't— not primarily to blow my own horn but just because I thought you might be interested. Mrs. Roosevelt told everyone what a versatile person I was, and it used to embarrass me to death. There is another girl, Miss Orndorff, up there now, and I surely hope she has as good a time as I did, but I'm afraid she won't as she doesn't like to swim or do any of the things that I liked to do, and for which there is every opportunity.

I must tell you about my buying a fur coat. Mrs. Scheider had said that if I really was thinking about getting a new coat this winter, she

would give me a letter to Mr. Ritter, of Ritter Bros., in N.Y.C.*
Inasmuch as I had to change trains in New York, I thought it would
be a good opportunity to get a coat. So, she gave me the letter, and I
found the place all right. I had expected just a nice shop, but it was
quite an imposing building, and the place was on the 14th floor. I
went in and was just about ready to turn around and flee. You should
have seen the joint—whew! One would never guess that it was a store;
the reception room was just beautiful—carpeted in a luxurious light
blue rug and decorated in gold and white. A very lovely girl sat at a
modernistic white desk and greeted me. On the floor was a perfectly
huge, gray Persian cat—a most aristocratic looking animal—which gave
the room much atmosphere.

I gave the girl the letter, and she disappeared, and pretty soon Mr.
Ritter came out, greeted me most profusely, and ushered me into a
private room—sort of a penthouse affair. The same beautiful, light
blue carpet was on the floor, and the furnishings were luxurious. There
were French doors leading out to a little garden, a running fountain,
and a gorgeous view of the city. I was wondering what in hell I had
gotten into and didn't know whether to go through with it or not, but
I thought, "Well, here I am; I might as well see it through."

Mr. Ritter then asked me what kind of a coat I was interested in,
and I told him one that would give me hard wear, that I could wear
every day, and that wasn't too expensive. He asked me what I wanted
to pay, and I said $200 was the maximum. He said he could give me
a coat for $150 that would retail anyplace for $375. Mrs. Scheider had
said that when she bought her coat, she purposely went all around to
the very best stores in New York to see the coats, and that you really
couldn't touch what he would give you for the price. He said he would
show me some coats, and pretty soon in came some girls all dressed
in black fur coats. They paraded around in front of me and opened up
the coats so I could see the linings while he explained the different
points of each. I was almost floored, never having shopped in a place
of that sort before; it was just like the movies!

I chose three that I thought I would like—black Persians—and then

*Ritter Bros., Inc., was located at 224 West 30th Street.

tried them on, but the black wasn't at all becoming, so I asked to see the grays, the natural color. So, the girls came parading around in those, and I found one I liked very much, tried it on, and was crazy about it. Mr. Ritter said that the natural color was far more expensive than the dyed lamb, so I just gulped and said, "How much?" He said that for Mrs. Roosevelt's and Mrs. Scheider's sake, he would make me a price of $225 on it, and he showed me the cost sheet on the coat; it had cost him $285 just to make it, and he said it would retail anyplace for $475. Of course, that was $25 over the maximum I had set, but it was the coat I liked, and he said it would be a lifetime proposition; that there was no wearing out a coat of that kind, and that he would give me four years' free service on it. I rather questioned the sleeves, as they had padded and built-up shoulders, and I told him that possibly twenty-five years from now that would be out of style. He said that I could send the coat back to him at any time, and he would take out the padding, make a perfectly plain sleeve, and it wouldn't spoil the coat in any way. It has just a small, turnover collar, which buttons up tight, is rather boxy, and is lined in a beautiful gray satin. It really is a honey, and I know I couldn't have gotten it retail anyplace in Washington for under $500. I gave him $50 down, and he never asked me one thing about how I wanted to pay for it or anything else. He just asked that I be sure to tell Mrs. Scheider what he had done for me, which I did, of course.

It was the most perfect setting you could ever imagine, with that beautiful Persian cat walking around and looking at herself in the mirrors, which, incidentally, lined the walls from floor to ceiling. There were cigarettes everyplace and very ritzy book matches in gold and blue covers to match the decorations. I was quite enjoying myself by the time I got out of the joint, but, believe me, it gave me a start when I first went in. I never had any idea that poor little me would be shopping in a penthouse! I know the place is good as the Roosevelts wouldn't buy there if it weren't; but nobody had warned me what a really ritzy establishment it was, and I just about passed out during the first few minutes.

After I got out of that place, I walked up to Rockefeller Center to see an exhibit I had wanted to see there and then ambled down Fifth

Avenue and went back to the station and took the 1:30 train for Washington. Bob met me, and we had dinner downtown and thence home. He had the house all slicked up—and two big bunches of gladiolas. Everything looked so nice. The only desperate situation was the laundry, but he had saved me one clean bath towel, which I appreciated. He certainly did well though, but it must have been a lot of hard work for him. He had lost 8 pounds and told me that from now on I would certainly have a halo around my head.

1939

The limelight is something I would never have sought, but I cannot say that I worry about it particularly now that I have had it. I just don't think about it.

ELEANOR ROOSEVELT, *If You Ask Me*

January 16, 1939

DEAR MOM,

Christmas at this place is bedlam, and we are only now beginning to get out from under. Next comes the President's balls and the March of Dimes—which are already coming in—and I suppose we'll get in another mess. This is some place to work.

The other night Bob and I went to the President's Reception for the Judiciary at the White House and had such a good time. It is a much more formal affair than the departmental reception to which we always have been invited before. There were some gorgeous clothes and headdresses and whatnot. After shaking hands with the President and Mrs. Roosevelt and getting something to eat, we had about an hour's dancing in the East Room with the Navy Orchestra playing— and they were good! Saw many people worth seeing, and the whole affair was really beautiful.

I think it really is a privilege to go to those things, even though we know they are far beyond us socially. I was hoping that Mrs. Roosevelt might not recognize me, as I am beginning to feel embarrassed because I have shaken hands with her so much. I thought, with a long line of people passing in front of her, that it would be just routine, but no chance. She greeted me with "Oh, hello, Dorothy, it is so nice to see you here!" I almost died; everyone around turned and looked at me, and I could have passed out. She is the darndest person— nothing ever gets by her.

I also went to the annual card party and tea of the Women's Democratic Club last Tuesday afternoon. Mrs. Helm had bought a table ($10.00) and given it to four of us to use. We left work at 2:00; it was a very nice function. It is also another place where the women are dolled up fit to kill. I never saw so many fancy hats in my life, and jewelry flashed all over the place.

[*June 8, 1939*]

DEAR FRAN,

Well! We have just seen the King and Queen of England, and I am thrilled to death. They are *so* good-looking. The Queen's pictures don't do her justice at all. We went out and lined up on the driveway as they drove out to go sightseeing. The President and the King were in the first car, and it just crawled by. Sir Ronald Lindsay, the British Ambassador, rode with them. Then came the Queen and Mrs. Roosevelt. The Queen is simply lovely and so gracious. She waved and smiled, and, for once in my life, I was in the first row to see something. Both the King and Queen weren't three feet from me, and I really had a thrill out of it. It was worth all of the trouble we have been to these last few weeks.

You can't imagine the preparations, the correspondence, the questions, the invitations, the people who offered to entertain, the people who sent in gifts, and the hubbub of getting ready at the White House. It was just exactly the way the average American home would have been if distinguished visitors were expected. Yesterday I went over to the White House, and it looked like a beehive on the lower floor. I think there must have been a hundred men scrubbing all the paint, woodwork, and floors, and shining up the brass; they were on ladders and on their knees and were just giving the place the grandest cleaning one ever saw. The housekeeper has had the jitters in the first degree, and if she ever lives through it, it will be a surprise.

This city has gone wild. The stores and schools are closed, and the Government departments closed from 10:00 to 2:00. One couldn't have found a square inch of space on the parade route—on the roofs, windows, or what have you—from eight o'clock on this morning. I went out the door and thought I would walk around to see the royal party come in, but one look at the mobs of people streaming by was enough for me. So, I came back in, climbed out on the ramp surrounding the second story of the office, and had a good view of them driving in the grounds and getting out of the cars.

The entourage was so colorful: the British people in their uniforms with bright, gold braid, some of them in red coats, the White House ushers and Secret Service men in high hats and cutaway coats, the soldiers and color guard standing at attention, all of the State Department men dressed up within an inch of their lives, and the diplomats in their uniforms. Couldn't see the King and Queen except from a distance, but this afternoon I was so close that I could have touched either one.

The city is overrun with policemen, the cavalry, and soldiers; the White House grounds are surrounded with a military guard standing at perfect attention; the streets and buildings are all decorated with the British and U.S. flags. There have been endless preparations from all branches of the District Government, and, not the least, from the White House.

All arrangements have been made for the picnic at Hyde Park. I think I wrote the last letter yesterday to the caretaker about the arrangement of the tables, counting the chairs, be sure this is done and that is done, tell so and so to be sure to do this and that, etc. We have received hams, cakes, champagne, wines, turkeys, even a live lamb, and have turned down hot dogs, buns, catering services, and everything imaginable.

I saw the cake yesterday that Madame Blanche, of New York, made for the formal dinner tonight. She is an artist in that line, the foremost in the profession, and, believe me, the cake was a work of art. It must have stood about four feet high, was lavishly decorated with red roses and white flowers, layer on layer, and on the top were four little white columns supporting the King's crown, all made out of sugar. It was gorgeous. They were taking the picture of it when I saw it. The programs for the musicale tonight are tied with the British ribbons and are very interesting.

I couldn't begin to tell you the funny letters we have had incidental to this visit. They have been a scream; everybody from bartenders to spiritualists have offered their services; famous stage people, unknowns, and children have offered to entertain; hundreds of people want the royal autographs, a picture, or a souvenir of the visit. And the dozens of letters we have received over the "hot dogs" question! People have taken it upon themselves to object—strenuously—because hot dogs are to be served at the picnic, and maybe you think we haven't heard about it! Every suggestion in the world has been sent: how to act in Their Majesties' presence, what to do, what to eat, and how to make them feel at ease, just as though the President and Mrs. Roosevelt didn't know how to entertain and weren't noted for their graciousness as a host and hostess. Everyone who has ever come in contact with the Roosevelts knows that there couldn't be two better people to make anyone feel perfectly comfortable and have a good time. But the Great American Public feels that things couldn't go off properly without instructions and suggestions from it. And we got 'em!

We may catch a glimpse of the King and Queen once more before they leave, but it undoubtedly will be very fleeting; however, we are satisfied after this afternoon. In the meantime, I still have loads of work to do.

Later:
Saw the King and Queen again last evening as they were leaving for the Embassy garden party. She certainly looked beautiful—all in white lace with a fluffy little white parasol and long white gloves.

George VI and Queen Elizabeth arrived in Washington on Thursday, June 8, after an extended stay in Canada. They were the first British sovereigns to travel to the Dominion or to the United States, and both visits were intended to strengthen the bonds between the English-speaking countries. Following a whirl of activities in Washington and a visit to New York City and the World's Fair, the royal couple continued northward to Hyde Park on Saturday evening.

After church on Sunday the famous "hot dog picnic" took place at the President's Top Cottage, with Mrs. Roosevelt, dressed in brown gingham, bustling about to make sure that all of the guests were served. Later the King and the President went for a swim in the pool at Val-Kill while the Queen and Mrs. Roosevelt looked on. In the evening the King and Queen departed for Canada from the Hyde Park railroad station. As their train moved out, the local people who had gathered to see them off began spontaneously to sing "Auld Lang Syne," creating a happy memory for Their Majesties to take back to England, which was then only three months away from war.

Dorothy Dow, of course, witnessed none of these happenings at Hyde Park: she did not come up to Val-Kill until July.

[*July 23, 1939*]

DEAR MOM,

I have had the most thrilling weekend. The President came up on Friday, and Mrs. Roosevelt asked me if I wanted to go over to the Big House for dinner with them that night. I told her that I didn't have any long dresses with me, but she said a short dress would be all right, and fortunately I did have one that looked pretty good, so I said I would go. I would rather have been shot, as I must say that I'm not used to dining with Presidents. However, Miss Thompson was going, too, so we both had some cocktails at the cottage, and then Schaffer, the White House chauffeur, drove us over to the Big House.

Mrs. R. met us on the front porch, and we went into the President's little office and had cocktails. It was very informal as there were just the President, Mrs. Roosevelt, Mrs. J. R. Roosevelt, Miss LeHand, the old family lawyer, Harry Hooker, and a cousin, Monroe Douglas Robinson. The President poured out a cocktail for us, and by the time I had downed that one, with the one I had already had at the cottage, I couldn't have felt uneasy if there had been any cause to be. However, these people are the grandest persons and made you feel as though they were simply delighted to have you, and that you have been accustomed all your life to dining with the President. He didn't have on a dinner coat—just an old, gray seersucker, sack suit that looked as though he had slept in it.

Then, we went in to dinner, and, of course, the service was grand. Two colored butlers serve and are perfection itself. The President entertained the whole table with a tale about one of his ancestors, and it was really a scream. He can tell a funny story so well, and the history that man knows is astounding. We had a clear soup, broiled chicken, boiled rice, string beans, beets, hot muffins, raspberries mixed in whipped cream, little cakes, demitasse, and cigarettes. After dinner the President went upstairs to work on a map, and the rest of us went out on the porch overlooking the Hudson and talked until after ten o'clock, when Schaffer called for us, and we went home.

Yesterday—Saturday—at one o'clock we had a picnic at the cottage to which the President came. There were also Mr. and Mrs. Carlin—he is the head of the United Feature Syndicate which handles Mrs. R.'s column—and their five kids; Alexander Woollcott; Frances Parkinson Keyes; the new librarian of the Library of Congress, Mr. MacLeish, and his wife; Frederic Delano, in the brightest blue shirt and the brightest red tie you could ever hope to see; some more Delanos from Boston; the minister of the Hyde Park Church, which the President attends, with his wife and three boys; Harry Hooker; Monroe Robinson; and all of us.

I was helping to pass some of the food, as the butlers and Mrs. R. were all so busy. I passed the President some macaroni and cheese; he greeted me as though he had known me all of his life. He couldn't make up his mind whether or not to take any of the macaroni and cheese, as he said it was very fattening; I told him it was *very* good, and he berated me up and down for being a temptress and then took two great big spoonfuls and said, "If Eleanor has anything to say about it, you will have to take the whole blame." He is a scream when he gets going and had everyone in stitches. Later he left and drove some of the guests around the estate, and, of course, the full quota of Secret Service men and New York State Police trailed around behind him. The atmosphere is quite different when he is here than when Mrs. R. is here alone.

At 5:30 Schaffer picked us up—he drives Car 102, a great, big, beautiful Cadillac with the President's seal on the door—and drove us over to the Big House, where we picked up the rest of the party to go to Secretary Morgenthau's for the annual clambake.

It was the first time I had ever ridden in a Presidential entourage, and it was very thrilling. First came three motorcycle policemen, then the President and the MacLeishes, who were riding with him; then a car full of Secret Service men; then our car in which were Mrs. R., Miss LeHand, Miss Thompson, and I. The motorcycles cleared the way and fairly pushed everyone off the road. When we got to Poughkeepsie, two State Troopers picked us up at the head of the procession, and every time the cars had to slow down, the Secret Service men jumped over the sides of their car and ran beside the President's car, or if the car stopped, they stood on each side of the President's car.

At the Nelson House we picked up all the rest of the cars—just the common herd: newspaper people, the group the President had brought from Washington, etc., and the whole procession went on to the Morgenthaus', which is about 25 miles from there.* It was the most thrilling ride I've ever had—people lined the streets and the road and cheered, and it was a work of art the way the motorcycle cops and the Secret Service men kept the road clear.

The Morgenthaus' place is gorgeous. The house looks as though it had been standing there for a couple of centuries, but, in reality, they built it only about fifteen years ago. It is southern style, with huge columns on the front porch, a wide center hall, and perfectly lovely rooms, decorations, and furnishings. The setting is perfect, with huge trees all around, swimming pool, tennis court, beautiful gardens, and a massive expanse of lawn, where the clambake was held, overlooking the Hudson River hills. Life in a place like that must really be heavenly.

We "chosen few" in the first two cars were taken into the library with the President and the Secretary to have cocktails. We sat around for a while and talked, and then we all went out on the lawn, where

*The Morgenthaus lived at "Fishkill Farms," Wiccopee, near East Fishkill, Dutchess County, New York.

the rest of the party had gathered. Tables were set in horseshoe style, with paper plates, cloths, and napkins. The centerpieces on the tables were apples—from their own trees—just beginning to turn red, and branches from the currant bushes. It was lovely with the red berries and green leaves over the green and red apples. There were also plates of raspberries and muffins on the tables.

Boy! What a feed they put on! I didn't like it much because I don't care for seafood, and, after the picnic at noon, I can't say that I was particularly hungry. We had clam broth; then they brought each one a wire basket filled with steamed clams; on top of that was a baked sweet potato and half of a broiled chicken. I ate a few clams and the chicken; then they brought around steaming, Golden Bantam, sweet corn—the first they had had from their farm—after that, each one got a half of a steamed lobster (I had quit eating by that time); then came watermelon, coffee, beer, cigars, cigarettes, and what have you. Lord! I never saw so much food in my life!

When we had finished eating, three colored entertainers came out; they played guitars, danced, and sang anything anyone requested. They finally had everybody singing and made the President sing a solo—which was surely something. He was having the time of his life.

After it got dark, we all went inside, and the entertainers turned out to be an orchestra for dancing, and we danced until about eleven o'clock. Mrs. Roosevelt, of course, organized a Virginia Reel, and the President sat there and called it and laughed so one could have heard him back at Hyde Park, I think. There were eleven couples in the set, and we kept going and kept going until we were all breathless— except Mrs. R., of course—and the President finally just sank back in his chair, with his tongue hanging out, and called quits.

After it was all over, we came back the same way we had gone, with the escorts, etc., and I still got a thrill out of it. All in all, it was a most successful weekend as far as I was concerned.

The thing that impressed me the most, though, was the lack of awe one feels around the President. I expected to be panic-stricken at the dinner at the Big House, but I would have to consciously think that he was the President of the United States, with the eyes of the whole world focused on him, to realize in whose presence I was. You couldn't possibly think of him as being anyone important without stopping to really think about it. The same was true at the picnic and at the Morgenthaus'. It doesn't make any difference who you are, or what you are, you seem to be just as important to him as the most important person he has ever met. I have never had much to do with him and was so glad of this chance to really meet him. Sometimes I wonder how in the world I ever got this job—hobnobbing with Presidents and their wives and relatives!

[*July 25, 1939*]

DEAR MOM,

I am boss today as Mrs. R. and Miss Thompson went to New York, so I'm running the shack. Been working most all day for a change. But I am contemplating going swimming pretty soon, as it is hotter'n the hinges of hell at the moment. I like it, though, as all of last week was cold and disagreeable.

Yesterday noon we went over to the Big House to witness the ceremony of deeding the land nearby to the U. S. for the building which is to house the records of this administration. Lots of big shots were there, and movies were taken of the President and Mrs. Roosevelt signing the deed. After he spoke, they took various shots of the field, pictures of the house, etc. It is very interesting to see a regular newsreel made. You will probably see it in the movies, and if you do, look for me in the group of people standing around the President's car. But I hope to heaven that I am not in it, and I think they didn't get in any of the people. I stood as far back from the car as I could because I don't want my mug in the movies. The President had a press conference afterward, which was very interesting. His trip west has been called off until the first of October.

I don't know yet how long I'm going to stay up here. I asked Miss Thompson how long she wanted me to stay, but she didn't give me any definite answer—she just said, "Just as long as you're happy, and Bob doesn't object." She said that she doesn't want to break up any homes but would rather have me than anyone else, and that I should stay until I feel I simply must go home. That is bad, as I don't want to stay up here all summer. I'm anxious right now to go home, and, still, I hate to appear overly anxious as they all are so nice to me. I had set August 5th as the deadline, but I suppose I will have to stay until the 12th, and then that will give Miss Orndorff, the girl who follows me, four weeks until they leave September 12th on a lecture trip.

I am going to try to get Bob to come up this weekend, and then I'll do whatever he says. I know he is terribly lonesome, but he is a good sport about it and doesn't urge me to do anything I don't want to do. Mrs. R. said she would like to have him come up—and Miss Thompson, too—so I think I'll call him tonight and urge him. He's funny though; he never wants to interfere with my "business," and I suppose he will think he is imposing, although Mrs. R. specifically asked that he come, saying that she would be delighted to have him, and that I could have as much time as I wanted to go around the country, etc. This is surely some job—I feel guilty drawing money for it.

But imagine what: I got a letter from the Interior Department today saying they had raised my salary from $2100 to $2200 annually. The shock was so great that I was almost speechless. I can't imagine whatever got into them, as seemingly they did it of their own free will. I hadn't asked for it, but it's about time—I'll say that. They surely don't get generous very often.

We are having the worst drought. Everything is completely dried up, and these poor country people without very deep wells are almost without water. Nelly's goes dry periodically, and it takes hours before any more water seeps in. The dust is terrific, and everyone just prays for rain.

(*Opposite*) Mrs. Roosevelt signing the deed to the United States of land at Hyde Park, N. Y., to be used as the site of the Franklin D. Roosevelt Library, while the President looks on, July 24, 1939. Credit: United Press International Photo.

[*July 31, 1939*]

DEAR FRAN,

Bob didn't get up this weekend, and I was very disappointed, but he thinks he is coming up next weekend, and I'll go home the following week, so this session will soon be over.

Mrs. Roosevelt asked me to stay for dinner Friday night; there was a young couple from the Youth Congress, Mrs. R., Miss Thompson, and a friend of hers. We had cocktails and dinner, and then I played the piano, and we all sang until about ten o'clock. Then we decided to go in swimming, as it was a glorious warm, moonlight night. It surely was fun, and Mrs. R. got a real kick out of it.

That reminds me: we had a good laugh out at the pool the other day. Some time ago Mrs. R. and I were talking, and she said she wished she could learn to go into the pool head first. In order to get into the water, she had just been sliding in over the edge. She is a pretty good swimmer, but that is as far as she had gone. I told her that I would be glad to teach her as I had done a lot of that sort of thing in the days when I taught physical education. She was delighted, so we started. I must say she was a good pupil and tried anything I asked her to. Finally, she could dive in—not only from the side of the pool but from the diving board as well. She was anxious to perform for the President, as he had said he didn't believe that she could do it.

One day he drove over from the Big House to the cottage and sat at the edge of the pool. I sat down on the grass beside him, and he said, "I understand that you are the one who taught her all this." I acknowledged the fact. So, Mrs. R. walked out on the board, got all set in the proper form, and went in—flat as could be. She could have been heard down at Poughkeepsie! I thought the President would explode laughing, and his hand came down on my shoulder so hard I almost fell over. Mrs. R. came up red in the face, with a really grim expression, said nothing, walked out on the board again, and did a perfect dive. We all gave her a big hand, and she was pretty proud of her accomplishment—which she certainly should have been.

Yesterday there was much company up here, and I got so sick of talking—it wearies me awfully—that I went off by myself and decided to go out to the pool and loll around in the hammock for a while. I no sooner got settled than the whole mob came trooping out, and that was the end of that. We had fun, although I ruined my right thumb in some way, and it is very sore. I can see that working is going to be a pleasure today! I don't want to say anything about it, as Mrs. R. would have me chasing down to a doctor, and I think it won't be necessary.

Mrs. R. is taking Miss Thompson and me to New York tomorrow to go through the General Motors Exhibit at the Fair. She also has a commercial broadcast to do, so we shall go to that; then, she is going to have dinner with the Morgenthaus and go to the ship with them, as they are going to Europe. Miss Thompson and I are going to have dinner together and spend the night in Mrs. R.'s apartment. Sounds like fun to me. I just hope that it doesn't get too darned hot.

[*August 3, 1939*]

DEAREST BOB,

The following is my usual blurb that is forthcoming every time I manage to do anything out of the ordinary, and it is all here, if you are interested. The World's Fair is really very interesting, and I would like to go back. I was very pleasantly surprised, as I had really expected it to be an ordeal. I think seeing it as we did made it doubly interesting because things are much easier to see if one has special attention on being taken through and doesn't have to buck the crowds.

We had the White House chauffeur and car and left Tuesday afternoon. We went down the Hudson River Parkway, which is a gorgeous drive, and when we reached the Fair grounds, of course all of the guards knew the car and the chauffeur and let us right through to the front of the Administration Building where cars aren't allowed to go. Officials popped out of the place and fell over Mrs. Roosevelt, asking to do this and to do that, to give special escorts, etc., which she turned down. She went in and bought our tickets, and we went out on the grounds to meet a friend of hers, Miss Hickok. From there we decided we had to have a cold drink, so we all went to the Danish Building where Mrs. R. hadn't been before. Watching the expressions on

Dorothy Dow teaching Mrs. Roosevelt to dive. Courtesy: Dorothy Dow
Butturff.

The splash is Mrs. Roosevelt! Courtesy: Dorothy Dow Butturff.

people's faces as we passed them was better than going to the movies. They would glance up, recognize Mrs. Roosevelt, and their mouths would drop open and their eyes would pop. The autograph hounds would come rushing up and had to be shooed away, and people with cameras were all trying to get pictures.

However, we made the Danish Building, and the head of the Danish restaurant was notified; he came galloping down into the lobby, bowing and scraping, and invited us up to a special air-cooled office, where one of the big shots of the Fair was telephoned and told that Mrs. R. was there, and we rather caught our breaths. Then we went up to the dining room, and such service I never saw. They wanted us to try everything on the menu, and all we wanted was a drink. The others had Danish iced coffee, but I stuck to lemonade. Then they brought around a huge cart of Danish pastry and insisted that we select something from that. We all did, and boy! Was it good! Then they wanted us to try the Danish cherry wine and brought us each a glass of that—delicious, too. Then the head man insisted that we try their famous dessert, which none of us wanted after that sweet pastry, but to appease him, we said we would take a little. They brought it in a huge punch bowl; it is a strained concoction made entirely from berries, and they filled soup plates with it, poured on cream heavy enough to cut, and sprinkled it with sliced nuts. My gosh! One spoonful was enough for me, but I ate it to be polite. Mrs. R. asked for the check, but the man wouldn't hear of it—he was honored to have us eat there and was only sorry we could eat so *little*, etc. So, with the continued bowing and scraping of all the waiters and powers that be, we left and looked around the exhibits—at least, we tried to see them.

Every place Mrs. R. moved a crowd would congregate, and what we actually saw was very little. Then Miss Thompson and I left to go to the General Motors Exhibit where the guest relations man was to take us through. Mrs. R. met the Morgenthaus for dinner, and we were on our own for a little while—thank heavens! We were supposed to meet Miss Hickok and Commander Flanagan at 8:15 for dinner, the thoughts of which fairly nauseated me after all that they had pushed down us at the Danish place.

The man at the G.M. Exhibit met us in front, took us right into the

building ahead of thousands of people waiting in line—kind of nice—
and we took the ride through the Town of Tomorrow, which is very
interesting. After we got off, he met us and took us through private
exhibits, private lounges, etc., and it was grand not having to buck
the crowds.

Before we went to the G.M. Exhibit, we went with Mrs. R. to the
housing exhibit with the Homes of Tomorrow, which was swell. Mrs.
R. stopped to buy the tickets, but the officials hopped on her and
said, "Right this way, right this way," and pushed us through a private gate. When we got in, though, the crowd recognized her, and
trying to get through those houses with a crowd following along behind
and autograph hounds trying to get to Mrs. R. was no mean job. I
couldn't see a thing because I was so busy trying to keep people who
asked for autographs away from Mrs. R., as she doesn't give autographs in public. Then we had to meet all the hostesses of the various
houses, etc. After we left Mrs. R., as I said, we went through the
G.M. Exhibit and then walked back to the French pavilion to meet
Miss Hickok, but we got mixed up in the place to meet and never did
see her, for which we were duly thankful, as neither one of us likes
her, and neither one of us wanted any dinner.

At 9:30 the fountains at the Court of Peace put on their display,
which was the most gorgeous thing I have ever seen. The lights and
sprays of water are all controlled by the music, and the fireworks are
interspersed; it was such a gorgeous sight that I was almost breathless. That alone is worth a trip to the Fair and is what Mrs. R. had
particularly wanted us to see. After that we went back to the Administration Building where Schaffer was waiting for us, and soon after
Mrs. R. and the Morgenthaus arrived. They got their car, and we
went to Mrs. R.'s apartment to spend the night.

In the morning after breakfast, Mrs. R. planned our day for us—as
usual. She wanted us to go back to the Fair and gave Miss Thompson
$20.00 for our expenses! I don't know what she thought we were going
to do for that amount of money, but she insisted that we take it. Miss
Thompson had to do the column, so I took a bus and went uptown on
Fifth Avenue and wandered around the stores for a while, getting
back about noon. Mrs. R. had appointments all day, so we went by

ourselves, but, thank heavens, with Schaffer and the car at our disposal. I think if there is anything in the luxury line that I would like to have more than a chauffeur, I don't know what it is. It is a godsend, especially in a big city. He drove us out to the Fair, and we went to the Italian pavilion for lunch. All of the dining rooms in the various foreign exhibits are perfectly gorgeous. Luncheon was $3.00, but we couldn't eat the whole layout, so just had spaghetti and some kind of Italian dessert, and that was almost $5.00 for the two of us.

After that we romped through the Italian, Venezuelan, Chilean, Polish, and League of Nations buildings, just to get a general idea of them, as it would take weeks to see all of the exhibits. Besides, it was rather warm, and we were tired from the night before. Then, we went back to the housing exhibit, and as Mrs. R. wasn't along, we could go through the houses leisurely, and they are very nice. I think I enjoyed that more than anything else outside of the G.M. Exhibit and the lighting display. After that we met Schaffer in front of the Administration Building, and he drove us back to the apartment where we both fairly collapsed from galloping around so much.

However, we cleaned up, and two people came for dinner; then we went to Radio City where Mrs. R. had a commercial broadcast with the Hobby Lobby program.* There the goggle-eyed spectators started in again, but the uniformed guards in the building formed sort of a circle around us, and we got right through and up to a private studio, where they all went over the script. Connie Boswell was on the program, too, but nobody else of any interest. Then the press men had to come in for interviews with Mrs. R. and to take pictures. From there she went down to the stage, and we went to what they call the Client's Booth—for the chosen few—to watch and hear the broadcast. I still think that watching one of those big broadcasts is one of the most interesting things there is to do. I was so scared and nervous for Mrs. R. I almost chewed my fingernails off, but she just takes such things as a matter of course and wasn't at all nervous about

*The Hobby Lobby program, which was first broadcast on the NBC radio network in 1937, featured unusual hobbies of ordinary people, with occasional guest appearances by celebrities. Its host was Dave Elman, for whom Mrs. Roosevelt was substituting.

Mrs. Roosevelt interviewing Connee Boswell on the Hobby Lobby radio
program, August 2, 1939. Credit: United Press International Photo.

it. Everything went well, and at the end we dashed out and went
down on the stage, but Mrs. R. was already surrounded with the
usual mob, and it was quite a few minutes before she could break
away.

Then she started out like a shot—and, believe me, that woman can
walk—and Miss Thompson got caught in the crowd; she called to me
to stay right behind Mrs. R. and to do my best. I wasn't a bit polite;

I just pushed everybody aside, and if anyone tried to stop her to tell his tale of woe, I would go up and get him away. Soon our "guard" met up with us again and took us down the stage elevator. All was well until we got down in the lobby, where we had another battle to get through. Schaffer was right outside the door with the car, and the three of us hopped in and were off. I just flopped down with a groan and said, "Whew! That's almost too much for me," and I thought Mrs. R. would die. She said, "What's the matter?" I was so exhausted I couldn't do anything but mop my face and try to collect my wits.

Of course, she and Miss Thompson are used to it, but it was my first experience in traveling with "royalty," and, while it was terribly thrilling and exciting, I must say it is extremely wearing. You feel quite grand when all gates and services are opened to you free of charge, and everyone is ready to jump at your slightest wish or desire, but it is only basking in reflected glory as far as I am concerned, and there is really much to contend with, too.

We came right back to Hyde Park last night, and I turned in with no ceremony whatever. I may have been more tired sometime in my life, but I don't remember when.

1940

One of the things I believe life intends
us to learn is an adaptability
to the new requirements that may come
to us at any moment.

ELEANOR ROOSEVELT, *My Days*

[*August 8, 1940*]

DEAR FRAN,

Boy! Such a day! Mrs. Roosevelt entertained the Democratic
Women's Clubs from some of the surrounding counties, and they
swarmed on the place like a flock of seven-year locusts! We expected
about 400 until the middle of the morning; then we were informed
that there would be over 800. We called everyplace within a radius
of 30 miles to get more food. Nelly got up at 4:00 this morning to
make 250 cupcakes, and I called her about 11:00 to ask if she could
make 200 more; she very willingly agreed. Then I had to call the
Women's Exchange in Rhinebeck—they were also making 250 cakes—
and told them to send all the food they could get together by 1:00.

On top of that, we had ordered from a woman in New York City
500 doughnuts and 1,000 cookies, which came on the 1:00 p.m. train.
In all, we managed to get 2600 pieces of food together by 4:00, and
Lord knows how many gallons of lemonade and iced tea. The poor
butlers were making crocks full of drinks until their backs were about
broken.

The horde arrived hours early, of course. Mrs. R. and Miss Thompson were over at the Big House for lunch, and I was left to hold the

fort and chase people to hell and gone. First, one of the State Troopers came to say that he had been sent to take care of the parking situation and wanted to know what to do. I said *I* didn't know what he should do; that I was sure he knew more about the situation than I did; that he should go right ahead and make his own plans, and that whatever he thought was best would be all right with all of us. All I did know was that they couldn't drive their cars right up to the cottage; they would have to put them some other place and walk up. So he went on his way.

Then the man came to put up the loud speaker equipment and wanted to know what to do. I said I didn't know; that I was sure he knew more about it than I did, and that he should go right ahead and string up his stuff wherever he thought was the proper place—he had done it before on several occasions.

Next, a newspaper reporter came from Poughkeepsie to cover the President's part in the meeting and asked me what he should do. I gave him the same answer; only I did tell him that he should go over to the Big House, as all publicity was handled by one of the President's aides who was over there. After I directed him how to get there, the head of the Democratic Committee came and wanted to talk to me about the program. To tell the truth, I didn't know one darned thing about it, but I sat and listened to all she told me and gave her as sensible answers as I could because I knew it would make little difference to either Mrs. R. or Miss Thompson.

Then, a few of the guests came and wanted to go to the bathroom. One of the maids came running in and asked me where they could go. I told her to tell them they would just have to wait until Mrs. R. got back, and we found out what arrangements had been made. I wouldn't let them in the house as they probably would have gone over it from top to bottom unless escorted to the bathroom and back again.

Then, Mrs. R. called and told me to tell the maids to start getting everything down on the picnic grounds and gave me a million other

(Opposite) Mrs. Roosevelt at the picnic given at Val-Kill August 8, 1940, for the Democratic Women's Clubs. Courtesy: Dorothy Dow Butturff.

instructions. Boy, what a peaceful day! Don't tell me I don't earn my money up here!

When the meeting started, the President drove over with Secretary Wallace; he sat up on the back of the seat and delivered a short greeting to everyone. He said he and Wallace were going to spend the next four years arguing over which was better—New York corn or Iowa corn! They make a swell looking pair, and the President has such a good sense of humor that one can't help but go for him in a big way. (He looked pretty well, too—much better than the last time I saw him. But don't read or tell this to anyone).

He drove away, the speeches started, and, in the meantime, all of the women started for the food. And such a scramble! Miss Thompson and I stationed ourselves at the table to serve the drinks, but finally I turned it over to someone else and went to help the maids try to get the food dished up and get it to the tables. I don't know why women in a group like that forget their manners and any upbringing they may have had. One would think they hadn't had anything to eat for months: they would grab things off the plates before we could put them on the tables. All in all, it was a great day!

When we finally could break away, Mrs. R., Mrs. Morgenthau, Miss Thompson, and I fell into the cottage, sat and looked at each other, and then had a good laugh over the whole business. Mrs. R. said, "That was just a little afternoon's diversion!" She certainly takes everything in her stride—nothing upsets her at all.

[*August 10, 1940*]

DEAR MOM,

Last night I ate dinner with the President; Secretary of the Navy, Frank Knox; some high-up Army and Navy men, and Colonel William J. Donovan, who had just returned from Europe with a lot of firsthand information about conditions over there. It was a picnic supper at Mrs. R.'s cottage. I sat on the left of the President and surely enjoyed it. He is a grand person and was in high good humor. We had hot dogs and hamburgers, which Mrs. R. broiled over the charcoal grate on her porch, macaroni and cheese, sweet corn, homemade ice cream, cake, and coffee. We ate at 7:00 and sat around until after 9:00. By then the mosquitoes had thoroughly chewed us all. Last year I was quite nervous over sitting next to the President, but this year I had no feeling in the matter whatsoever; he is so easy to be with. I certainly get a kick out of him; he is so full of fun.

It is so interesting to hear the foreign news from people who have been over there, and who really know the situation firsthand. The newspapers are so unreliable that I never believe anything I read in them anymore. Colonel Donovan is of the opinion that Great Britain is going to be able to hold out against Germany, and Madame Tabouis, a French journalist who was here for lunch the other day, also had the same opinion and gave good reasons for thinking so. She was tremendously interesting as she had had to flee France when the Nazis came in because her newspaper had been writing so strongly against the Nazis that they were after her hide. If she goes back, she will be arrested at once. She has no idea where her husband and only son are, and she had to leave her daughter, very ill, in a Paris hospital and has had no word from her. We also had some officials from ex-Loyalist Spain here.

Had supper the other night with Mrs. Morgenthau, Mrs. J. R. Roosevelt, etc., and afterward went to a play put on here by a group of Vassar girls and college boys, calling themselves the Valley Vagabonds; they write plays concerning the Hudson Valley traditions.

Tonight Mrs. R. is taking Miss Thompson, Joe Lash, a house guest, and me to the Berkshire Symphonic Festival at Stockbridge, Mass. It is supposed to be a wonderful musical festival, and people come from miles around. The seats are $5.00 apiece, so it should be good. Wish I could spend $20.00 as easily as Mrs. R. does. I had to make three long-distance calls before I finally got our reservations; they are in a box, but we had to take them as they were all that were left.

Tomorrow, Sunday afternoon, Mrs. R. is giving all of the children in the neighborhood a little party; they are from 6 months to 10 years old. Ought to be really something doing then.

[*mid-August, 1940*]

DEAR FRAN,

Have been enjoying my stay up here, but it has been too cool for swimming. We went to the Berkshire Symphonic Festival the other night. It is held in a huge Music Shed at Tanglewood, where the Boston Symphony Orchestra gives concerts. It was a wonderful occasion, and I more than enjoyed it. We took a picnic supper along and ate it in a cow pasture on the way.

Going anyplace with Mrs. Roosevelt is always a shock to me. We get so accustomed to her around here that we forget she is a personality until we go someplace like that Festival; then the police open the way for her car, we drive right up to where we are going, plow through lines of clapping people, and the flashbulbs are popping from every direction, people are trying to shake hands with her, and the newspaper men hover about—it is quite startling. I really don't like it, as I feel so conspicuous that it is rather embarrassing.

We had a box, and the poor woman wasn't seated more than two minutes at any time when the orchestra wasn't playing, as people would come up to shake hands, etc. She drove her own car, so afterward we left like a shot—jumped in the car, the police made way for her, and we were off. Got home about 1:00 a.m. She's funny, too; she would greet someone who had come to shake hands and talk as though she had known him all her life. After he had gone, I'd ask her who he was, and she would say, "I haven't the *slightest* idea!" Some she knew, some she knew the faces but not the names, and some she didn't know at all but evidently should have known.

August 20, 1940

DEAR FRAN,

I'm surprised to hear that you are going to vote for Willkie, but I suppose there is no changing you black Republicans. However, let me say this—don't form your opinions from columnists like David Lawrence, whose clipping you enclosed. His is only one man's opinion, and he would do anything to smear the President. If you want to read columnists, read those which are both for and against. But I suppose the only paper you see is a Republican one, which naturally would have only the Republican columnists.

I read everything I possibly can on Willkie, as I know nothing much about him. I listen to him speak whenever I can, but I still can't see where he has anything for which I would care to vote. Government is a business, and he has had no experience whatever in that business. He knows nothing about Congress or foreign affairs. While I agree with you that there is more than F.D.R. and more than one man who could run this country, I still think it can be run better by someone who has had his fingers in this foreign business ever since its inception and knows the ins and outs of the whole matter. I'm afraid that Willkie would find himself very much in a fog if he got in—with no experience in back of him on how to handle Congress. He would find that he needed great tact, diplomacy, and every other ability. However, this is a free country, and I'm sure everyone has a right to vote for whomever he pleases.

Later:

I suppose you heard Willkie give his acceptance speech the other day. Wonder what you thought of it. I am sure that your reaction probably wasn't the same as ours. Personally, I thought it was very amusing; the guy didn't have one thing to offer that isn't being done at present or hasn't been tried and failed. I didn't expect much but did hope for a little more than that.

Secretary Ickes really took a blast out of him last night, and when they begin to uncover his past activities, he is really going to be "exposed." His attitude toward public utilities, his involvement with the Insull business,* his statements about the people of the South, and his testimony before the Congressional committee are really going

---

*Samuel Insull (1859–1938) was an American public utilities magnate who built and managed utilities in five thousand communities in thirty-two states, having assets of over two and one-half billion dollars, before his spectacular failure in April 1932, when he was forced into receivership and thousands of small investors lost their savings. He fled to Greece but was exonerated on all charges of fraud and embezzlement at a trial in 1934. Nevertheless, his name became a symbol of frantic and unsavory financing.

to do a lot of damage to that guy. I suppose, too, if he gets in, labor is going to quit hollering for higher wages and shorter hours, and capital is going to give it anything it wants! I wonder what the man would do, with his lack of experience in government and in handling Congress, when he tried to get some of his ideas through.

He was pretty safe in challenging the President to public debates, as he knows the President couldn't possibly accept the challenge, and it is a good thing for Willkie that he can't. The President could mop up the floor with that guy in 15 minutes as he knows, from long experience, the various pressure groups, the demands of the people, and the difficulties with Congress. Willkie is only a raw recruit and couldn't possibly know the answers. I surely wish I could work in the campaign, as it must be very exciting. Just hearing them talk about it gets me all thrilled, and I crave to be in it. However, the Hatch Bill* would prevent me from doing a darned thing, even if I did have the time. Mrs. Roosevelt says that I am "completely Hatched!"

August 30, 1940

DEAREST BOB,

I've been holding the fort alone since Sunday, and things really have been buzzing. The other afternoon I was absolutely all alone—the maids had all gone to town, the chauffeur was off, the yard boy, Bill, had his day off—and things happened so fast and furiously that I didn't get time to go to the bathroom and almost burst before I got there! There were about six long-distance 'phone calls, myriads of telegrams, and arrangements to have three people met at the station, two of whom I finally had to meet myself, as I couldn't get anybody else. This is the craziest job! I'm everything: housekeeper, receptionist, hostess, secretary, and what have you.

And yesterday I certainly had *some* day. In the first place, Mrs. R.

*The Hatch Act, sponsored by Carl Hatch, Senator from New Mexico, 1933–41, was signed, reluctantly, by President Roosevelt on August 2, 1939. It forbade campaign solicitation of funds from, or electioneering by, federal employees and excluded all but top policy makers from active politics. A 1940 amendment brought under the act all state and local employees paid in full or in part by federal funds.

gave me all the work to do about assigning rooms at the Big House for the Norwegian house guests and royalty they are entertaining—also making the table plan for the big lunch they had. She dictated the rooms to me but went so darned fast that, as I am not familiar with the Big House at all, I didn't dare miss a word, and it was something! Then, I went upstairs to do that, and she came up with pages of stuff—picnic today, picnic tomorrow, guests for Sunday and Monday, menus up to Thursday, memos to Schaffer, to the help in the Big House, the help in her apartment, memos to the girls here at the cottage, food to order for all the picnics and through Monday, people to call, to write to, etc., and then she calmly announced that we were all going to the Dutchess County Fair with the President, and I should be ready at 1:45 when Schaffer would pick me up at Nelly's! Such a woman!

Anyhow, I worked like a sucker to get everything done that was necessary and was ready to go to the Fair. I always get a thrill out of going anyplace when the President goes because I like to watch the motorcycle escort and the Secret Service men. All the kids were put in the car with me—three of Hall Roosevelt's girls from Michigan, ranging from about 8 to 15 years, the two little Norwegian princesses, aged 8 and 10, and their governess, and the little Norwegian Count something or other,* about 10 years old. I rode in front with Schaffer. The President had Princess Martha, the mother, the lady-in-waiting, and Franklin, Jr. Mrs. R. drove her own car with Miss Thompson and some other guests.

We got to the Fair at Rhinebeck and watched the horse show for well over an hour, and I loved it. It is the first time I had ever been to a horse show, and Monte Snyder, the President's chauffeur, who

* Son of Countess Ragin Ostgaard.

(*Overleaf*) President and Mrs. Roosevelt at the Dutchess County Fair, Rhinebeck, N. Y., August 29, 1940. In the automobile with the President are Princess Martha of Norway, her two daughters, and Countess Ostgaard's son. Mrs. Roosevelt is standing at the side of the car. Courtesy: Franklin D. Roosevelt Library.

knows a lot about horses, stood beside me for quite a while and explained the various gaits to me, and it was so interesting. The horses are beautiful; they just seemed to know they were showing off and acted so smart. They had jumpers and all kinds of different classes. Then they had a show horse, Silver Nip, who did all sorts of tricks for entertainment, and he was a honey.

When we started back we went through the amusement center, and the governess said she thought it was a shame that the children couldn't stop there. I said I didn't see any reason why they couldn't, so while we were held up in traffic, I ran back and asked Mrs. R. She said she had no objection at all if it was all right with Princess Martha. Evidently, they already had her consent, so Schaffer pulled out of line, and we started with these six kids. The little girls understand English fairly well if you speak very slowly, but they can't speak it at all and would start jabbering at me in Norwegian, and you know how much Norwegian I understand! Oh—it was great stuff! The governess both understood and spoke English well, so we got along fine.

The kids were so excited they wouldn't wait for us to buy tickets; they just got on the Whip, and I had to dash around and buy the tickets. When we got them off of that, they went on the merry-go-round; then they split—some on the Ferris wheel and some in automobiles. Schaffer was grand, and with him, the governess, and me, we managed to keep them more or less together, and they had a grand time. We stayed over an hour and then bought them all balloons, but I was glad when they were once more back in the car. Needless to say, I felt rather a heavy responsibility, taking care of royalty, but I noticed that a State Trooper, standing well in the background, followed us everywhere we went on the grounds, so that made me feel better, to say the least.

Mrs. R. had given me $10.00 for the tickets and things, and I don't mind telling you there wasn't enough to wink at when we left. Got back to the Big House at 6:00, dumped them there, and came over to the cottage. Everyone was having tea here, including the President, and Mrs. R. came out and asked me to come in and have some, but I refused as I felt so dirty and messy. Then she asked me to stay and have dinner at the cottage with Miss Thompson, as she wasn't going over to the Big House, so I did that. We mixed a couple of martinis, unlaxed, had a leisurely dinner, talked a while, and I got home about 10:30—exhausted!

We get so embroiled up here with royalty, Presidents, Cabinet members, etc., that they don't make any more impression on me than the WPA people, some of whom also have come for visits. It is a great place, and I surely enjoy it.

Last Saturday was the annual newspaper picnic here at the cottage, and it simply poured all evening, so we had to have it inside—about 50 people—and it was messy! The President came over, and we had tables, food, and drinks all over the house, but everything went well, and everyone had a good time in spite of the wet weather.

Got up here early this morning to try to do some of the things I had to leave yesterday. There is a picnic at noon. Incidentally, at the last picnic we had, I was talking to Mrs. Waldo, who is quite a cat enthusiast. They are wealthy people from Connecticut—he owns a couple of newspapers or something—and she told me about a book that they enjoyed so much and said she would send me a copy. And, by gosh, she did! Got it yesterday—called *Puss in Books*. It is an anthology on cats. It looks grand, and I can hardly wait to get at it.

Must stop now; have just been informed that the picnic is to be at the President's cottage, which means carting all the stuff up the hill— and to cap the climax, it is raining. Nuts!

[ca. September 6, 1940]

DEAREST BOB,

Today we have another picnic, Saturday a tea at the Big House for the teachers of the Hyde Park School District—about 50—and at night is the annual clambake at the Morgenthaus', to which we all go, the same as last year. That is fun.

It has finally cleared after a week of rain, but it is quite cool. I suppose Mrs. R. will be dragging me in swimming again when she gets back. It is too cold for me to enjoy it, and I protest vigorously, but she shouts and hollers for me all over the house when she is ready to go, and nothing will do but I must go, too. However, I think it is a little too cold even for her today, but I swear she is steam heated as nothing seems to bother her. The little Norwegian children have been over every day, and the cold air and cold water don't seem to bother them at all. I think I'm getting too old for such foolishness; I like my water warm! I've been playing a lot of badminton with Mrs. R. and like the game a lot. She is certainly a good sport.

September 9, 1940

DEAREST BOB,

If the next time you see me I'm speaking with a foreign accent and expect you to bow, scrape, and curtsy, don't be surprised. Would you like to know with whom I ate Sunday dinner yesterday over at the Big House? The President, Mrs. Roosevelt, Empress Zita of Austria and her four children, the Archduke Otto, Prince Felix, Prince Ferdinand, Princess Adelhaide, the Crown Princess Martha of Norway, Countess Ostgaard, Franklin, Jr., and Ethel, Secretary of Commerce Harry Hopkins, and Miss Thompson! If you can think of any more imposing array, I'd like to know about it. I almost died! The only reason I ate there was because of necessity, and I don't mind telling you that I had no desire to do so.

Miss Thompson was howling around all morning that she had to go, and I was gloating at her uneasiness when Mrs. R. called up and told me that I should stand by and be ready to come over in case the Austrians brought an extra person with them because, if they did, that would mean 13 at the table, which could never be. So, I was to be ready to be the 14th if necessary. Of course, Miss Thompson had a good laugh on me, and I told her, when she went over to the Big House early, to please plead my cause and get me out of it if there was any way possible, as I surely did *not* want to go. She told me to go home, change my clothes, and be ready by 12:45, as they would know by that time whether or not I would have to go. So I did, praying every minute that I could stay at Nelly's. But she called and said, "You have to do it." And she sent Monte and the President's car for me.

I went over, and all of them were sitting on the porch, but Mrs. R.

was perfectly swell; she knew it was an ordeal, so she came running out to meet me, introduced me all around, and it really wasn't bad at all. I can't say I enjoyed it, as I have such trouble understanding foreigners even when they speak English fairly well, but I sat between Princess Adelhaide and Miss Thompson, and it was possible to keep up an inane conversation of sorts. And, then, the President engages the whole table in talk a great deal, and Franklin, Jr., is priceless.

The children were most ordinary looking—they ranged from about 18 to 30, I would say—but the Empress was quite picturesque in black drapes and a long dress. Of course, I'm getting used to the Norwegians now, so they don't bother me. The little Norwegian children were brought out on the porch to meet the Austrians, and every one stood up, and they went around and shook hands and curtsied to each one. And the Norwegian lady-in-waiting, when they said goodbye, made a deep curtsy to each Austrian. Even little Prince Harald—3 years old—went around, shook hands, and made a deep bow from his waist to each of us. Funny business!

Afterward, coming back over to the cottage, Mrs. R. thanked me very much for being willing to come over. I told her it was a labor of love, and she said, "It surely was!" I think she didn't enjoy it any more than anybody else, but it was quite an experience, and I'm glad now that I went. I am reading a book about the Empress Zita and King Karl of Austria called *Imperial Twilight,* and it makes having met them just that much more interesting. I wish that I had read the book first.

The night before, Saturday night, was the clambake at Secretary Morgenthau's. Of course, the Norwegian royalty were there, the Roosevelts, Harry Hopkins, and the hoi polloi. We had the same food as last year, the huge bonfire in the middle of the horseshoe tables, a perfect night, the same colored entertainers, and the same dance inside, with the Virginia Reel. However, there weren't so many there, and, for some reason, it seemed nicer than last year. We had a lot of fun.

I really have been stepping out a little high, don't you think? I guess some people would be pretty set up about it, but, somehow, I don't feel a bit different than I did before!

Henry and his friend, Roy Cheney, are here—back from their fish-ing trip on the St. Lawrence. Haven't seen them yet but understand that they had a good catch. Mrs. R. has gone to New York for the day; tomorrow she goes seaplaning all over the State of New York to see NYA projects;* Wednesday she goes to New York again, and, then, she says, the rest of the week she is going to relax. I'll believe it when I see it!

The Norwegian royalty leave today, which will be one less worry, so it should be a fairly calm week for us. And next Saturday morning I leave for home. Um-m-m.

[*September 11, 1940*]

DEAREST BOB,

Well, I guess my plans have changed again. I won't be home until Monday afternoon. Mrs. R. sat down and worked out her schedule and found that she would, in all probability, not be here but an odd day or two for a couple of weeks, and Miss Thompson is going with her. So Miss Thompson couldn't see any sense in Mollie coming up here and twiddling her thumbs. She said she would have the mail all sent down to Washington, and we could handle it there. Consequently, she wanted me to stay over Sunday, if I could, for the general cleanup and to help clear out some books, etc., and she 'phoned Mollie not to come up until later in the month.

Miss Thompson said you would probably kill her for keeping me here over Sunday when we could have the day together. She amuses me; she is so afraid she is asking me to do something I might not want to do or something to which you would object. I told her that we had had nothing at all planned for Sunday, so I was sure you could bear up if I didn't get home until Monday.

---

*One of Mrs. Roosevelt's special interests was the National Youth Administration, established in 1934 by executive order to provide work for unemployed young people. Headed by Aubrey Williams, the agency gave part-time work to two million students and 2.6 million youths not in school until the program was terminated in 1942. Among the NYA projects in New York State were Camp Jane Addams (for girls) at Bear Mountain Park and a camp for boys at Lake Hill.

Mrs. R. told me the other night that she hates to see me leave—which I take as quite a compliment. With all the people she knows and all she does, I don't see how she would even know that I exist other than as a useful person to take care of details for her.

Worked yesterday. Mrs. R. was at the Big House, but Henry was here. They asked me to stay and have lunch with them. We had an old-fashioned before lunch, and we all felt quite hilarious. Had lots of fun—the three of us giggled through the whole meal. Mrs. R. came over in the afternoon and at about 5:30 came up and asked me if I wanted to put on my suit and play a game. I said I would play the way I was, and it tickled her to death as it was cold and rainy, and she knew I wasn't taking any chances of having to swim. She said she was going to put on her suit, but she was in her bedroom about one minute and then came out and said she had decided to play in her dress—and I had the laugh on her. We played three games of bad-minton and one of deck tennis and had lots of fun. Didn't get home for dinner until after 7:00.

Today I play chauffeur as Schaffer has gone to Campobello, and it is Bill's day off. I know I have to meet Mrs. R. at 8:30 tonight, and I have to take Diana (Harry Hopkins's daughter) to the doctor this afternoon, get some eggs and cream for the cook, and, I suppose, do a million other things before the day is over. Right now, I'm super-vising Diana, who is helping (?) me get up the mail. I showed her how to fold letters, put them in the envelopes, and stamp them, and she is simply delighted.

Miss Thompson says she has a new name for me—"The Fitter-inner."

[*September 12, 1940*]

DEAREST BOB,

I got here six weeks ago tonight, and it has seemed like a short time—looking back on it—but I wish I were going back to Washington on Saturday. Personally, I don't see any reason why I couldn't, because I know there will be very little work done around here on

Sunday. However, Miss Thompson seems to think I can be useful in the cleanup. But I think she just wants me to stay until they go. So, I guess I can stand it until Monday.

We worked most of yesterday, and I ate both my lunch and dinner here at the cottage with Miss Thompson and Diana Hopkins. At 8:30 we were to meet Mrs. R. at the station and take her to the Jewish Community Center. We allowed plenty of time to get there but were held up when we ran into a fire and a dumb policeman who knew nothing about rerouting traffic. By the time we arrived at the station we were late. About twelve men descended on us and asked if we were looking for Mrs. R. We said "Yes," and they said that she couldn't wait; she had taken a taxi, and we were to follow her.

So, we went on to the Community Center and were there about 1½ hours. Mrs. R. spoke; then we grabbed her afterward, and she drove us home. There was an awful crowd of people. Going home, she said she never could get the lights on her car straight—asked me if I had any trouble. I didn't know what she was talking about. Then, it came out that she never knew when the bright lights were on and when they were dim. So, I showed her that when the bright lights were on, a little red dot came on at the top of the speedometer. She was absolutely amazed—had never noticed the red dot before and was so delighted to find out. I told her that I would take her out some day and show her how to drive her car! It really is a honey to drive—but if you think the Ford is the only body that rattles, you are sadly mistaken. Hers is a new, big Buick, and Schaffer drives a Cadillac, and they both squeak and rattle worse than our Ford ever did.

It is so cold up here today that my hands are just about frozen. I wish I had some heavy clothes, but there is no use getting anything now, as I'm sure I'll be home in a few days. Diana is running around here with a heavy coat on and shivering, and I'm bundled up as much as possible. It certainly seems to me that we haven't had any summer at all. It has been too cold to swim much or to play strenuously as we did the previous years.

1941

Human relationships, like life itself,
can never remain static.
They grow or they diminish.
But, in either case, they change.

ELEANOR ROOSEVELT, *You Learn by Living*

Dorothy Dow's letters from Val-Kill in the summer of 1941 sound a note very different from those of previous years: she is disenchanted and critical of Mrs. Roosevelt's circle of friends. Probably the heat of that summer and the discomforts of her pregnancy affected Dorothy's outlook more than she realized, but it seems equally true that, as she wrote to her husband, "things aren't the way they used to be."

By the summer of 1941 the Nazi march of conquest was dominating the attention of the world, although public opinion in the United States was still greatly divided. Pacifism appealed strongly to the idealistic young; isolationism appealed just as strongly to many of their elders. Nevertheless, Congress had reluctantly passed a one-year Selective Service Act on September 6, 1940, and the first draftees went off to camp for basic training in late October. The Roosevelt sons had not waited to be drafted. By the summer of 1941 all four were in the armed forces: James in the Marines, Elliott in the Air Corps, Franklin, Jr., and John in the Navy.

All through 1941 the apparatus of war was being set in place amid secret wrangles and open conflicts between the president and Congress. Passage of the Lend Lease Act in March provoked the greatest debate, for many realized that there could be no turning back afterward. Indeed, Senator Vandenberg termed it "the suicide of the Republic." It was soon followed by agreements permitting the United States to establish bases in Greenland and Iceland for the convoys of merchant ships that would carry supplies to Britain and by a presidential order directing American warships to protect those convoys as they crossed the Atlantic. How much the president confided in Mrs. Roosevelt about such matters it is impossible to say. She was careful not to ask questions or pry into the secrets of diplomacy and preparations for war lest she inadvertently reveal something not for public knowledge, but, as she wrote in her *Autobiography*, it was impossible not to know when important matters were afoot or to remain unaware of the seriousness of the international situation.

Her inability to help in this critical period upset her. As early as June 1940 Malvina Thompson had written to Anna Boettiger that her mother was "quite uncontented . . . She has wanted desperately to be given something really concrete and worthwhile to do in this emergency, and no one has found anything for her. They are all afraid of political implications, etc., and I think she is discouraged and a bit annoyed about it." And, in fact, Mrs. Roosevelt was given nothing definite to do until late September 1941 when she became assistant to the head of the Office of Civilian Defense, New York's Mayor La Guardia.

But there was more than the absence of worthwhile work to trouble Eleanor Roosevelt in the summer of 1941. For one thing, the president had been very ill from May to July: he had had intestinal flu and had undergone two transfusions made necessary by a severe iron deficiency anemia. During June he suffered intermittently with a sore throat and low grade infection. He tired easily and was, Mrs. Roosevelt said, "*very* edgy." She worried about him, telephoning daily from Campobello.

June was a bad month in every way. Early in the month Missy LeHand had been paralyzed by a stroke from which she never recovered, although she lingered on until August 1944. Germany attacked the Soviet Union on June 22, while at home the Sleeping Car Porters Union and NAACP threatened to march on Washington on July 4. They predicted that from fifty thousand to one hundred thousand black men would march that day if the government failed to give guarantees of nondiscrimination in federal hiring. Only the president's establishment of a Fair Employment Practices Commission on June 25 averted the march. And Mrs. Roosevelt had also to think about Sara Roosevelt, the president's mother, and her brother, Hall. The elder Mrs. Roosevelt was ill for three weeks in late May and early June, narrowly escaping a stroke; her condition became worse over the summer, and she died on September 6. Hall Roosevelt's alcoholism had for years caused his sister much anxiety, but in the summer of 1941 he was deteriorating rapidly; he died on September 25 of cirrhosis of the liver.

With so many worries, Eleanor Roosevelt behaved characteristically in her display of frenetic activity. She believed that work of any sort brought relief to a troubled mind. "If I feel depressed," she once said, "I go to work. Work is always an antidote for depression." Not everyone, of course, responded in that way to the feeling of being trapped by events: some went about their duties glumly; some chattered endlessly, but in that last summer before the war everyone sensed the coming of change. Undoubtedly, Mrs. Roosevelt's restless activity, as well as Miss Thompson's depressed state of mind and the general lack of enthusiasm pervading Val-Kill, heightened Dorothy's impression that everything was now different, and colored the letters she wrote that summer.

March 11, 1941

DEAR MOM,

With good luck and the grace of God, you will be a grandmother next fall! I haven't told Mr. Magee as yet and don't know how long I shall work. The doctor said that I could work until the seventh month without doing any harm. I told Miss Thompson, and she is simply delighted. She was quite funny. She was so pleased over it, and yet about every other word was "Are you going to resign? You aren't going to quit, are you? I'm going to miss you like hell. Don't know how we'll get along, etc."

Naturally, I do want to quit as this is a strenuous existence, and with a child, even with capable help, it would be very difficult. But it would be foolish for me to resign until I see what complications might arise in the future.

While I was talking to Miss Thompson, Mrs. Roosevelt came in, so we told her, and she was tickled pink. Miss Thompson wants me to go up to Hyde Park this summer, but I told her I didn't want to, as by then I would look like a sack of potatoes. Mrs. R. said, "Tommyrot, you can go and hide in the bushes if you want to!" Miss Thompson said she wouldn't make me work, but that I might want a change for a couple of weeks, and she could fix it up to detail me to Hyde Park if I wanted to go and it was all right with the doctor. However, I think I wouldn't be very comfortable up there this summer as there are too many people around, and I would be too self-conscious. We finally left it as an open subject.

Miss Thompson said that she wanted to buy all the baby clothes! She simply adores getting the necessary things for a baby and asked if I please would give her that much pleasure. Mrs. Roosevelt also wants to give us something; she has a passion for a certain kind of screened-in crib that is very expensive and about the most useful thing one could get. She said that it is "portable, foldable, absolutely safe for months, as there is nothing the baby can get his head stuck in, and he can't fall out, and would I like that?" I was so taken back that I didn't know what to say, as I haven't given any such things a thought. Perhaps I'd better start thinking.

Monday noon
[June 30, 1941]

DEAREST BOB,

Well, I arrived safely. It was hotter'n hell for a while yesterday driving up, but, at that, I think just as comfortable as on the train jaunting across New York. After we hit the parkway out of New York, it was grand, and I must say that Schaffer was most solicitous. This service is too much for me! We got to Nelly's at seven o'clock, and she was delighted to see me. Brought Schaffer in and bought him his dinner at Nelly's. Her place is really nice. I didn't take my old room. She said I could have whichever one I wanted, and I decided it would be much nicer to take one of the new rooms—it is small with only a single bed in it—*but* it is right next door to the bathroom, which is the primary consideration at the moment. I have the bath all to myself, which is pretty nice after what I had to put up with last year; it has a shower, too.

Schaffer stopped for me this morning to bring me up to the cottage. They didn't get in from Campobello until late last night and were eating breakfast on Mrs. Roosevelt's porch, so I went out there to say hello to them. Miss Thompson looks terribly tired, and she says she is and that she feels so depressed all of the time. Gosh, I wouldn't have her job for anything in the world. She was telling me what she had to do at Campobello. Mrs. R. seems terribly restless and nervous. If she doesn't wear herself to a frazzle it won't be her fault. Henry is here for just one day, and thus far he hasn't been able to say two words to Malvina.

I am in the new recreation house, made out of the old forge, and it is really beautiful. Henry had it done at a cost of about $2,500. I have a big room, and the place is all insulated, so it is nice and cool. At one end of the room are a sink and shelves and also a lavatory (which is handy), so that when they give a dance or party, all the essentials will be right here. It is certainly much better than that room upstairs, and it is easier going in to Miss Thompson, too, than running up and down stairs.

Mrs. James Roosevelt and Jimmy are here for a few days, and Miss Thompson just brought Mrs. James* in to meet me. I don't blame Jimmy for going for her in a big way as she certainly is a good-looking girl and seems terribly nice.

Babies still seem to appear on the horizon. Miss Thompson told me that Franklin and Ethel are expecting another; Ruth (Elliott's wife) is having another, and Betty Winsor (Elliott's first wife) is having another. I'm beginning to feel right in the swim of things.

I think they are going to take the President's mother to Campobello

*This was James Roosevelt's second wife, Romelle Schneider.

on July 7th; that, at least, is the present plan. I suppose they will be gone for a week. Miss Thompson said she hasn't any idea what goes on after that. She asked me how long I would stay, and I said that I would stay for three weeks or until they got back, and would be here so that when Prudence came, I could show her the works. Miss Thompson said she would so much rather I would be here when they are away as I know the workings of the place and can do the ordering and get a plumber, etc., if anything should go berserk. I've been pretty busy this morning trying to check up on supplies and see what is here, what's not here, and getting my office arranged. Lots of mail to get out, too.

Mrs. R. has a new Buick—a convertible, close-couple job*—gray inside and out and is really a hot-looking number. Just between you and me—Mr. Baruch gave it to her. She has her last year's Buick, too. Wish I could have a car to drive as I hate to depend on others. When they go away, I probably can have the old Buick. When we get organized, I'll be able to snag something, I'm sure.

Tuesday a.m.
[July 1, 1941]

DEAREST BOB,

Gosh, it surely is hot up here. Worse today than yesterday, but my office in the new building really is nice and cool. I know it is at least 10 degrees cooler than the house, so I stay out here most of the time.

It seems as though I have been up here for a long time, as it is so easy to get back into the swing of things. Yesterday afternoon Schaffer drove Henry, Malvina, and me over to the Library dedication exercises—and it was really boiling. Frank Walker, Archivist Connor, a

---

*A car with a rumble seat.

(*Opposite*) President Roosevelt speaking at the dedication of the Franklin D. Roosevelt Library, Hyde Park, N.Y., June 30, 1941. Mrs. Roosevelt, with a white band around her hair, is sitting in the second row from the speaker. Courtesy: Franklin D. Roosevelt Library.

man from Harvard,* and the President gave short talks. The President really looks awful, I think. I haven't seen him for a long time—not at all since he has been sick—and I swear he looked 15 years older than the last time I saw him. His hair was whiter, his face thin and drawn, and it was really shocking. He must have been quite sick.

The Norwegian royalty are here for a week or so. They were there, and the President drove them over to the cottage afterward, and we had to give the whole outfit some soft drinks. Then they all went swimming. We took Henry to the station, came back, and chewed the rag for a while, and then Schaffer took me home at 6:30. Have had quite a lot of work to do and still haven't things organized very well.

Very confidentially—the President told Mrs. James Roosevelt that he didn't see how we could possibly stay out of this war very much longer. He said he thinks we are going to be driven into it or see the whole place over there go to hell. He must be under a terrible strain.

I don't know yet what the lay of the land is as far as the bosses are concerned. They plan to take the President's mother to Campobello starting next Saturday—will be gone a week at least—then back here for an indeterminate time. Then they will have to go back to Campobello, and there is some plan in the wind for taking a trip around the Gaspé Peninsula in August, so I don't know what is going on.

Mrs. Roosevelt just seems to be in a swivet. She is so different from what she used to be. She can't be still or be alone for a minute, and I think even Miss Thompson is getting terribly fed up with chasing around with her. She told me about a couple of good fights she has had with her when she came so close to just picking up and walking out that it wasn't even funny. She says she thinks she has been with her too long—that it isn't for anyone to stay so long on one job.† Mrs. R. looks very tired, I think, and there isn't the enthusiasm around here for anything that there used to be. I haven't even been near the swimming pool but understand that Miss Cook has had it all sur-

---

*Professor Samuel Eliot Morison.
†Malvina Thompson had worked full-time for Mrs. Roosevelt since 1927.

rounded with trees, a fence, and a terrace leading down to it from her house, so when Mrs. R. or her guests use the pool, they really feel as though they are intruding on Miss Cook's property. Great stuff! Mrs. R. said that if she had money enough, she would have another pool of her own built.

I'm awfully glad I came up here now. Nobody pays the least bit of attention to my shape, and it doesn't bother me at all. Went over in that crowd yesterday and never even thought of it. Miss Thompson asked me yesterday if I were going back to the office when I left here, and I said, "No." She said, "Then you ought to stay up here just as long as you feel you can if this is really your swan song." Since I'm earning good money, and it probably will be the last I'll earn for some time, I suppose I should make the most of it.

Later:

Had to go for lunch and now have to stay at the house and answer 'phone calls until they get back from the Big House. G-d-m, it's boiling around here! I'll bet our kid is getting sunburned!

Friday
July 4, [1941]

DEAREST BOB,

I suppose you have a vacation today. I didn't realize that it was the Fourth of July until the mailman failed to show up this morning. That is the trouble with this job: every day is the same. We don't get any vacations, and I wouldn't know what to do with one if I had it, so I guess it is all right.

I think I have decided to stay until they leave July 27—if it is all right with you, and nothing unforeseen happens. They leave then until sometime in August, and I think Prudence won't come up until they get back. I said that it made no difference to me in the least— whatever Miss Thompson wanted to do was o.k. If she wanted Prudence to come up and get broken in before they left on the 27th, I would leave earlier, but she said she didn't want her here when they

weren't here, as she wasn't familiar enough with the place or its workings, and she wanted me to stay as long as I wanted to and felt that I
should, especially since I didn't expect to go back to the office.

It has cooled off, and I'm wearing my red jacket today. Seems like
heaven after all that heat. Has rained most of the day, but it was most
welcome. I didn't have to go to the picnic with the President and
royalty this noon. They had to have it on the porch, and I would have
made 13 at the table, which is prohibited, so Mrs. Roosevelt told me
she recalled her invitation, which was all right with me, I must say.
That is one thing I like about them up here: they really treat me like
one of the family, as they know it doesn't hurt my feelings not to be
invited, or to stay out after I am invited, or to fill in. Malvina gets it
all the time, too, and it makes one feel much easier than if they were
always trying to save one's feelings. Henry said he would gladly change
places with me, but I don't relish talking to these furriners: I can't
understand them. The Norwegian kids were over this morning
playing in the recreation room here. I spoke to them and their
governess, whom I met last year; they aren't so bad, but the others
give me fits.

Nelly is surely having a big time today—the Fourth. Business started
about seven o'clock this morning, and when I got down to breakfast,
the dining room was full, and people were waiting around for a place
to sit down. It was still rushing when I went down for lunch, and she
said she hadn't sat down a minute. I made my own bed and picked
up my room, as I knew it would be hard for her to get at it. The little
room I have next to the bath is really swell—so much quieter than
the room I used to have where I would hear all the cars, kitchen, and
dining room noises.

Mrs. Roosevelt is on a tear this afternoon. She's moving all of Earl
Miller's stuff out of his room, bag and baggage. I think she is mad at
him, and it sounds as if she is tearing the place to pieces. Such a life
as these people lead!

I really have been terribly busy, and by 6:30 when I quit, I don't
feel like writing many more letters. Haven't written to anyone but
you since I came up. Hope you aren't having too bad a time at home.
Maybe I'm kidding myself—you probably are enjoying it!

Saturday p.m.
July 5, 1941

DEAREST BOB,

I am holding down Miss Thompson's desk while she and Henry have gone to Hyde Park to mail some packages and gallivant a little bit. This is the darndest typewriter. I don't see how she uses it. When they go to Campobello next week, I'm going to have mine moved in here, as I will have to stay in the house in order to answer the 'phone, etc.

Yesterday afternoon we went over to the President's office in the new Library and watched him broadcast his Fourth of July message. It was very interesting to see the men set up the battery of cameras, microphones, etc., and get everything focused and all set. The President is terribly patient and would do anything over and over again so that the men could get things right. The Norwegian royalty and kids were there, also the President's mother and some family friends, and the room was packed and jammed.

Got a note this morning from the office giving me the office news, which doesn't amount to much. Somehow, I have no regrets at leaving that place. If I have to go back, I think I shall try to go somewhere from under Mr. Magee's nose. Miss Thompson was saying that I would have the same privileges that she gives Muriel and Prudence about staying off whenever they had to on account of their families. I don't know, though; personally, I hope I don't have to go back or want to go back. I rather feel that I have done my hitch.

Mrs. Roosevelt was just over here "settling" the place. My! She gets so busy it is funny.

My shoes look like hell again, but what can one expect along that country road. I walk it usually twice a day and ride it twice a day. Wish I had a car here, but it probably is just as well that I haven't, as life is necessarily much calmer without one.

I'll bet that I get awfully fat. I don't know that it makes much difference, though, as I haven't much of a shape anymore to spoil. So, I might as well gain 30 pounds as 20! I wish this business of having a baby were all over, but I think I'll be wishing it even more in another month. Sure takes a long time.

Have been here a week already. Hardly seems possible. The time will go fast, and I might as well stay as long as I can and make the waiting time afterward that much shorter.

You probably won't get this until a day late, as Schaffer had to drive the Norwegians to their summer home on the Cape, and nobody will take the mail in, more than likely, so it will have to wait until tomorrow morning.

Sunday evening, 8:15
[July 6, 1941]

DEAREST BOB,

What a day this has been! I'm absolutely exhausted and am writing this lying down, so you probably won't be able to read it. Sundays certainly are no days of rest up here. They are going to New York tomorrow and then to Campobello for 10 days, so they were cleaning up all the work and have left me with more pesky things to do. I have to write invitations to a whole mob for a tea on the 17th, order all the food, etc., see that the chairs and such are in place at the Big House; then, get turkeys and hams, order a birthday cake, and get things in order for Hall's party July 19th. Marie Morgan, the one who is going to have the baby, is coming next Friday, and I have to get her settled, eat lunch with her, and see that she is generally taken care of.

On the 17th more guests are coming, and Mrs. Roosevelt said that I should take care of them, order the lunch, etc.! Cripes! Then, to beat all, when I have some spare time, she wants me to catalogue all of her books, and I haven't the faintest idea how to do it. I have to hold down Malvina's desk so as to get the 'phone calls, and that is such a hard place to work as everything is inconvenient and a mess. Looks as though I'm in for a good time the next few days.

The detail on this job is horrible. Sometimes I wonder why I do it with a perfectly good husband to support me. The only reason I can figure out is that I must be a little bit crazy! I'll be glad when it is all over, and I can let down my hair and relax for a while. I don't see how Malvina ever stands it.

Sis, Nelly's cat, is up here in my room. She is a nice puss and makes me feel quite at home. She's very affectionate and seems to have taken quite a liking to me. Wonder how much I weigh. I feel huge, although everyone tells me I look anything but.

Had to eat lunch at Nelly's this noon with Hall Roosevelt and Mrs. Raset. He's nuts, I must say. As far as I'm concerned all these people can have all they have, and all that goes with it, and welcome to it. I wouldn't change places with a darned one of them! I would rather be poor, unknown, and happy!

[July 7, 1941]

DEAREST BOB,

They all left this morning in a great furor and a cloud of dust for Campobello and will be gone until the 17th. Left me enough work—everything from selecting and arranging for linoleum in "my" office in the playhouse to cataloguing books, and loads of mail to get out—so I won't be wondering what to do with myself. I'm going to eat lunch up here every noon so I won't have to trek way down to Nelly's. I would just as soon walk it morning and night, but four times a day is too much, especially when it is hot. Mrs. Roosevelt threw directions at me for 15 minutes this morning—everything from having mouse traps set in her living room to getting the piano tuned. Then they started out, and she forgot her pocketbook and had to turn around and come back for it. I've been signing and getting out mail ever since. I wouldn't change places with these people for anything in the world.

There is a very nice dog up here—Earl Miller's—and her name is Taps. She is an Irish setter, and I surely would love to have one like her. She is so affectionate and quiet, and just stays outdoors all day and causes no commotion whatever. She loves to be petted and looks up at me with her liquid eyes; I really could go for a dog like that. Nelly has a new dog, too—another police dog that she still calls Rex. The dog she had last year was killed on the road. This is a puppy less than a year old and is a nice pooch, too, but not so nice as Taps.

I can drive Mrs. R.'s last year's Buick while they are gone, so I may go into town someday just for a change. Don't care particularly about going but may find something for excitement—go to a movie or something. But the country suits me fine, and the weather has been glorious the last few days.

I can't get over your Sunday morning breakfast! If my being away will cause you to eat five pieces of bacon and three pieces of toast, I had darned sight better stay away for a while. You never do such a thing when I am home. Maybe you burn it better than I do!

This seems to be quite a letter, and I haven't said anything either, so think I'll quit before I don't say anything more.

Friday a.m.
[July 18, 1941]

DEAREST BOB,

Well, I'm back in the playhouse again and glad to be here. Mrs. Roosevelt is seaplaning around New York State today to see NYA projects, so we are here alone. Malvina has been talking a blue streak ever since I got here about their trip, the Roosevelt kids, how this one feels about that one, and how mad she gets at Mrs. R. Gosh, I certainly am glad I am not embroiled in that outfit any closer than I am. I am perfectly willing to stand on the sidelines, do my work, go home, and forget about them. I should think people who try to worm their way inside and try to be somebody would be terribly unhappy. I honestly think that Malvina is sick to death of the whole business, and she even gets awfully mad at Mrs. R.

I get tired of listening to the gossip; I think they are all a bunch of hypocrites! Yesterday Mrs. Morgenthau came over before the tea, and of all the petty gossip you ever listened to! They just grab at anything, run this person down and that person down, try to be terribly democratic, etc., but when it arrives at a real issue, they are the biggest snobs in the world. Everyone is always perfectly grand to me, but, believe me, I know the whole outfit well enough to take it just as it is given and not expect any more. It doesn't pay to get set up about it.

The tea at the Big House went off well yesterday; the food arrived in good time, everybody came, and there were no hitches, thank heavens, as I was left with all the arrangements. I went over with Malvina and Mrs. Morgenthau in the Secretary's car. The Hampton singers were grand, and the movie was good. We had had seven people for lunch—which Mrs. R. hadn't ordered before she left—so I had to tell the cook what to have to eat, etc. Gosh, what a job! You know, I think it is going to be a lot of fun just to stay home, raise a kid, and run my own house. I honestly think I've had all of this I want and will have no regrets leaving it. You chase around in big cars, with chauffeurs and servants and everybody to wait on you, and meet all of these people with big names—met Mrs. Vincent Astor yesterday (now Mrs. Lytle Hull)—but it certainly means absolutely nothing in my life. I think they all lead terribly superficial lives. They all fawn over Mrs. R. and are so sweet and slobbering, even to me, that I could spit in their faces, as I know there isn't one bit of real feeling in the whole business. Malvina is the only one I don't suspect, as I really do think she likes me, and there is nothing artificial about her.

Tomorrow is Hall's birthday. Mrs. R. called him up yesterday and gave him the devil, and things are going on as they are arranged. Thank heavens, that is out of my hands. I can't cope with the drunken fool. I'll bet it will be a mess, and I'm going to stay out of it as much as I can.

I think Henry is coming up, and whether he is going back Sunday, and whether Schaffer is going to Washington, I don't know. They still don't know if they are going around the Gaspé, but, in any case, they are going back to Campobello on the 27th.

Saturday, 8:10 p.m.
[July 19, 1941]

DEAREST BOB,

I didn't get time to write you even a line today. Reason? It was Hall Roosevelt's birthday party, and one more day like this and, believe me, I'd go home tomorrow! I have just finished eating my dinner from a tray in my room because the big oaf has some of the people downstairs for dinner, and Nelly knew I had no desire to see any more of any of them. I could have kissed her when she brought up my dinner.

It was surely some party, and Hall was terrible. He was so drunk he could hardly stand up and had to be called twice from his shack to come over to eat. You should have seen him—no socks, old moccasins, old wash pants and shirt. Then, between courses he went out and tried to get in his car to go back for another drink. George Bye came and told me, and I said to go out and drag him in if necessary, but not to tell Mrs. R. They finally got him in, but he never ate a bite, and he made such a rumpus it was disgusting. I felt so sorry for Mrs. R. that I could have wept. She got a stoical look on her face, went ahead and took care of everybody, and completely ignored him.

As I told you, we ordered all the food; then he said he was bringing it, and Mrs. R. called him and told him he couldn't. But, by Gosh, about eleven o'clock in walked three caterers with food for 50 people. I honestly thought that Malvina was going to faint. The caterers took over Malvina's kitchen, the girls were already preparing things in Mrs. R.'s kitchen, and such an amount of food you *never* saw. Personally, I couldn't eat a thing—had one slice of turkey, one piece of cake, and a cup of coffee. I noticed that neither Mrs. R. nor Malvina ate anything either. I think we were all feeling about the same.

While the eating was going on, they had the "Gay Nineties Quartette" entertain, and they were fine. Then, George Bye and the Deans had set up a peep show in the playhouse; they had banners and balloons, and it was all very clever. There were quarts of champagne, and we were all supposed to drink a toast to Hall. I left mine sitting on the mantelpiece, as I couldn't drink it.

We were all exhausted by the time everyone had gone. Malvina and I were talking it over afterward—the awful expense, the waste of food, the time and effort put in by all of us and the Byes and the Deans—and that goop would have been happier, I think, with a jug of whiskey and a cheese sandwich in his own shack. I wish he'd die, and I think he will before long. I think everyone would rest easier. It's absolutely sickening to see a man like that just go to complete ruin. Anyhow, you can see by the above why I had dinner in my room. If I had gone down, I know he would have insisted that I join them, and I had had *enough* of the whole outfit.

This afternoon they used my office as a dressing room, and when I came back to finish my work, I found cigars on my typewriter, champagne bottles on my letters, water all over the floor, the sink stuffed up with cigarette butts and half full of water. I just turned around, walked out, and got Alice, Georgie, and Bill to come in with mops and brooms and clean up the place. Tomorrow I'll rewrite what was ruined. Deliver me from these so-called "parties." I'm telling you, I wouldn't change our mode of living for all the money in the world. Well, enough of this raving! After a day with the extremely wealthy and "aristocrats" of our country, I keep thinking how lucky I am to be what I am and to have just plain Robert Butturff for a husband!

Tomorrow there is a mob coming for lunch—a sober bunch—and I haven't had anything to do with it. It will have to be served picnic style. I hope I don't have to stay.

> Monday p.m.
> [July 21, 1941]

DEAREST BOB,

Just finished lunch—another picnic style affair. Honestly, I'm so sick of them! It's kind of funny—Mrs. R. doesn't want me to go down to Nelly's at noon but wants me to stay at the cottage to tend the coffee urn and help serve the people. Malvina always wants me to stay, too, so I do and work twice as hard as if I went to Nelly's! I usually pour the coffee, Mrs. R. does the meat, and Malvina, the vegetables. Then everyone gets a plate and stands or sits around and tries to get rid of the food without spilling it.

Tomorrow there is another bunch coming, and Saturday there is a huge picnic for the United Feature Syndicate. I was just checking on the number, and Mr. Carlin says they are one hundred strong! I hope to heaven some of them can't come. Wednesday and Thursday Mrs. R. and Malvina will be in Washington, and it ought to be fairly peaceful around here, but I suppose they will leave me with the arrangements for the picnic on Saturday to tend to. Sunday they are off to Campobello for about ten days, thank heavens, and then maybe you will come up, and we will have a peaceful time by ourselves. I have to laugh when I think of Mrs. R.'s statement to me this winter: "You

could go hide in the bushes when anyone is around if you want to."
I'd like to see myself try it. But I will say that it would certainly have
been foolish to stay home because of the way I look, as nobody pays
the slightest attention, and I am not the least bit self-conscious.

Wednesday a.m.
[July 23, 1941]

DEAREST BOB,

My bosses left for New York early this morning and won't be back
until Friday morning. I don't know what is on the schedule now. A
call from Campobello came yesterday, saying that old Mrs. Roosevelt
isn't so well, and she doesn't know whether she wants to stay up there
or come back here. Mrs. R. cancelled two engagements and said she
may have to go direct to Campobello to bring the old lady home if
she decides she must come, so heaven only knows what is going on.
In any case, though, I'm sure they will be away beginning Sunday as
they will either keep their former plans or be on the way over to bring
the old lady back. Anyhow, it won't make any difference if they are
here or not if you want to come up. I just think we would enjoy it
more by ourselves.

They certainly watch over me up here. It was hot yesterday; Malvina and I had gone to Poughkeepsie and then to Rhinebeck, as there
wasn't a great deal to do. There was another big picnic scheduled for
six o'clock, of which I wanted no part. About five o'clock I was so
goldarned sleepy I could hardly keep my eyes open, and I told Malvina that if she didn't want me anymore, I thought I would go home
as I was so sleepy. She asked me if I didn't want to stay for supper,
and I said, "No," and as they were leaving early this morning, I told
her that if there was anything she wanted me to do, just to leave a
memo on her desk and I would tend to it. So Schaffer took me down;
I lay down and slept until six o'clock. Had dinner at seven, and only
by sheer will power could I keep awake until ten o'clock. Went to
bed then and never opened my eyes until eight o'clock this morning.

Well, this morning when I got up here, I found a note from Malvina saying she was so concerned over me because I hadn't felt well

A picnic at Val-Kill. Courtesy: Miss Deborah Dows and Franklin D. Roosevelt Library. Credit: Drawing by Olin Dows.

last night, that she didn't blame me for not wanting to face another picnic, but that she didn't want me to go home, not to bother about her or the work or anything, to tell the mailman to forward all mail to Washington, and so on. My gosh! All because I got sleepy!

This afternoon I am going down to Luckey Platt's* and blow myself to a shampoo, fingerwave, and manicure. Nothing much to do around here in the work line—I could do the books but don't feel like it. Maybe I *am* getting lazy!

*Poughkeepsie's leading department store.

Monday a.m.
August 4, 1941

DEAREST BOB,

Guess I'll get this line off to you, and probably it will be the last. I hope so, as I want to go home. Got a wire from Malvina yesterday saying that they would be in sometime tomorrow, and then I'm clearing out just as soon as I can. I don't know whether or not she has told Prudence to come up, but, in any case, I'm starting to agitate my home-going.

I played hostess all day yesterday, Sunday, to four university students from Campobello—two boys from Seattle, one from Indiana, and a girl from Connecticut College for Women. They were really a lot of fun, and I enjoyed them. There was nothing sophisticated or blasé about them; they simply bubbled with enthusiasm and were so thrilled at having a chance to see everything. More like the kids I've always known than those who usually migrate up here.

They were to have left right after breakfast yesterday morning, but as they hadn't come in until about 3:30 a.m., they asked me if they could hang around during the day and leave about midnight last night. They had been in some terrible traffic and didn't want to face the Sunday traffic back to Washington. I knew that Mrs. R. would want them to stay, so I said, "Sure," and consulted with Nancy in the kitchen to arrange menus and to see how much food she had, etc. They went swimming, and then, as the boys were Catholics, they went to church. Afterward I took them over to the Big House, and then we came back and had lunch. Then we went over to the Library and back for another swim. Dinner was at 7:00, and I went home about eight o'clock, thinking they would go to bed early if there was nothing to do. However, Nancy said they were up and around until all hours, but they were on their way at 6:30 this morning. I never saw people eat so much in my life—three and four helpings of everything—and I was beginning to worry that the kitchen supplies wouldn't hold out. But they certainly enjoyed their visit, and I think that probably, with just me here, they felt much freer to act themselves with no restraints.

Last night the 7:00 p.m. gas closing time went into effect, and I guess that Nelly was really busy just before that time. She said that between 6:30 and 7:00 cars were lined up all the way to Poughkeepsie at the various stations, and at her pumps she and Karl both pumped gas. The load was so heavy that they blew out three fuses, and there was some excitement. At 7:00 prompt she closed down to comply with the law.

Those kids yesterday had planned to start for Washington at midnight after they figured the traffic had died down. But I happened to remember that they would be able to get no gas, and I thought it was terribly foolish to start with one tank of gas and no chance of getting any more, so that is why I told them to spend the night and start early in the morning.

I wonder how much good the gas curfew will do. Very little, I should think.

Tuesday a.m.
August 5, 1941

DEAREST BOB,

Well, here is another letter instead of me! However, now I know definitely when I'll be home—Saturday afternoon—probably around five o'clock or thereabouts, as I'll leave here in the morning. Got a letter from Malvina yesterday saying that if I thought it was "perfectly safe," would I stay until Saturday or Sunday and have Prudence come up on Friday so I could take her around. I thought there was really no reason why a couple of days more wouldn't be "perfectly safe," so I shall stay. Boy, what a stretch—from June 29th to August 9th! I called Prudence yesterday and arranged to meet her Friday morning, so my homecoming is now definite—and am I glad! I can hardly wait to get home even though it means cooking and housework again; I think I'll welcome it.

Malvina just called from New York and said she was taking the train up and would I meet her this noon. Mrs. R. is driving up with Joe Lash later on in the day. Evidently, she has had all she wants of that. Henry and Roy Cheney are coming up this evening sometime. The influx begins again, but, thank heavens, I'll soon be out of it. It has been the most glorious weather, though. It rained for three days after you left but has been clear and cool ever since. I hope it stays this way.

I called up Stockbridge, Mass., and reserved tickets for the Berkshire Festival on Thursday night—the same thing I went to last year with Mrs. R. Mrs. Morgenthau and Joan, Mrs. R., Joe Lash, and Malvina are going. Mrs. R. asked me to go, too, but I'm not. I simply loved it last year, as it is in the most perfect setting, and the music is marvellous, but they plan to take a picnic supper and eat along the roadside, as they did last year, and that is definitely an uncomfortable procedure for me now. Then, too, it is quite a long trip; Mrs. R. is a lousy driver, and I get jittery and would be no asset to the party. Too bad Prudence isn't here so she could go, as I know she would enjoy it.

No more to write about now.

Wednesday a.m.
August 6, 1941

DEAREST BOB,

Well, I really do think this is the last letter. I certainly hope so. It seems to me that I can hardly wait to get away. Mrs. R. arrived last night with Joe Lash, and just now Trude Pratt and her young daughter have come. She is good-looking, tall and blond. Malvina says Trude's husband isn't a bad-looking man—nothing to set the world on fire—but she says if she or I had the choice—as far as appearance and general manners are concerned—we wouldn't hesitate in the least between Pratt and Joe: we'd vote for Pratt. I can't imagine why Mrs. R. doesn't see it that way.

Malvina took the train up from New York yesterday, and I met her at noon. We had lunch together and talked over the trip and what not. Mrs. R. let Joe Lash drive most of the way down, and he is a very inexperienced driver. Malvina said that she had a knot in her stomach that she thought was going to kill her—she was so scared. She said his driving was perfectly awful—that is why she took the train up: she simply couldn't bear it anymore.

Henry came at 5:15, and we went down to meet him. However,

just as we were starting out, Hall Roosevelt came over to swim, and he was so drunk that he could hardly get out of the car. He fell out, staggered over to the door, and almost insisted that he take us into town. Of course, we insisted otherwise, got in the car, and beat it. He was sprawled out on the ground, playing with Taps when we left, and his guests were sitting in the car, looking rather blank and askance and wondering what to do now.

Henry left about 9:30 this morning. He doesn't like to be up here anymore at all, and I certainly don't blame him. There is nothing for him to do—Malvina doesn't have time to talk to him, and with all these other things going on, it doesn't make it very pleasant. Things aren't the way they used to be.

The linoleum man arrived this morning and is working all around my feet. However, I think he will finally finish now, and I can get this place straightened out for Prudence. Malvina tells me about every hour that she just hates to see me go, but she realizes that I really should now. I imagine she does rather hate to see me go, as she can spill all the things that bother her, knowing they won't go any further, and we can kind of get the things that don't set so well out of our systems together. I can't say, though, that I hate to go—I can hardly wait!

1945

As always happens in life,
something was coming to an end and
something new was beginning.

ELEANOR ROOSEVELT, *Autobiography*

In 1945 war ended and peace began, but no one could pick up where
he left off on December 7, 1941. Almost four years—and a lifetime—
had passed before the dropping of the first atomic bomb on Hiro-
shima on August 6, followed by Japan's capitulation on August 14.
Germany had surrendered three months earlier, and rationing, which
began in 1942, of sugar, coffee, meat, shoes, rubber, gasoline, and
other critical war materials, soon came to an end. The manufacture of
automobiles began again, houses were built once more, and factories
could not produce goods fast enough to meet the long repressed desires
of consumers. The Charter of the United Nations was born, and the
boys who had gone off to war came home—if they came home—men.

But Franklin Roosevelt, who had struggled first with economic
depression and then with global war, had not lived to witness the
victory: he had died suddenly on April 12. The avalanche of mail that
followed his death brought Dorothy Dow back to Hyde Park—for the
last time—to help Miss Thompson deal with it.

There had been great changes in Dorothy's life in the intervening
years. Her daughter, Frances Elizabeth, was born on September 10,
1941. When she was about seven months old, her parents discovered
that she suffered from cerebral palsy. At first they cared for her at

home, but when she was three, the doctors advised them to place her in the Children's Rehabilitation Institute in Baltimore where, it was hoped, therapy might bring about improvement. There Dorothy and her husband visited their pretty little daughter every Sunday.

Dorothy had not planned to go back to work after her child was born but found it necessary to do so less than a year later to help with the expense of her daughter's care. But Francie was never far from Dorothy's thoughts. In the spring and summer of 1945 public and private sadness mingled with the world's rejoicing.

Saturday p.m.
April 14, 1945

DEAR MOM,

I suppose that you can guess what a terrible shock the President's death was to all of us. I don't know when I have ever felt so stunned and completely bowled over as I was Thursday night. Everything was as usual when we left the office Thursday at 5:30. I stopped at the grocery store on the way home, and the clerk said he had heard a report that the President was dead. I passed it off, as such rumors come a nickel a dozen around here all of the time, but he turned on the radio, and the news almost took me off my feet. I went right home and called Miss Thompson to see if there were anything I could do back at the office, but she said, "No. Mrs. Roosevelt is leaving at 7:00 for Warm Springs, and I shall stay here to take care of things at this end." Bob and I just sat and listened to the radio until after midnight, and when the immensity of the thing began to sink in, it was unbelievable. At first, I could only think: what will happen to the world in general? Then, gradually, it began to sink in that there would be no more Mrs. Roosevelt or Miss Thompson to work for; everything I had left on my desk was completely dead; we could answer no more mail, as Mrs. Roosevelt was no longer our boss and had no right to use White House stationery or to speak with White House background; everything we had left in the office—files, gifts, manuscripts, books, stuff in the Christmas closet—would have to be moved out of there.

The next day when we came to work there was certainly a pall over everything. Everyone who worked in the White House had a real, personal affection for the Roosevelts, and we all felt as though we had lost a friend as well as a world personality. There wasn't much we could do all day except to answer the telephone and tell people they couldn't come to the funeral, etc. I started to clean out some books and things in the afternoon, just to keep busy, as the gloom was so thick you could cut it with a knife.

Today, Saturday, they brought the President's body back. I have been to many different things in this city and at the White House, but nothing that was so solemn or stirring as the processional and the whole occasion. Of course, we can't go to the funeral—it is to be in the East Room, and there is only room for the officials and family— but this morning they let us go out and stand along the drive by the front portico when the body was taken in.

As far as one could see across Lafayette Park opposite the White House, it was just a sea of faces. At 10:00 a.m. when the train pulled into the station, St. John's Church near the White House began tolling the bell. The parade route was lined all the way with service men and policemen in mourning, and the procession was something I shall never forget. With the thousands of people we could see, there wasn't a sound among them even long before the procession arrived. A guard of honor of Marines, soldiers and sailors, and a band were stationed on the grounds in front of the portico.

The procession was led by a service band; next came divisions of Marines, the Army and Navy; then some armored equipment, more bands, Waves, Wacs, and Spars, and finally the guard of honor, with flags, and the caisson, drawn by six horses, bearing the flag-covered casket, while formations of bombing planes flew over the route. Everything was just ghastly still except for the distant roll of drums, and the solemnity and immensity of the thing was almost overwhelming. I think that—especially for us who had so often seen him drive in the driveway there, waving his hat, smiling and bowing to everyone, with people cheering and hollering—the contrast was indescribable.

They stopped the caisson right in front of the portico. Mrs. Roosevelt, Anna, and General Elliott Roosevelt were in the next car and had to get out and stand for the photographers. The four daughters-in-law were in the next car, and the following cars all pulled into the driveway, and the people got out. The Cabinet members, Secretaries, and old friends of the President slowly walked up to the house and stood outside while the armed forces presented arms, and the band played the "Star Spangled Banner"; then the coffin was taken into the house.

Josephus Daniels was standing right beside me. He was Secretary of the Navy during the First World War when the President was Assistant Secretary of the Navy, so he was Franklin Roosevelt's "boss" and has been a close friend and adviser ever since. He is an old, old man—well into his 80s—and he looked completely beaten. Secretary Morgenthau was next to him, and he also was a close personal friend. And there were others who were closely connected with the President. Their grief was something terrible to see. It just didn't seem as though it all could be real; it seemed that you were looking at something that was just a dream.

What it all will mean to us here I don't know. We will probably stay on just as before, but, personally, I simply can't imagine not working for Mrs. Roosevelt and Miss Thompson. One thing I do know: whatever happens to me the rest of my life, I feel privileged beyond words to have had the close contact with people like the Roosevelts. It has been an experience for which I shall always be grateful. There has never been, and probably never will be, a more colorful administration, nor ever a time when so much history has been made, and even to have been a small part of it is a privilege.

Miss Thompson said that they would try to get out as soon as possible, so I suppose that next week we shall be in it head over heels trying to get things packed.

I can't imagine what Mrs. Truman will be like. She probably will be just nothing after Mrs. Roosevelt. And who her secretary will be

(Overleaf) President Roosevelt's coffin is carried into the White House, April 14, 1945. Mrs. Roosevelt, escorted by Vice Admiral Wilson Brown and a White House usher, follows. Courtesy: Franklin D. Roosevelt Library.

is anybody's guess. Things won't be the same again, as there is a great deal of difference between just working and working for someone because one has a real affection and admiration for her. Nobody could have been finer or more considerate than Miss Thompson, and the activities that Mrs. Roosevelt was always engaged in were interesting and, through the correspondence, brought in a wealth of information that one couldn't help but absorb. I imagine Mrs. Truman won't do anything of that sort; she just isn't the caliber to do it, and I think she wouldn't have the drive that Mrs. Roosevelt has. However, I have a daughter to work for, so shall stay on come what may.

It is about 2:00 p.m. now, and people are still milling around the park across the street. They just come and stand and look, although there is nothing to see. At noon yesterday I went downtown for a few minutes, and everyone on the street was terribly solemn. Small groups of people would gather and talk, but you couldn't help but sense that some great calamity had occurred. I think people in Washington were particularly fond of the President as a person because he always gave everyone the feeling that he was glad to be here and was always so friendly.

Well, enough of this; you probably don't share my feelings about the Roosevelts, but if you don't, the only reason is that you never knew them.

Saturday p.m.
[April 21, 1945]

DEAR MOM,

Gosh, what a week this has been! It seems as though years and years must have passed since the President died, and it is really just a little over a week. So much has happened in such a short time that it seems almost unbelievable.

I think that I wrote you right after they brought the President's body back to the White House. That afternoon, just before the funeral, they let us go up to the East Room to see it. I never saw such gorgeous flowers in my life. There must have been $20,000 worth, at least, and Carter—in the bouquet room—said there were still about

$2,000 worth of flowers downstairs that they couldn't bring up. The East Room is immense—over 80 feet long and about 40 feet wide—and it was lined on all four sides and almost to the ceiling with the most gorgeous displays of flowers you ever saw. One set piece from some king stood about five feet high and was made up of orchids and white roses. We all just gasped when we went in as none of us had ever seen such a display. The odor was almost sickening.

They had the casket, unopened and draped with a flag, in the center of one side of the room, and four servicemen stood at attention at each corner of it. The center of the room had the gold chairs placed for the funeral service. Only a very few were given seats in the East Room for the service, but the house was wired in the various rooms, so we went up to the Green Room and listened to the service there. We were in distinguished company: Jim Farley, Governor Stassen, all the high government officials, etc.

They left that night at 11:00 p.m. for Hyde Park, and Miss Thompson told me that on the way up the whole route was guarded by soldiers stationed every few yards. She said she couldn't even pretend to sleep, and even after they left Philadelphia in the wee small hours of the morning—about 3:00 a.m.—and went on up to New York, the tracks were lined with people—the men standing with their hats off, and the people just looking to see the train pass. The casket was in the last car, and they left the lights on and curtains up so that people could see it as the train went by.

They left for Washington immediately after the service at Hyde Park and got back here on Monday morning. Mrs. Roosevelt announced that they wanted to be out of the house by Friday. Everybody gasped, as we didn't see how we could ever get everything packed and sent by that time. Nobody but Mrs. Roosevelt would have set such a short deadline, but we all made it. You can't imagine the terrible upheaval it has been. I have always admired Mrs. Roosevelt, but my admiration for her has gone up 100% since all of this happened. I think the woman must be made of steel. After all she had been through, all the traveling, all she had to do from Thursday night, when he died in Warm Springs, until she returned to the White House Monday morning, including two perfectly awful and solemn processions and services, she came back and pitched right into the moving without so much as a minute's rest. She is the most completely self-disciplined person I have ever seen. I met her in the hall Monday morning and had to ask her a question about something, and, while she looked terribly tired and worn, she was her same pleasant self and as efficient as ever.

You have no conception of what moving meant. Not only did it entail all the personal accumulations of twelve years, but it also meant getting all of the President's things together and digging out all the closets. In both the President's and Mrs. Roosevelt's offices it meant boxing all the files. We had to get together all the manuscripts and articles she has written for all these years, all her "My Day" originals and copies, boxes of books, old records, etc.

Then we had to go up to the third floor to take care of the Christmas closet—packed 36 big boxes of toys alone. We threw out so much junk that accumulated for years on shelves and in corners that we were just black from top to bottom from fighting the dirt and the dust.

After that we went down to the storeroom in the basement and cleaned that out. That was where all the gifts were stored that were sent in but were of no material value. They were always kept a year before they were destroyed, and we had tried to keep to that schedule more or less, but when we finally delved into the innermost recesses, we found stuff that we never knew existed: crates of old phonograph records, a whole pile of pictures and paintings, boxes of china, etc. All of that had to be thrown out, given away, or boxed for Hyde Park. Every package and box had to be tagged so that it would go to the right place when it got up there.

A big moving company, Day and Meyer from New York, were working throughout the house crating all the personal pictures and ship models of the President, all his books, his clothes, etc., and everywhere you would go in the house there was pounding, packing, and tumult until you thought you would scream.

And with all of this, the 'phone still kept ringing, business had to be tended to pretty much as usual, and letters were coming in at the rate of about 5,000 a day. Thus far this office has looked through about 25,000 letters, merely to pick out the personal ones and open all of them to see if there was money in them. I didn't have to do that, thank heavens. Many people sent money to go to Warm Springs as a memorial to the President. In fact, Mr. Magee told me yesterday that they had already taken out of the letters over $4,000 in small contributions; the largest was a check for $500.

By the time we had taken down, thrown out, sorted, boxed, tagged, lifted, hauled, and what have you all day, we were completely exhausted by night. However, everything was done and on its way by Friday night. Mrs. Roosevelt, Mrs. Boettiger, Colonel James and his wife, Mrs. John Roosevelt, and Miss Thompson received all the members of the staff at 3:30 Friday afternoon to say goodbye, and it certainly was a sad occasion. Miss Thompson was weeping openly, but Mrs. Roosevelt was just as steady as ever, although she did look very tired. They were to take the 6:00 p.m. train to New York, and as I watched them leave the house at 5:30 it surely gave me the dumps. They had two sedans and a station wagon for their luggage. Mrs. Roosevelt was in deep mourning with a veil, and all the children and Miss Thompson were with her. It must have been awfully hard to leave the place for the last time after such a long residence. The ushers and butlers came out on the porch with them, and, as they drove off, waved to them and then just stood—looking.

So that is the end of that. However, I think I shall see them again. Miss Thompson found out that the government would allow one detail to go with them to help with the receiving end of all that junk, and she asked me if I would be willing to go up to Hyde Park. She said she would rather have me than anyone, and, of course, I said I would go. They have certainly been real friends to me, and I shall be more than glad to do anything I can to help them. They are coming back to Washington the first of May for Anna's birthday, and Miss Thompson is going to break up her apartment; then they want me to go back to Hyde Park with them for about a month, or as long as they need me.

I was just sick thinking about Miss Thompson facing all that stuff alone up at Hyde Park, not knowing where anything was, having to get used to doing everything herself, besides making the difficult adjustment, and I was surely glad when they told me that it was permissible for the government to detail me up there so I wouldn't have to take leave and could get my per diem. I don't know how long I'll stay—probably a month—and it won't be a joy ride, I can tell you, because the amount of stuff they will have to go through and dispose of is tremendous. The condolences continue to arrive from all over the world, and while most of them are not acknowledged, they have to be opened and the personal ones answered.

Today we are cleaning up the loose ends. I met Mrs. Truman's secretary the other day; her name is Miss Reathel Odum. She is about 30, I think, and seems all right, but is nobody startling, and I know she is completely inexperienced in this line of work. She was on Truman's staff in the Senate, so they just detailed her to Mrs. Truman. Mrs. Truman has said that she wants things to go right on as they have been, the mail should be handled the same way, etc., so I think we'll just continue, but it won't be very inspirational.

Mr. Magee said he wanted me to go over and work with Miss Odum a while when she is ready, as she had to be broken in and wanted some help. I am sure Mrs. Truman doesn't plan to do one thing, though, and it will all be very deadly, but I must work, so I have no choice. At least, the White House itself is a pleasant place to work. The experience with the Roosevelts can never be duplicated, I know, so nothing will be a disappointment. I wonder if things ever will return to normal again.

[*ca. May 5–6, 1945*]

DEAR MOM,

Things have settled down here into a dead calm. And I do mean *dead!* It is almost impossible to believe, after all the business and the rush and scurrying under Mrs. Roosevelt, that things could vanish so completely as they have in this office. Mrs. Truman apparently meant what she said when she stated that she was going to do *nothing*. It might pick up after the thirty-day mourning period; at least, we are hoping so, as we shall go stark raving crazy if something doesn't happen.

Last week Mrs. Truman's secretary, Miss Odum, called me over to go through some of the mail with her. They are staying at the Blair

House, which is a lovely, old, historical house across from the State Department. The Government bought it just as it was and has kept it for the entertainment of foreign representatives who visit this country. They moved the Trumans into the Blair House out of their small apartment when he took office. I had never been inside the Blair House, so I was glad of the chance to see it. It is just a comfortable, lovely old home; all the furniture is over a hundred years old, and it is a place where one could settle down in great comfort.

The butler took me up to the fourth floor where Mrs. Truman and Miss Odum were working. I told Mrs. Truman that it was the first time I had ever been in the Blair House and what a lovely place I thought it was. She said, "It certainly is. How I wish we could stay here! It is so much more like that to which we've been accustomed than *that* place across the street. I just dread moving over there." I said that I didn't blame her in the least, as the White House leaves much to be desired. I really feel sorry for the Trumans. When the Roosevelts were in the White House it was o.k., as they had a large family, many grandchildren, and innumerable friends, who kept the house full and buzzing all of the time. But the Trumans will just rattle around in the place, and I know they must dread the move.

Miss Odum told me that she didn't know anything about her job; she was afraid she was going to be more or less of a companion to Mrs. Truman and Margaret; that she was just an upstart and had never worked for Mrs. Truman and was unfamiliar with her method of writing and working. Poor Mrs. Truman was loaded under a pile of mail on her desk, and Miss Odum was trying to answer all of it in longhand. I said that it was foolish for her to do that when our office was over there just to take care of correspondence. She had a pile of mail that had come for Margaret and piles of stuff that had come for Mrs. Truman, so I suggested that she let me take the whole business and get it answered along the same lines as such letters had always been answered. Then, if she wanted something else, it would be easy to change or note whatever else she might want. She was tickled to death, so I went back to the office with both arms loaded and felt like a fool coming out of the Blair House. People hang around waiting to see something, and they were crowding around the place at that time because there were 17 Russians next door who had come for the peace conference. One of the policemen had to help me through, as I was severely handicapped with all the mail I had taken.

Anyhow, all we have are mere thank-yous and congratulations, etc., and in comparison, very little of that. I am doing all of Margaret Truman's stuff, turning down the wise guys, daters, etc., but there isn't much of anything. Mrs. Roosevelt and Miss Thompson have been in the city this week, and I have been busier doing things that were left over for them than with anything for the new people. I am going up to Hyde Park next Thursday, May 10th, and probably shall stay about a month.

I hate to go and leave Bob and Francie for so long, but they really are in a mess up there, and I feel I should go. I think I can help better than anyone else; at least, I know where things were when they left this office and also can do correspondence quickly. Malvina told me that they had washbaskets full of mail that hasn't even been opened, and it all must be opened since people send in money for Warm Springs as a memorial to the President. I think I'm not going to lack for something to do.

Friday p.m.
May 11, 1945

DEAREST BOB,

Will just dash this off to let you know that I arrived safely and have been so darned busy ever since that I haven't had a minute to write a line. Mrs. Roosevelt and Malvina came up on the same train with me from New York, although I didn't know it until we got to Poughkeepsie as I was riding pullman and they were riding coach! Schaffer met us, and we came right out to the cottage and started in at once going through mail. There were nine big mail bags full since they had left here. Had dinner with them, and we continued working until 9:30 when Schaffer took me down to Nelly's. Her place is the same, and Nelly is as individual as always. I have the big front room, and she and I are the only ones there, so it is nice.

Have just about frozen since I've been here. It snowed yesterday, and it is just terribly cold today. I have on my wool blouse that I tucked in at the last moment, my suit coat, and have been wearing a tweed coat belonging to Mrs. R. in order to do any work at all in the playhouse. I have just gotten the files in some sort of order. Mrs. R. has been out there unpacking all afternoon, and we have been trying to find places for things.

Fala is here, and he follows us all around—from playhouse to house and back again. Poor dog—he wants so much to go for a walk or something, and we don't dare let him loose, as Mrs. R. says he has strong hunting instincts, and she is afraid that he will wander off in the woods. He is surely a nice dog.

I told Mrs. R. and Malvina on our way out to the cottage yesterday that we all got fired, and they were aghast. However, they both said not to worry; Mrs. R. said she would speak to Secretary Ickes, who is coming up tomorrow, and also to Mrs. McMillin of the Civil Service Commission, who had said that Mrs. R. could send anyone to her, and she would place him or her in a good position. Mrs. R. also said that Mr. Morgenthau could be counted on. So I'm not worrying about the situation. I think I'll get something and at my present salary.

It seems so good to be up here again. I feel almost as though I had never left the place, as things are just as usual. Ate lunch up here today but hope to go down for dinner tonight. We are all going to the Hyde Park Church Sunday for the memorial service for V-E Day. Wish to heaven I had packed my black hat.

There are about 25,000 pieces of mail that have to be slit and opened to see what they are and if they contain money. That playhouse looks like something!

May 12, 1945

DEAREST BOB,

Just had tea with Secretary and Mrs. Ickes and Jonathan Daniels, and the conversation was most interesting as it hinged on President Truman, et al. They are all going up to Miss Delano's for dinner, and I'm going home and try to get a little of this work done. Gosh! This is the hardest place to work I ever saw. Malvina talks a lot about this and that, people, etc., which is all interesting and pleasant, but the work surely suffers, and there is such a whale of a lot of it to do. I don't see how we can begin to touch it in a month unless we really get down and do a serious job on it. Too many distractions! However, I take some stuff home at night, open the letters that have come, and look into them for money, personal notes, etc. I can do more in two hours at home than I can in two days up here. Then, too, Fala demands a lot of attention; he is the cutest dog and is always begging for a walk or for a tidbit or for some head rubbing.

Wish you could be up here to have some of Nelly's good cooking. You have no idea how wonderful it seems just to be called to a meal without giving a thought to food, its preparation, or cleaning up afterward. This morning at breakfast I had orange juice, three strips of bacon, one fried egg, two pieces of toast, and two cups of coffee; for lunch at the cottage (I eat up here every noon), we had a good substantial meal; I can't imagine that I'll want much dinner, but I suppose I'll manage that, too!

I'm going to walk home tonight, and it will seem good, as I haven't walked since I've been here. It has warmed up a little today, thank heavens. Mrs. R. gave me a pair of pink leather bedroom slippers with white fur around the tops, and, believe me, I was glad to have them last night.

I'm dying to hear from Catherine to learn what has gone on in the office. We were all talking about the upset today at tea, and, of course, Mr. Daniels knew all about it and said he thinks they are going to be sorry. However, apparently they are keeping some of the "political" appointees in the office and most of the Civil Service bunch, but he wasn't sure, as he has stayed out of it entirely. Mrs. R. certainly is very indignant about the whole business and says she is sure Mrs. Truman is going to be sorry later on that, for instance, she fired so many of the household staff. She says it is all right now, but when the entertaining starts, Mrs. Truman is going to run into all sorts of difficulties. Mrs. R. feels the same way about the office staff, too.

I must make an effort to listen to a radio. They take six newspapers up here, and I never get a chance to see any of them, so I haven't the faintest idea what is going on in the world—not that it makes much difference, I guess.

Well, think I'll sign off and get started. This house is certainly in an uproar, and I feel sorry not to have accomplished more, but what can you do when your bosses won't let you? I'm willing, but it is certainly difficult.

Sunday, 5:15 p.m.
May 13, 1945

DEAREST BOB,

It has poured all day here, but I got up here this morning as usual and worked until time to go to church. Then Mrs. R., Elliott, who is up here until tomorrow morning, Mrs. Roosevelt Roosevelt, Malvina, and I went over to Hyde Park to church. It has been such a long time since I've been to church on a Sunday morning that I almost felt like a stranger in a strange land. It was very nice, though. The church is about 150 years old and was established and is maintained by the wealthy people along the Hudson in this section.* This Hudson River Valley is surely a closed corporation. All of the people who have big estates along the shores are old-timers: the Morgans, Vanderbilts, Rogers, Ogden Mills, Livingstons, etc. Most of the people are dead now, and the children have moved to other parts, but the form of living seems to go on somehow.

Came home and worked until dinner time; then had dinner here with Mrs. R., Elliott, and Malvina. Elliott was very interesting, telling some of the many things he has done, and the condition of things in Europe when he left. I think he is not going back; he isn't discharged, but he has had 44 months of overseas duty, so he is to be stationed in this country. He is a nice fellow, but he certainly hasn't the charm the other boys have. He said that two years ago the NBC

---

*St. James Episcopal Church in Hyde Park was established in 1811 by Dr. Samuel Bard and others. Franklin D. Roosevelt became a vestryman in 1906 and senior warden in 1928, in which capacity he served until his death.

offered him $3,000 a week to do a fifteen-minute news broadcast three times a week, and that there would be no limitations on his holding another job. Wish we could make money like that! However, Malvina said afterward that the NBC probably wouldn't continue the offer now that the President is no longer here.

Malvina is certainly disturbed about all of us being let out. She and Mrs. R. talk about it all the time. They tried to get all they could out of Jonathan Daniels and Secretary Ickes yesterday when they were here, but, of course, they didn't have anything to do with it. I told Malvina that I would hate to go to the Interior because of the god-awful hours, and she said that Ickes would probably give me anything he could, but that he undoubtedly wouldn't be there too long, and it might mean another upset. She suggested that she write to Mrs. McMillin of the Civil Service, as she is bending over backwards to find places for everybody and wants to help in that way. She would probably be able to place me almost anywhere I wanted to go, and I think that would be better, too. Malvina was talking particularly about me to Jonathan Daniels last night on her way up to Miss Delano's for dinner, and he said he was sure that "anyone as good as I was" could get any place and just what I wanted, as people were howling for good secretaries—ones who could take a little responsibility. Be that as it may, it remains to be seen, but I'm not worrying in the least.

What department do you think it would be best for me to get into? Of course, Secretary Morgenthau would take care of me in the Treasury, and I know Ellen Woodward could be depended on in Social Security. Do you think either of these would be good, or do you think I should go back to the Interior?

Later:

Mrs. Roosevelt came in and said she would take me home as it was still raining, so I grabbed my hat and took the ride. Had a terrible time convincing Fala, who was soaking wet, that he had to ride in the back seat. When we eat, he always sits and begs for food, does his tricks, and pleads for a little snack. Of course, we all feed him, and he is quite a baby.

The interior of St. James Church, Hyde Park, N. Y. The Roosevelt pew is the third from the front on the left side; the Roosevelt memorial plaque is to the right of the chancel. Courtesy: Miss Deborah Dows and Franklin D. Roosevelt Library. Credit: Drawing by Olin Dows.

Think I'd better do a little work. I bring it home and work here, too. It is certainly terrific, and I still say there is no harder place to try to do things than that cottage.

Monday, 6:30 p.m.
May 14, 1945

DEAREST BOB,

Honestly, you can't imagine the amount of mail that continues to stream in here. I made up my mind this morning that I was at least going to open all of today's mail and glance at it to see what went to the Library, what was to be thrown away, and what had to be answered. I sat in one spot for almost four hours doing nothing but that, and I don't think I got through half of it. Then I gave up as I was thoroughly tired of the job. Saturday's mail still sits in one of the chairs absolutely untouched except that the personals were gleaned out of it. And the playhouse is piled six feet high all along one wall. I can't see how we'll even make a dent in it. I not only work all day, I take my "homework" home every night and put shorthand notes on the ones to be answered, so I can dash them off in the morning when I get up here. Or I take a suitcase of the old stuff just to open and get the money out. It is most discouraging, to say the least.

About 4:30 this afternoon we knocked off, and Malvina made us a scotch and soda, which either helped or hindered the rest of our efforts—it is hard to say which—but it really tasted good as we were dragged out. We eat lunch and start in immediately afterward. Of course, I will say, we do have our conversational moments, but those are rather necessary as a letdown once in a while. Mrs. R. is just as busy over at the Big House and breaking in a new yard man, etc., and still we seem to get nowhere.

It is anybody's guess when or if letters get mailed in this mess. Sometimes the outgoing mail seems to remain there for almost all day. Both the postman and Schaffer seem to pass it up, so I don't know when it goes out.

My 'phone number at the cottage is Poughkeepsie 959. At Nelly's it is Poughkeepsie 21-F-4.

Think I'll go home—and *walk!* This business of getting no exercise is rather bad, and when Schaffer takes me back and forth, it means that I don't get any action at all. Nelly informed me that she is having "chicking" tonight, and I bet it will be good. You should see the way I eat up here! I'm almost ashamed of me, but it surely tastes good.

Tuesday p.m.
May 15, 1945

DEAREST BOB,

Malvina and I have just finished a lemonade (with a dash of gin in it), and it is after six o'clock. Think I'll write this and go home. We have worked like the devil all day and are really beginning to see the light, although the playhouse is still sky high in letters and mail that will have to be opened. This is some job, believe me!

Had lunch with Mrs. Roosevelt, Mrs. J. R. Roosevelt, and Malvina. Yesterday at lunch the subject of picnics came up, and I told Mrs. R. about the resin potatoes* I had last summer out at Fran's on the picnic. She had never heard of such a procedure and was completely entranced. She had me repeat everything a couple of times and said she would be tremendously interested in installing some such thing on the grounds here. But, of course, she can't do it this year because there are no steaks or picnic foods available, and she doesn't plan on having any large groups.

Mrs. R. is going to have her piano tuned so I can play on it. I'd play on it tuned or untuned if I had a minute, but she thinks it ought to be tuned before I use it as I might not like it! Of all things!

Fala was so cute today. He can't be out alone, as they are afraid he will try to go over to the Big House, or his hunting instincts will rise to the surface, and he will run away. The other night he did get out,

---

*Resin potatoes were a favorite dish in Wausau, Wisconsin, where Dorothy Dow often visited her sister. To prepare them, a large black iron kettle was heated over an outdoor fireplace until it was red hot. Large backing potatoes were then placed into the kettle where they cooked quickly. When done, they were removed with tongs, wrapped in pieces of newspaper, and placed on each person's plate. When opened, the potatoes were dry and fluffy.

and Malvina said they had everybody out looking for him and calling and whistling. She called people down the road to keep their eyes out for him, but no Fala. Finally, Miss Cook found him out back of the hedge that goes around her garden, with his nose right outside of a woodchuck hole—within easy hearing distance of all the calls for him—but he wouldn't move. She had to drag him in by the collar. So Mrs. R. conceived the idea that she would have a wire pen made for him—sort of enclose her front yard with wire so he couldn't get out. It was done, and Fala was deposited out there while we were in for lunch. Mrs. R. kept saying that she supposed his feelings were hurt— being kept outside when he knew it was lunch time, etc. As soon as we had finished eating, she went out to let him in, and Fala met her at the back door! The little devil couldn't get around the wire, so he just jumped in the pond, swam around the enclosure until he could get up on the land again, and so was free. He came in and was just wild. He ran back and forth around the rooms and jumped and turned over, just as much as to say that he knew he had pulled a fast one. He is really an awfully cute dog, and does he ever want attention!

Schaffer goes home on Thursday, and we are surely going to miss him. They have a colored boy working around now who is supposed to be able to drive, but he won't take the place of Schaffer, I'm sure.

Think I'll go out and get my homework: I always work 2 or 3 hours in the evening opening mail after I get down to my room. There is no end to this stuff.

Mrs. R. autographed another picture for me. It's a Karsh photograph that I like very much, and Malvina said I could have one of the leather frames with the White House crest to put it in if I wanted to—which I do.

Wednesday, 5:30 p.m.
May 16, 1945

DEAREST BOB,

I shouldn't stop to do this, I suppose, but I'm so tired of working I could pop. Malvina has been pounding the typewriter a mile a minute

Mrs. Roosevelt with Fala at Val-Kill. Courtesy: Franklin D. Roosevelt
Library.

ever since about 2:00 p.m. today, and she shows no sign of letting up. Me—I'm weary! I couldn't pretend to keep up with that pair! Mrs. R. has been packing, unpacking, sorting silver, dishes, bedding, etc. all day, too, and she is still at it. I wouldn't dare think of going home until somebody around here stops, as I'd feel guilty. I always take work home to do at night, opening letters, etc., but I usually fall in bed at 11:00, but Mrs. R. and Malvina usually don't go to bed until about 1:00 a.m.

Everything up here is the same as usual. Poor Mrs. R. has been working like a Trojan trying to get things out of the Big House so it can be turned over to the Government on June 15th. She was over there all morning, dividing linen, silver, glasses, etc., and is now out in the playhouse putting away china, getting pictures hung, and what have you. Settling an estate like this is a real job, and it is doubly complicated because the boys can't get home. Jimmy and Elliott were here for a while, but everything just hangs fire.

I swear, if you didn't see the work up here, you wouldn't believe it. It is a full month since the President died, and letters of condolence are still pouring in. I think everyone who wrote when he died is now writing again on the first anniversary of his death—or sending Mrs. R. Mother's Day cards—anything to swell the total! We aren't answering anything but the very personal ones, sending out cards to officials, and just opening, looking into, and sending the rest to the FDR Library archives, or throwing them in the fireplace, whichever we think is the more appropriate place. I wish to heaven people would affix their affection and attentions on Mrs. Truman now. You just have no conception of what the President's death meant to people. It still amazes me, even thought I don't take the time to read the letters. The foreign mail has been tremendous—from all parts of the world— both the very great and the very low have just swamped us with messages. It is quite a revelation: how much one man could mean to so many people.

Everything has to be opened, as so much money has been sent in for the infantile paralysis fund as a memorial to the President. I, personally, have taken about $3,000 out of the letters, and we have hardly started on the accumulation. I have lunch up here at the cottage with

Mrs. R. and Malvina every day, as that doesn't take as much time as going back to Nelly's. Miss Laura Delano, the President's cousin, joined us this noon; she is a character.

I had a letter from Mr. Magee today, and he said everything was different now. He, Tunie, Mr. Smith, Mr. Charlton, Georgia, and I were to remain. The rest will stay until they are properly placed. What gave them the change of heart I'll never know. I'm glad I didn't worry about it, but I don't know that I'm too happy about remaining in that place. It is the easiest way out, I suppose. Sometimes I think I'd like a real job, but anything else would probably have its undesirable features, and, at least, the known is far less fearful than the unknown.

Mrs. R. just brought me in a vase of beautiful carnations "to have something nice to look at while I'm working."

7:30 p.m.:

We all signed off after I'd finished the above and had a Scotch and soda. Mrs. R. came in and said her back ached and her feet hurt. Malvina just groaned when she moved, so I think I wasn't any worse off than they were. Schaffer left tonight and cried when he said good-bye to everybody.

Friday p.m.
May 18, 1945

DEAREST BOB,

It has poured again all day. I don't see where the rain comes from. It seems funny to hear how hot it is in Washington because it has just begun to warm up a bit here, although I'm still wearing my suit. We won't know how to act if it ever quits raining. It just keeps coming down in torrents. Mrs. R. left for New York right after we had lunch today, and Malvina and I are trying to catch up a little on the mail. I have just finished my quota, and thus this.

Went out in the playhouse this morning and decided that if I cleared all packages, pamphlets, and newspapers out of the stack of mail there, and sent them on their way to the Library, it would make the outlook a bit less discouraging; so I worked a couple of hours out there, and it does help. However, it will take hours and hours just to open and quickly glance at the contents of all the mail. I work a couple of hours every night in my room and only do about 150 letters, and there are thousands! The one encouraging factor is that the current mail is beginning to die down, and much of that which is still coming in is because of the President, so we hope that when the mail hits the usual run, it won't be too much for Malvina to handle alone. I suppose, though, by that time people will all write on some other subject.

Malvina received a letter from Mr. Magee this morning, giving the present office setup, and he was certainly all cheer and light. Think the aspect of things has changed a great deal. I only wish that I could feel happier about staying on there. I think, though, it is the thing to do, as it does have its advantages, and I don't care about making a career for myself—all I want is the money for Francie. If they want me, I suppose I should stay.

9:30 p.m.:

Had to quit as Malvina was tired of working and wanted me to try the piano, which, of course, I was glad to do. Then she made some martinis, and we both had two and talked and talked out on the porch. Then we took Fala for a walk, and I surely was dizzy—I still feel woozy after four hours, a full dinner, and much conversation with Nelly. I surely can't drink and keep my feet under me. I don't like it but can hardly refuse under the circumstances. Mrs. R. had gone to New York, so we just relaxed, and it is the first time since I've been up here, so I think we had it coming. I brought my "homework" home, so I think I'd better start slitting envelopes. I'm glad that no one will have to go through this when I die!

Saturday, 6:30 p.m.
May 19, 1945

DEAREST BOB,

I don't know for sure, but I think I'm going to freeze to death—or float away. It has just poured all day, with a high wind, and is colder than the devil. I'm so sick of it I could scream. We sit huddled around the fireplace most of the time, and I can't work in the playhouse more than a short while, yet I have so much I want to do out there. Fortunately, there is enough to do inside, too, so it doesn't make a whole lot of difference, I suppose.

There is certainly never a dull moment in these parts! Mrs. R. hired a man a few days ago—through the U.S. Employment Service—to be a grounds man, do the driving, etc. I never did like his looks and wouldn't have trusted him ten minutes out of my sight, but they thought he was all right. Mrs. R. is very gullible, you know, and thinks everyone is honest. When Schaffer was here, he kept this James in line, and before Schaffer left, he took him all over Poughkeepsie and showed him what to do, etc.

Yesterday James was to take Mrs. R. down to the train at 2:30 as she went to New York. He said her Buick had a slow leak in one of the tires and suggested that they go in that car instead of the Ford, so that he could stop at the garage and get it repaired. So he left, with letters to mail and the column to file. By the time I went home he hadn't come back, and Malvina greeted me this morning with the fact that he still hadn't returned. She called the sheriff's office and reported the car as stolen. They sent a man up here for details, searched James's room over the stable and found no clothes except a hat and a pair of lady's shoes, and then sent out radio messages to the State Police to look for the car.

They found it very soon—about 75 miles down and across the river—completely wrecked. The accident had occurred at 2:15 this morning when he had run into the back of a big truck. There were five people with him; three girls and one man were killed; one man and James were seriously injured and in the hospital, and the car is a complete wreck—just a bunch of tin, the sheriff said.

So Malvina had to call the insurance company in Boston, had to consent to James's arrest, since they said that would protect Mrs. R. to some extent as far as the insurance was concerned, call Mrs. R. to tell her, and she was all jittery and upset over it. Now we are down to the President's Ford, which has been converted, with nobody to drive it but me at the moment. I'll have to go to file the column and

179

meet Mrs. R. at the station tomorrow. They had applied for a C ration
but only have an A now,* and the Buick was filled with gas, so that
much is gone.

Believe me, I *still* say that people who want a lot of money and
places such as this are certainly welcome to them. Malvina said, "I
wish to hell she would sell the whole establishment and settle herself
in the apartment in New York." The brook has been running into the
cellar all day—the sump pump went on the fritz—and men have
been down there trying to keep it fairly shallow, at least. And the
gutters are stopped up in places. Gosh, it is one damn thing after
another!

Then, to beat all, we have Fala in our care, and Malvina said all
that had to occur now was for him to get lost, strayed, or stolen, and
she would put on her hat and walk out. We have been taking turns
taking him out for a walk—in the pouring rain. There are things I like
to do better than take dogs for a walk—even such a famous dog as
Fala—but that comes with it, I guess. He is a darling pup, though. I
ran with him this noon all the way from the cottage down to the bridge;
his little, old, short legs went a mile a minute, and he was just puffing
when we got back, but I think he liked it. He just came to me now,
woofed, showed his teeth, and woofed again: it is his supper time.
Malvina has gone to perform those chores. It's a wonder we get anything done in the secretarial line, but somehow we do.

7:30 p.m.:

Have just finished my dinner, and now I'm going to wash my hair.
Then I'll have to do some homework as we are getting no place fast

---

*Gasoline rationing was made nationwide late in 1942. All passenger car owners
were eligible to receive small, equal "A" rations for personal necessary driving.
Supplemental "B" rations were granted to persons needing additional gasoline to
carry on an occupation not considered essential to the war effort or to the public
welfare by the gasoline eligibility committee of the Office of Price Administration.
"B" rations were limited to an average of approximately 400 miles per month. "C"
rations, which were unlimited, were granted only to persons who needed additional
gasoline in connection with occupations deemed by the committee to be essential to
the war effort or to the public welfare.

with the accumulation. I could do three times as much in a regular office, but this place is terrific. I should think Malvina would go mad, and I guess sometimes she thinks she is.

Sunday, 6:30 p.m.
May 20, 1945

DEAREST BOB,

Just finished tea with Mrs. R., Malvina, and Ruth Cowan, who is an AP war correspondent just back after 2½ years overseas. She is very pleasant and has some interesting stories to tell.

The biggest news, however, is that the sun has been shining all day, and it has been around 70°, so it has been most enjoyable. We have a girl here from the neighborhood, Sheila Linaka, who came up today to help open some of the accumulated mail. I started her on papers and pamphlets in the playhouse, then had to go to town and file the column and meet Mrs. R. and Miss Cowan at the train. Came back and worked with Sheila until 1:30 when I had dinner with the folks, and we all had a grand time. Everybody was feeling in high spirits for some reason—I still think it must have been the sunshine—and we all had a lot of fun. Then Sheila and I worked on mail again until 5:30 when we both came in and had tea with everybody. We moved our work outdoors on the porch of the playhouse today, and I must be so full of vitamin D from sitting in the sun that I'll probably collapse with a sunstroke or something similar tonight. I'm going to try to stay in the sun and work whenever I am doing anything that makes it possible. However, it probably will rain without ceasing for the next ten days.

Now that Mrs. R. is home, Fala just goes out and comes in as he pleases, so that little chore of taking him for a walk is over, thank heavens. That I don't like to do! Gosh, he's a cute pup, though. I think he would never run away as he always seems happy enough to get in the house whenever anybody comes in.

This life up here is queer business. I can hardly connect all that has happened to us—Francie with all her troubles, etc., since I was up here last—to my present life. It just takes you completely away from your ordinary way of living, and, I suppose, because of that, it seems rather like a vacation even though I have been working plenty hard. I still can't think of Mrs. R. as being anybody extra special, although when I do settle down and try to realize it, I sometimes wonder how on earth I ever got to cavorting around with such people!

I think Mrs. R. likes me, too, as she is very friendly and treats me just as she does Malvina. She is so glad that I can drive, and so am I. I have just put her car in the garage for the night. I hope to heaven she lets me do the little driving that is necessary until such time as she gets somebody whom she knows she can trust with a car. I think it is foolish to turn over a car and the keys to some fellow about whom you know absolutely nothing. I'd trust him with lesser things for a while. As long as I'm here, it wouldn't take more than an hour a day to run into town with the column and mail and do the few odd errands that have to be done. And she'll have a car when I'm through. I don't know, though—she's funny about asking anyone to do anything extra, and I suppose she will think she is imposing on me.

Monday, 6:00 p.m.
May 21, 1945

DEAREST BOB,

Just finished tea with Mrs. R., Ruth Cowan, Malvina, Joe Lash, and Trude, and now I am completely disorganized for any more work. I made up my mind this afternoon that I was going to dig in and work like a sucker, but I defy anyone to do it in this place. Malvina comes in to talk about every two minutes, and people ask you questions. Then Ruth Cowan came in, sort of at loose ends, as Mrs. R. was picking up Joe and Trude. So I put her to work helping me sort the money that we have gathered in for infantile paralysis memorials, as I was determined to get that sent on its way if nothing else. And that is all I did. We have about $2,500. I shudder to think of how much must be still lying out in the playhouse in unopened letters.

Malvina finally got to unpacking her trunk and suitcases today and gave me some clothes, which she thought Gram or Mom might be able to use. They are real nice, so I just took anything, as I know

Gram can make over things. Also, Malvina told me that if I saw anything I would particularly like to have to let her know. I knew there was a leather scrapbook that we had packed, which I was fairly drooling over when it came in, so I asked her if I could have that, and she said, "Sure." It will be swell for my White House accumulation. It is a beautiful book with double cellophane pages, so things can just be slipped in instead of pasted, and you can't buy those now.

Malvina got a letter from Tunie Orndorff today. She had offered to pay her train fare and her board at Nelly's if she wanted to come up on her vacation and help her out a little, but Tunie said she couldn't come. Malvina is headed for a tough time if she is going to swing this job alone. Right now she is convinced that she can't do it, but, of course, it is still too early to evaluate it until it settles down to normal. I told her that I am afraid she will get too ruthless in not answering letters—just because she couldn't do it by herself—and, in that way, shut off the mail so entirely that it wouldn't be of any value to Mrs. R. in the column. Anyone who writes a "voice of the people" column like Mrs. R.'s must depend a great deal upon her "fan" mail, but if what does come in is not answered, mail will disappear, and that isn't good for a columnist.

I suggested to her today that she bundle up the stuff on which there is no fire and send those letters down to me to answer. I could do it easily and also get the filing in order, and do many odd jobs that would relieve her a good bit, at least during this summer. When they get down to New York, I'm sure they will have to hire another person. But she may find my plan would be too much trouble. Anyhow, I made the suggestion, so she can do as she likes.

Think I'll go out and get my homework and go on home. It is useless to try to do any more around here. I will be glad when this tour of duty is over even though I enjoy being up here.

May 22, 1945
6:30 p.m.

DEAREST BOB,

Been a dull day, and, just for a change, it is pouring again, and I am marooned here until it quits—if ever. Malvina and I have just had a whiskey and water, and I have been trying to urge her to marry Henry. I really think she would like to if he could transfer to New York, but I don't know whether she would ever get up her nerve. She says she would feel foolish getting married at her age!

We really have been working very hard. Mrs. R. took a group of wealthy people over to Wiltwyck School in an effort to get money from them for the school, and then they came back for a buffet lunch out on her porch—the first of the season—and we didn't eat until about 2:00. It was nice, but I could spare it. Joe and Trude are here, which complicates matters. That is an attachment I certainly cannot understand.

Mrs. R. still hasn't bumped up against the facts of life, but I think it won't be long now. She can't get the pump for the pool repaired and is having seven fits all at once. They simply can't get the parts, but she can't understand that. She is also going to come a cropper on the gas situation if she doesn't slow up a bit on driving the car. It would be good for her to bump up against a stone wall and find out what other people have been going through, as she doesn't know what it is all about.

I wish it would stop raining long enough for me to go home, as I've had enough of this for the day. I'm beginning to feel a little better about the way we are getting work out the last couple of days. We are really beginning to see the light, and I think by the time the month is over we should be pretty well out of the woods.

Well, Joe and Trude are out in the kitchen getting themselves a drink. I hope they leave me out of it. I don't know *how* Malvina stands this constant stream of company running through her place all the time. I'd lose my mind!

> *Wednesday, 8:00 p.m.*
> *May 23, 1945*

DEAREST BOB,

Ann Gillis of the NBC came up this afternoon, and Mrs. R. asked me if I would take her and Ruth Cowan over to the Big House and to the grave. I was glad to, as I've been wanting to go over, and both Malvina and I were completely no good for work. This business of working seven days a week and every night is no good, as you soon get so weary that you lie down on the job because you need a change.

We went all through the Big House. Mrs. R. has all the china, linens, silver, and glassware out to be distributed and packed for the children; upstairs all of the President's clothes were laid out in his room; his suits (about 25 of them) were in the closet, and it was really very sad. It gave one a feeling not only of the loss of the President, but also that it is really the end of an era that will be no more. I doubt if those old family estates will ever exist again. It's a good thing the Government is going to take the Big House over, as I can't imagine what would happen to all that stuff if Mrs. R. had to dispose of it. After we had gone through the house, we went out to the grave. It is certainly in a beautiful spot and has a military guard on duty all of the time.

This noon at lunch a Mr. Lewis was here. I understand that he is filthy rich, and I think he must be, as he has a house at Palm Beach, a farm in Florida, a house in Chicago, and an apartment in New York. He was a very nice man, though—about 65—and I surely liked him. We talked about farming.

Tomorrow morning I have to drive Mrs. R. and Ruth to town to catch the 9:31 train, and then I'm going to get a few things I want for myself.

I'll surely be glad to go home. A month of this existence is plenty— enjoyable as it is—but there are always too many people, and too much food. I have three big meals a day—far more than I want—but it is put in front of me, so I have to eat it. Mrs. R. has a fit at noon if I don't each much, and Nelly has another one at night if I leave any- thing, so I just cram it in and wish to heaven I could eat as I want to. I ought to gain a few pounds if overstuffing will do it. Well, it won't be long now: another couple of weeks, and this will be over. I will have done my duty, earned about $100 extra, and had a real change— almost a vacation—out of it. It's the end of all this, and I rather hate to see it, as I have enjoyed it even though it has its drawbacks.

Thursday, 9:00 p.m.
May 24, 1945

DEAREST BOB,

I took Mrs. R. and Ann Gillis to the 9:30 train this morning, so Malvina, Ruth Cowan, and I have been alone all day. We set Ruth to opening the "accumulation," and I must say she did a wonderful job and kept at it all day. About 5:30 Malvina made some martinis, and we each had two. Malvina was telling tales about the 1932 election, and then we got into a heavy discussion of the Russian situation. About 7:00 p.m. I got up and went home. Ruth is very interesting as she has been overseas as a war correspondent for over two years. And with a couple of drinks under her belt, she let loose.

After I left Mrs. R. this morning, I went uptown and did some errands. I bought myself some flannel pajamas. I have darned near frozen in those silk nightgowns, so I blew in $2.98 for comfort. Now, I suppose, the temperature will immediately go up to about 90°. Gosh, it has been cold up here! I got Mrs. R.'s facsimile stamp for franking mail today, so we have been going to town stamping up mail.

I am going to write Miss Warren and ask her to call me collect after Francie has her tonsils out, so I will know how things are going. I'll call you as soon as I hear from her. Gosh, how I dread it. I hope that there is something sometime that happens to that child that will be a happy occasion—something to be enjoyed instead of dreaded. It seems to me as though her whole life has been just one dreaded and heart-breaking event after another. Well, if we can get over the tonsils and hip braces there just *can't* be anything more for a while. I wish I could take things the way you do. You accept Francie just as she is and love her for whatever she might be at the moment, and I seem to be just agonizing over her all the time.

Guess I'll read a little mail and then go to bed. Have to take Ruth to the 9:30 a.m. train tomorrow. When I put the car in the garage tonight, Fala came tearing from the pond as fast as his little, short legs would carry him. So, I let him in the front seat, and he sat up there as big as life, and I rode him around to the garage. Then he waited while I locked the doors and walked back with me. I never really liked Scotties much, but I can see now what an appeal they have. He is very smart and affectionate and very friendly. I don't wonder the President was crazy about him.

I've been here two weeks today, which means two more weeks to go, and then home. That will be wonderful, although I know I am going to hate to say a final goodbye to all this. It really has been a wonderful experience.

May 26, 1945

DEAREST BOB,

Anna and John Boettiger are here this weekend to go over things at the Big House. They came back to the cottage for lunch—Mrs. R. had lunch at the Morgans. Anna is the grandest person; she is so real, has nothing superficial about her, has no inhibitions of any kind, and is a lot of fun. The conversation at lunch was mostly about Joe and Trude (how she hates them!), and Mrs. R.'s peculiarities. Anna and her mother argue like everything, and when Mrs. R. gets stubborn and won't listen to her, the war is on. I surely wonder sometimes how I ever got mixed up in this outfit! It certainly is way out and far beyond me, but I enjoy it for a while—in small doses. However, a month will be plenty, enjoyable as it is, as there is too much of everything: too much to eat and drink, too many people, and too many things around.

Anna's mother irks the soul out of her on lots of things. You should hear her when she gets started and when she really lets her hair down. She gets so mad at some of Mrs. R's ideas. One funny thing that Anna told about this noon: she said that Mrs. R. was going through some of the President's things and came across a lot of his canes. He had had canes given to him by everybody under the sun, and she was sorting out the best ones to give to the Library. She said, in all seriousness, "I'm going to take these two back over to the cottage for Tommy and me as we might need them sometime." I thought Malvina was going to die. She said she always knew she was a doddering old fool but really didn't think she had reached the stage of needing a cane to get around!

I have come to the conclusion that settling an estate like this is some job! I went over to the Big House with a couple of house guests the other day, and Mrs. R. has everything sitting out on tables and beds, trying to divide it: silver, china, glassware, priceless heirlooms of the family, besides all of the President's clothes, paintings, gifts from foreign governments, etc. You never saw such an array of things in your life, and the estate is tied up so that nothing belonging to the family can be given outside the family unless it is given to the FDR Library, so all that has to be checked.

Mrs. R. looks very tired, too, and I think she is. I had to laugh at her the other day at lunch. I was asking her about Mrs. Parish, a cousin of hers, who is a very old lady. She has been ailing for many years (imaginary, Mrs. R. says), and she is about the only living relative Mrs. R. has on her side of the family. She is extremely wealthy, has a house on Fifth Avenue, a place in Orange, and another house at Newport. Mrs. R. has always been most conscientious about going to see her every time she is in New York, and she said that on this last visit Mrs. Parish was having a fit because she couldn't get two servants she wanted and insisted that she had to go to her house in Orange the first of June. Mrs. R. tried to convince her that it would be better to stay in New York, but she would have none of it. So, Mrs. R. said, telling about it in a rather weary voice, "Oh, well, I didn't argue too much because I think it will be easier to go to Orange once every two weeks to see her than it would be to settle another estate."

Sunday, 6:00 p.m.
May 27, 1945

DEAREST BOB,

Have been working all day in the playhouse with Sheila Linaka, opening the accumulation, and, believe me, I'm tired of it. She took a suitcase of mail home to work on during the week. I wish to heaven that we could get rid of that stuff. This noon we had dinner here, and they asked Sheila to stay, too. She was rather embarrassed, I think, but Anna is such a swell person she would make anyone feel at ease. Anna and John and the four of us had a martini before dinner, and

Sheila took one, but I noticed that she didn't do much with it. She is so quiet that it wears me out trying to keep up a conversation with her—or even casually talk once in a while. She is a good worker, though, and I'm glad they have her working on the accumulation, as I don't think we would ever get through otherwise.

Two more weeks of this, and then I'll be home. Malvina is really worried about how she is going to swing the job alone, and I think she can well be, as I don't see how she is going to do it unless things quiet down an awful lot. It is so much different having to do all the detail work, and, of course, I don't think Mrs. R. has any conception of how much time it does take. However, Malvina says she is going to insist upon help if she finds it is too staggering, and I hope she sticks to it.

Monday, 6:15 p.m.
May 28, 1945

DEAREST BOB,

It is hard to get any personal letters written up here as there is so much to do between "interruptions." I never saw such a place! It is almost impossible to settle down and try to get through any extended piece of work. I start early and work late, but there is still much to do. However, done or not, I think I shall come back to Washington at the end of a month for two reasons: one, I am anxious to see you and Francie, and, two, it makes little difference how long I stay—the evil day is coming when Malvina will have to swing it alone, and I can't see that a few days more or less will make any difference. I hope we can finish opening the accumulation, at least, so all she will have is the current mail, but even that will be a big job. It is amazing the amount of money that has been sent in for the infantile paralysis fund as a memorial to the President. I sent about $2,100 to the Foundation a few days ago and almost $4,000 today. I think there has been over $10,000 altogether, and Lord knows how much is lying in the unopened letters. If all Malvina had to do was to work, it wouldn't be so bad, but when she has to be housekeeper, entertainer, buffer for all quarrels and arguments for everyone on the place, I don't see how she is going to handle it. However, that isn't my worry.

Had a very interesting person for lunch today, Mme. Genevieve Tabouis, a French woman in this country, who has been publishing "Pour la Victoire" ever since the war began. She has just come back from four weeks at the San Francisco conference, and her outlook is certainly a gloomy one. She says the Indians are fighting among themselves; there are three Spanish factions fighting among themselves; and she trusts the Russians like nothing. She is sure that they are out for all they can get. She also told some very interesting incidents about the people in her own country: the different factions there; how each one hates the other; how hate seems to be governing the entire world, and one's word of honor has no meaning whatever.

She escaped from France at the beginning of the war through the aid of a British friend, as the Nazis were on her trail because she published a newspaper there that was very much anti-Nazi. Her husband had a huge chain of radio stations, and he remained. She has a daughter over there, too, who is an invalid with tuberculosis of the spine, and Mme. Tabouis has no idea what has happened to her. She intends to go back to France the middle of June and doesn't know what will be facing her: arrest, whether she will be allowed to come back here, what she will find has happened to her family, or how she will be treated. Gosh! When she finished talking, I was surely glad I was an American. It takes something like that to make one appreciate it.

I'll be glad to get back to civilization again. I never hear the radio, just glance at the papers spasmodically, and hardly know what is going on in the world.

Tuesday, 7:00 p.m.
May 29, 1945

DEAREST BOB,

Postmaster General Walker and his wife are here for the Memorial Day services at the grave tomorrow, so I cleared out before they began to gather for cocktails, as I looked like such a mess. The Roosevelt Home Club is having services at the grave, so I suppose we'll go over in the morning.

By the way, Mrs. R. nailed me this morning on gas rationing coupons, and I told her what I thought, but inasmuch as you always handle it, I really wasn't very sure. She has an A and B book for the Ford. Are those coupons issued for a three-month period from date of issue? She got them May 18th; will they have to last until August 18th? She has 15 B coupons and, I think, 12 A coupons. She wanted to know how many miles the Ford got on a gallon of gas, and I said about fifteen, so she figured she has enough gas for about fifteen miles a day. I think she is going to get a C card, too. I hope I told her correctly; let me know if I didn't, as she is going on my say-so.

Malvina and I had our usual Scotch and water tonight before I left. We always have one, and it doesn't get me as dizzy as it did at first. Gosh, when the Boettigers were here, we always had a drink before lunch, too. I don't like that because it is too hard to get back to work in the afternoon. In any case, I wouldn't care if I never saw any of it. I can see how people would drink a lot, though, when there are many people around and there is always an ample supply of liquor handy.

I think I am gaining weight. Lord knows I should, with about nine hours sleep a night, tremendous meals, and some liquor thrown in. You know, this isn't a bad way to earn about $12.00 a day. Why can't it be in Washington!

8:00 p.m.:

I think I'll be home sometime week after next. Malvina wants to go to Washington on the 7th to get her dental work finished, and she won't be back until the 11th, so I said I'd hold down the fort and go sometime during that week. I'm anxious to get home. I really feel that it is a dirty trick on you—running off like this—but this will end it all, I know. It has helped Malvina a great deal, been a vacation for me, and besides I have earned a lot of extra money. I agree with you, though—it *is* more fun to be together.

Memorial Day, 12:00
[*May 30, 1945*]

DEAREST BOB,

We have just returned from the service at the President's grave, and it was a very moving occasion. Postmaster General and Mrs. Walker, Major Harry Hooker, Mrs. R., Malvina, and I went over together from here. The Roosevelt Home Club put on the service, which was lovely. It is such a beautiful spot. There were just the friends and neighbors from around Hyde Park. It was very sad, especially for us who had often attended the annual meeting of the Roosevelt Home Club and had watched the President at his best. He always loved those occasions and would really give out in his talks and handshaking. There were many beautiful wreaths—one from Bernard Baruch, one from the Warm Springs patients, and one from a company of Air Corps men over in Europe someplace—and also innumerable sprays from friends and close associates. I have the program, and I suppose that is the last—really the last—of the Roosevelt regime. It makes me feel very sad.

I still can't see how Mrs. Roosevelt carries on as she does. I have never seen such a stoic. All of us were in tears—or near it—and she stood there with not a flicker of emotion showing in her face. She greeted and thanked everyone afterward and said something to all the returned service men from Hyde Park whom she had known throughout the years and who came up to express their sympathy, and still she never changed. Major Hooker, Malvina, and I went up to the Big House and sat on the porch in the sun to get thawed out while she went over to Mrs. J. R. Roosevelt's house to see her, as she has been very ill. When she returned to pick us up, a delegation from West Point was just arriving to place a wreath from President Truman on the grave, so we had to go back again and stand through that— taps and all—before we came back here. I don't know how she does it. It is a good lesson to us lesser folk in how to bear things that must be borne. Now she is back over here and has begun to write her daily column just as though nothing had occurred.

4:00 p.m.:

Guess I'll finish this now. Earl Miller dropped in before lunch, and now he, Mrs. R., and Malvina are chewing the rag in Malvina's sitting room, so I just came to my "office" and finished my work. We had quite a luncheon today: Mr. Shipman and Dr. Nixon, who are heads of the FDR Library, Major Hooker, Earl Miller, and the three of us. I find it so interesting listening to these people who have been overseas or in actual contact with the war and peace negotiations. It is discouraging and pessimistic to say the least. I just wonder how anything will ever come out of all this.

Incidentally, Earl Miller's wife just had a baby girl last Friday— the lucky devil! Of course, he is beaming, but Malvina says she thinks it is more because he has won so many bets that it was going to be a girl than for any particular feeling of attachment to the baby. He and his wife are at swords' points all the time; in fact, I think she is about to divorce him. Gosh! People have everything in the world to be happy about, and then, apparently, are perfectly miserable. They surely don't appreciate a well and healthy child, I know that.

The company in the next room seems to be dispersing, so I'll quit this for now.

May 31, 1945

DEAREST BOB,

Fala is so cute. Mrs. R. is in New York today, so he hangs around us. Malvina just yelled to me, "Dorothy, Fala is acting silly and showing his teeth! What's he want?" I thought that he probably wanted to go out, but nothing doing—he headed toward the kitchen as he thought it was time to eat. Whenever he wants anything, he comes up to you, shows his teeth, sniffs, snorts, and sometimes sits up on his hind legs;

(*Overleaf*) Memorial Day services at the grave of President Roosevelt, Hyde Park, N.Y., 1945. Postmaster General Frank C. Walker is at the podium, while Mrs. Roosevelt stands at the far left. Courtesy: Franklin D. Roosevelt Library.

then it's anyone's guess what he is after. But when he gets you out of your chair, he shows you without any difficulty just what he wants. We have just now let him out on his own; the only time we have to take him on a leash is in the morning, so as to be sure he does his stuff every day. Mrs. Roosevelt babies him like everything.

Did a lot of chores and errands this morning after I left Mrs. R. at the station, but, at that, I got back by 10:30. The mail was perfectly tremendous again as there wasn't a delivery yesterday, and we didn't finish opening it until after 3:00 p.m.

It's still freezing cold in these parts—just like March. The wind has been blowing a gale all day, and this morning when I went in town I had on my suit and Malvina's heavy top coat. I wonder if spring will *ever* come! It probably will turn insufferably hot with no notice, and then we shall perish!

June 2, 1945

DEAREST BOB,

Yesterday I didn't get a letter off to you. We were raising a storm around here trying to get rid of a lot of old accumulations. Then, I had to go to town in the afternoon to file the column and do the errands, and by the time I got back and went to work in the playhouse again on the old Albany files, which we are trying to dispose of, it was 6:30 before we woke up to the fact that the day had gone. Came in and had a cocktail, and I took a pack of letters home to put shorthand notes on so I could get them written quickly today, and it was midnight before I finished those, so your letter was never written.

Today we have been trying to dig out Malvina's living room, and it looks so clean now that neither one of us feels comfortable in it. We wrapped stuff to be sent to the kids and everybody else, and got rid of things that have been sitting around for days. Now, as soon as I finish this, I'm going to work like the devil on current letters. Everything is way ahead of me. Gosh! There is no end to it. I don't know how Malvina is going to do everything herself, but I still hope it won't be so bad when the accumulation is done.

Well, I must get to work, as I have to leave here at 5:30 to pick

Mrs. R. up at the station. It is freezing cold yet, and raining again. I have never seen such weather. You talk about white shoes, and I can hardly imagine such a thing. What you need up here are high-top boots!

Sunday, 10:30 p.m.
June 3, 1945

DEAREST BOB,

I just got home from the cottage. Mrs. R. asked me to stay for supper and play hymns afterward. To tell the truth, I could spare it, but it is fun, and Mrs. R. seems to enjoy it. She has the most horrible voice, and Malvina's is worse, but that's unimportant. Mrs. Kermit Roosevelt is here, so the four of us had the usual scrambled egg supper, and then I played for about 1½ hours. I don't know how I dare when I never touch a piano from one year to the next, but I enjoy it so much that it seems to give me the courage.

Mrs. R. was talking about Jimmy and Rommie; it is too much to write, but I'll tell you about it when I get home. Sheila Linaka came up to help open mail today. I was working on the old Albany files, going through them and throwing things away, and I got just filthy. In the afternoon I took Mrs. R., Mrs. Kermit Roosevelt, and Malvina over to the Big House and then went down to Poughkeepsie to file the column.

About 6:30 Fala was lost; we yelled and hollered; I took the car and drove down to the main road, yelling and honking the horn—but no pup. It was way past his dinner time, and he usually is right on the spot for that. Mrs. R. was quite upset, and I really was worried, too. I went out, looked back of the hedge and all around and couldn't see any trace of him. About half an hour later he came tearing around the corner of the house on two legs, looking like a drowned rat. He couldn't have been very far and probably had been watching a woodchuck hole and didn't want to come. Honestly, that dog is more trouble than a baby.

These extracurricular activities surely keep me busy. Mrs. R. has now hired another colored fellow, a much higher type of man than before, and I hope he can do the errand running and chauffeuring before too long. I don't mind, but my regular work suffers, and I won't be here much longer.

Monday, 6:15 p.m.
June 4, 1945

DEAREST BOB,

Today has been rather hectic. Mrs. R. was in a big rush this morning, and Mrs. Kermit Roosevelt had to be taken to the train, so Mrs. R. had us all in a swivet before we got going. The new colored man, James, went with me today so I could show him the ropes—what he will have to do and where to go. He does not know Poughkeepsie at all, so he will have a problem. He is a very nice fellow, though, well-spoken, smart, but I'm afraid that he is too high a type of man to want to do the job he is supposed to do here. However, that remains to be seen. He has evidently been a butler or houseman: this morning when he went into town with me, he was pressed and brushed and shined and fairly sparkled.

Had to take Mrs. R. over to the Big House, then take Mrs. Kermit Roosevelt to the station, then go to Western Union to file the column, then go to the gas station to argue over a coupon I gave him on Saturday for gas and have the tires checked, then to the grocer's for a huge order of groceries, then to the bank, then to the baker's, then to the Post Office, then back to the Big House for Mrs. R., then to the farm, and finally back to the cottage at almost noon. I told Malvina that I was certainly a big help to *her*. However, I hope this fellow will be able to take over in a couple of days, so it will give me more time.

Malvina is going down to Washington with Mrs. R. Wednesday afternoon, so I will have a few days of freedom in which I hope to accomplish a lot. I suppose, though, the place will fall apart, Fala will get lost, or something equally diverting will happen.

It is time for me to go on home. Malvina wants to have a drink, but I don't feel like it tonight. Would just like to get home and relax. It's still rainy and cold. I've gotten now to the point where I don't ever expect anything else. I just borrow clothes and keep on wearing them.

I think I shall write Mr. Magee and tell him I'll be back to work a week from Thursday—the 14th, I guess—and then try to get reservations for that Wednesday. There is no point in my staying up here any longer, as we never get caught up anyhow. The accumulation will be done, and that is about all that I can do on such things. All the rest is just current mail, and that goes on constantly.

Tuesday, 8:00 p.m.
June 5, 1945

DEAREST BOB,

We got stuck to go to tea this afternoon, so I didn't get my letter written. Today was just about like all the others. I'm still playing chauffeur, as James doesn't have his license yet, so I spent the morning running around doing the daily chores. I take James with me so he will know where to go and what to do.

Mrs. R., Malvina, and I were alone for lunch, so we swallowed it in a hurry and then worked like hell until 5:30, when Mrs. R. insisted that we come in for tea—much as we didn't want to. I have a new assignment for the next three nights: I am to sleep up at the cottage so Fala will have company while Mrs. R. and Malvina are in Washington. He is used to sleeping in a room with someone, so I'll have to play nursemaid to the dog. If he runs away or causes me any trouble, I'll be *very* severe with him. Honestly, the responsibility for the hound is worrisome to say the least. But I don't mind staying at the cottage as I'll be alone, except for the servants, and can play the piano and do whatever I like.

Tomorrow when I take the folks to the station, I think I'll ask for reservations for Wednesday, June 13. No more to write about, and I must get to my homework. You don't quit this job at 5:30! It will seem good to get back to some regular hours and free Sundays again. I don't know how Malvina stands such a grind; it would drive me nuts.

Wednesday p.m.
June 6, 1945

DEAREST BOB,

Holy smokes! This place closely resembles a three-ring circus. I can think of nothing else comparable. Mrs. R., Malvina, and Lucy (the cook) were going to New York. Alice had her afternoon off, so she went into town, and if it wasn't a grand scramble getting out of here I never saw one. All morning I was getting instructions about Fala, a demonstration on how he is to be combed and brushed every day, strict instructions on what and how he is to be fed, the proper temperature of the food, etc. I tell you, the weight of responsibility for that hound bears heavily! I told Malvina that I would try to remember just how I took care of Francie when she was a baby and do the same for Fala. By gosh, if he runs away or cuts up with some of his pranks, he'll hear about it from me!

We all gulped our lunch and such a to-do. Mrs. R. threw a few bills at me with which to buy something at a bake sale in Hyde Park on Saturday and for anything else we might need. And, could I get my own supper tonight because the girls are both gone? Then, what to do when Elliott arrives on Saturday; do this, do that; today's shopping list—a mile long. Lord! By the time we left them at the station I didn't know which end was up. James went along to do the driving, as he has his license now, so that was some help, but he doesn't know his way around yet, so I had to stay with him to buy the groceries, etc.

We finally arrived home to find little Fala completely desolate at having been left alone. I have just turned him out, and I hope he stays around here. I still say there is no job in the world like this! You never know what you will be called on to do. And you should just see this place: mail strewn all over everywhere—the morning mail hasn't even been opened—and stuff piled high to go over to the Library. I can't even see the bed in which I'm going to sleep because it is so full of junk. Thank goodness, I'll have three days alone and can approach this mess in an orderly manner, which is more than I can do when Malvina or Mrs. R. is here. Malvina is so unsystematic that I don't know how she ever gets anything done. It drives me crazy, but I work the way I want to, and she does likewise, and somehow it does get done. The first thing I'm going to do is to call the Library and have somebody come over here to remove all the accumulation that goes over there. That will at least give the place some semblance of order.

I think Mrs. R. will mention the cerebral palsied children whenever she has a chance. However, it takes something special—a visit or letters or something—to give her an opening. I know, though, from talking to her about Francie, that she is really interested. She told me the other day that she hadn't been aware of our situation until Malvina told her what a struggle we were having with Francie, so I'm sure she won't miss a chance.

Malvina and Mrs. R. want to send me mail, let me do it at home during the summer, and pay me so much an hour for the time I put on it. I think it is their only solution, as they can't get any help up here. I told them I would do it gladly—which I will—but, honestly, *when* am I going to find time? However, they say that time can be found for everything if you really want to, and I am so familiar with the work that it won't bother me. You can help in opening the mail and possibly with the writing if I dictate the answers. Between us I think we can do it, and the extra money will come in handy. We'll just have to let the house go and see this through. They have been so swell to me that I would really like to do it, and so much of the mail should be answered before Malvina ever sees it if it is going to be of any help to her. Then, too, the policy now is somewhat different, and I know from being up here how ruthless to be: what to throw away, what goes to the Library, the setup of the files, etc. Don't you think we can manage it? In the fall when they move to New York, I think Mrs. R. will set up an office and hire a young girl to work into the job, which is what she should do.

I think I'll take Fala and go down to Nelly's for dinner tonight. I don't see any point in fussing around here. Have to walk the damn dog anyhow, so I might as well walk him for a purpose.

Now I'm going to light a fire in the fireplace, settle down to some peace and quiet, and try to get the morning's mail opened. The calm of the place is almost more than I can bear!

June 7, 1945

DEAREST BOB,

I wanted to go down to Nelly's to change my clothes after lunch, so I took Mrs. R.'s bicycle and rode down, and was it ever fun! She has an English bicycle with a high seat and a hand brake, and you can really go on the thing. I thought I would probably break my neck, but after the first two minutes, I felt as though I'd never been off one. Funny how you never forget how to do things once you learn.

Must go out and hunt up my pup. He has been pretty good, but this morning he went out when we got up and didn't come back all morning. Finally, along came Griffin, one of the yard men, with Fala on a long rope. He had found him way down the road playing with some other dogs so thought he had better bring him home. He is something. These sunny days he wants to stay out all day, so I let him. Lord knows, it rained for a month, and I think the sun ought to be good for him.

June 8, 1945

DEAREST BOB,

My "responsibility"—by name Fala—has been a very good little dog. I put his blanket right beside my bed last night, and he slept there, without budging I guess, the whole night through. In fact, I had to wake him up at quarter of eight when I got up—he was still pounding his ear. The sun has been shining all day—for a change— and he has been out every minute but has been real good, just lying around near the back of the house, so I have had no trouble with him. I combed and brushed him, fed him, watered him, and I guess that was all I was supposed to do to him.

I took Mrs. R.'s bike tonight and was riding on it, and Fala had a swell time. He thought it was great fun and would tear along beside me as fast as his little legs would carry him. He is in now and has completely passed out. He even goes in the bedroom where it is dark. He's just like a kid.

June 14, 1945

DEAR MOM,

Got back to Washington last night and came to work at the office today. I surely hated to leave Hyde Park as it seemed so final this time, although both Mrs. Roosevelt and Malvina insisted that Bob and I should come up on our vacation whenever we can. And if I could manage to get another detail from the office, they wanted me to do so. However, I'm ready to stay put for a while because traveling is horrible between Washington and New York.

Before I left Hyde Park Elliott, Faye,* and her little boy, "Scoop," arrived. Elliott went on to Washington, but Faye and Scoop were at the cottage. They plan to live in the President's cottage on top of the hill for the summer, so Faye was going to try to get it ready for occupancy. She is the grandest person! She is as easy to know as a next-door neighbor, is very vivacious, and works like the devil, both with Scoop and at the cottage. One would never know that she is a movie actress to see her working around there! At night for dinner she did get cleaned up, though, and looked very nice. She came in and helped me open mail, and the last night I was there I had dinner at the cottage with Mrs. Roosevelt, Faye, Malvina, and Scoop. We had cocktails before dinner and were feeling pretty gay, so we had lots of fun.

Faye is going to do a broadcast next Tuesday night from 8:30 to 9:00 over CBS, so I had been helping her with the arrangements during the day and told her I was going to be listening on Tuesday night. She said she didn't know what she was going to get into, but they are paying her $1,000, so she thought she would take a chance. I said that I wished somebody would pay me $1,000 for a broadcast; then I'd do it, too. Malvina piped up and said, "Dearie, you could get a lot more than $1,000 if you would tell all you know about the Roosevelts!" I said that gave me an idea, and Mrs. Roosevelt said she would be very much interested in what I might say,

---

*Faye Emerson, movie and television actress, who married Elliott Roosevelt in 1944, as his third wife.

and would I give her a sample? At that, we quit the horseplay!

There is no work here at the office: Mrs. Truman isn't getting a thing as yet. Malvina is going to send as much of Mrs. Roosevelt's mail as she can down to me, and I'm going to do it for her this summer. But this job at the White House is going to be deadly!

June 18, 1945

DEAR FRAN,

Today is "Eisenhower Day," and we are all off at 11:00 to see the parade. Eisenhower is returning, and they are giving him a big blowout. Think I'll go out back to watch as I can't look with any joy on getting into the huge crowd today. He is coming to the White House at 2:30, and I suppose I could go over in the lobby to see him, but, somehow, I'm no celebrity chaser—seen too many of them, I think.

The work in the office is stupid now. Mrs. Truman gets no mail at all. They have agreed to let me work on Mrs. Roosevelt's mail when Malvina sends it down, so that will give me something to do, which pleases me. I can't stand this inactivity, and there probably won't be much of anything all summer, as Mrs. Truman is in Independence, and I know, from having been at Hyde Park and seen the mail that continues to come up there, that people are still writing to Mrs. Roosevelt and not to Mrs. Truman.

We went out in the rose garden Saturday and watched the President present a medal. President Truman is a nice little fellow and seems to be terribly anxious to be friendly and unassuming; he buzzes around and in and out, but he makes no impression on me whatever. It just doesn't seem that he could be President of the United States. There was always a kind of aura around President Roosevelt. I suppose it was mainly because of his affliction and inability to get around without a retinue along, but seeing him never failed to give me a thrill no matter how often it occurred.

I would like to be back at Hyde Park again, now that hot weather is upon us. It was so cold and rainy all the time I was up there that I didn't get a single swim or do anything outside, but, then, there was so much work that there would have been little opportunity to do

President Roosevelt's "Top Cottage," Hyde Park, N.Y. Courtesy: Miss
Deborah Dows and Franklin D. Roosevelt Library. Credit: Drawing by
Olin Dows.

anything anyhow. Mrs. Roosevelt wants me to come back if at all possible later in the summer, but I think I've left my family enough for one year.

Later:

We have just received word that President Truman is going to give Eisenhower a medal at 2:30 this afternoon, and we are all invited, so that will be nice. Will really be able to see the General then.

Monday, 7:30 p.m.
July 23, 1945

DEAREST BOB,

Well, here I am, and it almost seems as though I had never left. Everybody seems to take me very much for granted and as part of the establishment, and life goes on as usual: the number of visitors and general confusion is just as great.

The trip was o.k. except that the train into New York was a half hour late, which gave me just a half hour to change stations and get the train to Poughkeepsie. I couldn't get a taxi at Penn Station: there were about four times as many people waiting as there were cabs, and I had just about despaired when I was able to elbow my way through and hop in a cab with no consideration for anyone else. I had exactly five minutes when I got to Grand Central. I fairly threw the money at the driver, a porter grabbed my bag, we *ran* at top speed, and I just got on as the train pulled out. Would have had a three-hour wait if I hadn't made it and probably would have had to stand all the way. There was standing room only in the coaches as it was.

James met me, and we went to the express office, but my bag wasn't there yet. Then we went to a drug store so I could buy a toothbrush and some toothpaste, which I had forgotten, then to Nelly's where I left my bag and hat, and on up to the cottage. Malvina and I had a drink and talked. She is quite harrassed, I think, not by the work so much as by the people. John Roosevelt and his wife are here, Elliott and Faye with their five children—by all their various husbands and wives—and a tutor for Bill Roosevelt. And I think Franklin, Jr., is coming Saturday. There has been a constant stream of visitors, and I think Malvina is looking forward to getting away. Then I will be here alone, which suits me fine.

I'll be so damned glad when this assignment is over, and I'll be home to stay. It certainly is not of my choice, but Malvina was so delighted to see me, and I think even Fala remembered me. However, there is no place like home. But I guess I can sweat this out. If you and Francie were here it would be swell, but I get lonesome.

Wednesday, 6:00 p.m.
July 25, 1945

DEAREST BOB,

I am so glad that I am established in the playhouse, as I am sure I would get nothing at all done if I had to stay in the cottage. This place resembles Grand Central Station as much as anyplace I know.

Today we had about 25 boys from the Wiltwyck School—colored kids—for a picnic lunch. Had to help serve the food, and with all the grandchildren under foot, there was great confusion. Those poor little devils surely deserve a good time. I was talking with Dr. Cooper, the head of the school, and he said that the kids were all sent to Wiltwyck after committing some of the worst crimes imaginable. They range in age from about seven to seventeen and are nice appearing boys, and they are certainly well behaved. Dr. Cooper said that a good proportion of them are mental cases, but they had to have those right along with the rest of them because there is no other place for them to be sent except to an insane asylum or state reformatory. These kids surely are born with three strikes against them, it seems. Dr. Cooper said that the homes these boys come from are mostly the lowest of the low, but still the boys are always anxious to go back and talk constantly about the week they will be allowed to spend at home. He said that in a great many of the homes the fathers are drunkards and the mothers prostitutes or worse. But still the children seem to think that that is the only thing that belongs to them, and they wait anxiously for their turn for a vacation. However, some parents are so terribly irresponsible the school can't allow the children to go to them, and, he said, it is a big problem to make the children realize that they are better off to stay at the school. Dr. Cooper is a fine person to talk with. I enjoyed it immensely.

At tea time Madame Chiang, Elliott and Faye, and the mob of kids came. Tonight Mr. and Mrs. Hannegan, and a couple more from the State Democratic Committee are coming for dinner and the night; tomorrow we all go to Hyde Park for the issuance of the Roosevelt stamp—speech making and whatnot—and then we all go to the Catholic Church for lunch—eighteen of us!

It will surely seem good when everybody goes away, and there is a little peace and quiet. I suppose I'll have to offer to take care of Fala as I think Mrs. R. plans to take him with her to New York because the maids will be away. Lord knows what she would do with him in her apartment in New York! But Malvina said she wouldn't ask me to take care of him. So, I'll offer, but I hope she turns me down. I would have to take him down to Nelly's with me at night and bring him back in the morning.

I think Mrs. R. promised Mme. Chiang that she would go to China, and she has already half-promised to go to Russia and India, so, as Malvina says, it looks like a long vacation for somebody. Mrs. R. intends to go alone, so maybe Malvina would get a break for a while. However, lots can happen between now and then.

Thursday p.m.
July 26, 1945

DEAR FRAN,

Today they opened the sale of the Roosevelt 1¢ stamp at the Hyde Park Post Office. All was great confusion—it was hot—and the usual rush. Eighteen of us went to the ceremonies—all the kids, Faye and Elliott, Mrs. R., Mr. Hannegan, the Postmaster General, and Mrs. Hannegan, Mr. Fitzgerald, the Chairman of the New York Democratic Committee, Malvina and I, and some others from New York. Even Fala went along. They were typical small-town ceremonies. Mr. Hannegan and Mrs. Roosevelt had to speak. There wasn't room on the platform for all of us, so Malvina and I took a couple of the kids

Issuance of the first Franklin D. Roosevelt memorial one-cent stamp at the Hyde Park Post Office, July 26, 1945. Mrs. Roosevelt is seated at the left of the podium; her daughter-in-law, Faye Emerson Roosevelt, sits next to her, with Elliott Roosevelt sitting beside her. At the right of the podium is Postmaster General Robert E. Hanngegan. Dorothy Dow stands in the rear at the far left. Fala is in front of the platform. Courtesy: Dorothy Dow Butturff.

and Fala in tow, and, somehow, we all got together again afterward.

You have no idea what it is like to go around with a "notable." Everybody stares at one as though he must be God Himself; they besiege one for pictures, autographs, and everything else. Poor Mrs. R. and Faye (because she is a movie actress) just had to shake people loose in order for us to drive off as the people crowded around them and around the car. But finally we got back to the Big House, and Mrs. R. took the guests through. Faye and I just plunked ourselves down in the first chairs available and sprawled, with the kids swarming around, until the sightseeing trip was over.

Then we all had to go back to the Town Hall in the village for a lunch that was being served by the Catholic Church. I took Faye's boy and Fala in hand, and everything went well. I kept Fala's leash on my arm, but he sat under the table and never moved the whole time, and Scoopy and I get along famously, so that wasn't too bad. However, we were all pretty tired and hot when we finally reached home.

Faye is the grandest person you could ever hope to meet. I like her far better than any of the Roosevelt boys or their wives. She is very vivacious and capable, and she takes those kids in hand like a veteran. Elliott's children just adore her, and they never seem to get on her nerves; she works like a Trojan. I certainly admire her and hope that the marriage works out. I think Elliott would be a little difficult to deal with, but Faye certainly seems to be able to manage him, too.

Friday, 8:45 p.m.
July 27, 1945

DEAREST BOB,

Today was a total loss as far as work was concerned, but then, I think most days will be until everyone goes away. I work out in the playhouse in an effort to be alone, but Scoop and David came in first crack, and I had one perched on each arm of my chair and tumbling over me for almost an hour. I suppose I could have chased them out, but they are such cute kids, and I enjoy them both so much that I didn't have the heart. David was three in January, and we all call him "Texas." He seems much older and tries so hard to be rough, tough stuff that you could just die watching him. Scoop is really my favorite, though. He is crazy about music, sings well, has wonderful rhythm, and he will sit quietly and talk or sing for a long time. He is five years old.

I finally got a few letters written, and then, at twelve o'clock, we went on a picnic—the whole gang. We went up to Tivoli, to the house where Mrs. R.'s grandmother lived and where she grew up. No one has lived there for years. The road and grounds have completely grown up in weeds and underbrush, and the house has almost completely fallen to pieces. It is on the Hudson, overlooking the Catskills—a most gorgeous view. We spread blankets down on the tall grass and tried to find a comfortable spot. The grass was so tall that Fala got lost in it. We had to make sandwiches, and the kids were starved by the time we got there, so it was all pretty messy, and, needless to say, it would have been easier to eat at home. Poor Faye works so hard to keep the children happy and out of mischief.

Mrs. R. told everybody the history of the house, and then we went in. It must have been a gorgeous place in its day; there are some furniture and dishes in it yet. Faye and Elliott went over the things and loaded the station wagon with what they wanted. The kids tramped all over the place—which was rather dangerous as the ceilings were falling and the floors rotting—but luckily nobody was hurt. But dirty! All of us were smudged and begrimed from top to bottom. There was no water on the place, so we had to come back as was, and we surely looked like a bunch of Okies! Faye and Elliott had the station wagon so loaded that furniture and linens were hanging out all around, and the kids were stuffed in every available corner. Chandler and Tony came with us. We had a good time laughing at ourselves, anyhow, and didn't get back until after 5:00. We opened the morning's mail and called it quits. It surely does seem good to get out in the sun and air so much; it makes you feel like a different person.

Well, I think I'll darn the holes in my swimming suit; I haven't been in swimming yet and seem to have lost my taste for it, but Mrs. R. and the kids are beginning to high-pressure me, so suppose I'll have to come to it.

We had *steak* for dinner—and swell! Nelly had found it in town this morning and was as proud of it as if it was solid gold. I did justice to it, too.

Saturday, 5:15 p.m.
July 28, 1945

DEAREST BOB,

Today has been very unexciting, at least, comparatively speaking. I have worked all day and really have accomplished something. It has poured all afternoon, and the kids are housebound, so I have had things very peaceful out here in the playhouse. Tony and Chandler haven't even braved the pool, and that is something! However, I wonder right now how I'm going to get over to the house without getting drowned.

Scoop and David came in this morning, both with their faces swollen from some poison ivy they got into on the picnic yesterday.

John Roosevelt and his wife, Anne, are here today, and Faye and Elliott have gone away for the weekend. So there were the three oldest children, Pixie, John, Anne, Mrs. R., Mrs. J. R. Roosevelt, Malvina and I for lunch, which seems like a crowd, but it wasn't as bad as usual. Franklin and Ethel are coming tonight—and Jimmie also—for over Sunday. They have to sign papers and such things to settle the estate.

I just wonder how you get my letters; they must come in bunches as they certainly get mailed at odd hours, and one never knows what the Hyde Park Post Office does, especially now: with the first day issue of the Roosevelt stamp, the poor people have been swamped.

I will be so glad to get home. I wish I could move this work to Washington, and then everything would be wonderful. I like it better than anything I have ever done, and it is a shame that it isn't possible

The house near Tivoli, New York, where Mrs. Roosevelt lived as a child with her grandmother, Mary Ludlow Hall. Courtesy: Franklin D. Roosevelt Library.

to continue. I hate to think of going back to that humdrum at the office again.

I surely wish I could be with you tomorrow when you go to see angel child. I don't suppose she'll even miss me, but I surely do miss her.

Sunday, 5:30 p.m.
July 29, 1945

DEAREST BOB,

Sunday here is the same as any other day. I worked all morning, and then Malvina and I had lunch with the big kids as Mrs. R., John, Anne, and James went to Miss Delano's. The kids are devils when their grandmother is out from underfoot, but we had fun anyhow. I came out to the playhouse this afternoon to do some more work, and they wouldn't let me in—had the door barricaded because they were playing war. I finally persuaded them that I wouldn't interrupt their game, so they let me in, but what a commotion! If anyone could work, he would either be deaf or a genius. I was glad when they all decided to go swimming. They are a noisy, energetic bunch, but just the same, I know we will miss them when they go. Haven't seen David or Scoop all day; I think their nurse kept them up at the Top Cottage as Faye and Elliott aren't here.

I think Malvina isn't going to get much of a vacation. Mrs. R. rules her completely and told her just what she should do: go to New York on Wednesday, do a few columns, leave Friday for Muriel's and stay until Tuesday, when she would have to go back to New York for a few more columns; then she could go back for a few days if she wanted to, but Malvina says "Nix!" Traveling isn't that much fun, and she would rather come back up here where the two of us could be alone and it would be far more restful than galloping hither and yon. However, she may go, later, up on the St. Lawrence with Henry.

August 1, 1945

DEAREST BOB,

Malvina and I are here alone, except for James Roosevelt, who came back this afternoon; he is working on the estate and will be here until Thursday. It is so peaceful it is hardly believable. I think Malvina would just like to stay on here with me and not go away at all. She says it is more of a rest and more enjoyable than anything else she could do, and I rather believe it. However, Mrs. Roosevelt runs her life, and she does just what Mrs. Roosevelt says, and she has it all planned out just where Malvina should go and for how long.

I took Lucy to the train this morning and then went uptown and had myself a shopping spree; got everything I went after, too, which is quite a feat. It's fun to shop in a town this size—no waiting for clerks, and no crowds.

Have managed to do a little work this afternoon as Malvina had to go over to the Big House with James, so I've been alone. Fala has been begging me on bended knees to take him outdoors, so I think I'll have to.

Thursday a.m.
August 2, 1945

DEAREST BOB,

James Roosevelt has been here going through everything to take what he wants, and it has kept us both busy, making lists, checking, etc. He is an awfully nice fellow. I think I like him better than any of the boys, and he is quite thrilled over the prospect of his new baby, which they expect in November. He sits and talks about possible names and, I think, has decided that if it is a girl, it will be Anna Rebecca, and if a boy, Anthony Michael—after Rommie's grandfather, who came over here as a refugee from Poland.

We—James, Malvina, and I—went down to Nelly's for dinner last night for steak, which she had wangled out of some dealer, and he was so entertaining, telling about when he first got news of his father's death and also some of his experiences. He didn't have to take boot training, as he took ROTC in college and then got his commission in the Reserve. However, he said, when the Marines finally do get through the horrors of boot training, they are the best-trained outfit going. He is going to get a medical discharge, and they have bought a house in Beverly Hills because they couldn't find one place to rent under $750 a month, which he wouldn't pay. He said that the house they bought has three bedrooms, is about fourteen years old, but is built in Eastern style with good walls, insulation, etc., instead of the way so many of those California houses are built.

Malvina goes today for about ten days—only about five days of which will be a vacation with Muriel—but I'm glad she is going to get away, at least. James wants me to go over to his father's grave with him this morning while he lays out Mr. Plog, who is supposed to be taking care of it and who does everything else but. I was over the other day and thought what a sad looking sight it was. It is beginning to sink, and the flowers and wreaths on it were all wilted and bedraggled, and I was wishing somebody would do something about it. When James went over yesterday he just about blew his top, and he is going to get a nurseryman to plant something green and nice looking to outline the grave and then tell Plog to keep flowers on it and keep them fresh. He wants me to go over occasionally and check up on it to see that he is doing it. It will be a good thing when they get the stone, I think, and get some kind of permanent care for the grave. You have no idea how desolate it looks—just a sunken spot in the middle of a big, grassy yard, covered with wilted flowers.

Guess I'd better get to work. I haven't done much the last couple of days because John and James have both been here, and we have been helping them. However, I know that when everyone goes I'll be able to concentrate on this business, and it won't take long to clean it up. All I need is some uninterrupted time.

Friday a.m.
August 3, 1945

DEAREST BOB,

I know for a fact that you will probably get about six letters all at once. I see that yesterday's mail is still sitting on the sideboard waiting for somebody to take it. We forgot it when I took James and Malvina to the train yesterday and thought that whoever met Elliott could take it, but we have had no word from Elliott—so there it is! And today this will have to go with the Hyde Park mailman, which means a couple of extra days.

I spent all yesterday morning running around with James so he could tell me and show me the things he wanted packed and shipped to him. The packers are coming on Monday or Tuesday, and I suppose I'll spend that day with them to be sure they get everything.

We had to go up over the stables, over the garage, then up to the Top Cottage, then over to the Big House, then to the Library, and it was after twelve when we got back. He gave me a check for $50 and showed me what he wanted done to his father's grave, so if Mr. Plog doesn't get going on that, I have to keep after him, too, and see that it is done. I will be glad to do it, though, as the condition of that grave gave me the horrors. James is certainly a fine fellow. I think he has all the other children beat for charm and common sense. We got back to the cottage for lunch, and then I took both James and Malvina to the 2:47 train, so now I am alone with *stacks* of work to do. James is going on to California, and Malvina won't be back until about a week from tomorrow.

I offered to take care of Fala while Mrs. R. was gone, so she wouldn't have to take him to New York with her. I took him down to Nelly's with me last night, and the poor pup was sort of bewildered. He didn't know what it was all about. I don't dare let him outside of the door without his leash down there because of the cars, and I had to take him out about six times during the evening. However, when I went to bed, he settled down in my room and was quiet all night and waited until I spoke to him this morning before he bothered me. Took him out, then ate breakfast, and then brought him up here. He is surely a nicely behaved little pup, although I can't say that I relish spending so much time on a dog. I suppose I ought to give him a bath before Mrs. R. gets home as he looks like a tramp.

I must get to work. I think Malvina has been so completely bored and fed up with this stuff that she didn't care whether she did much or not before she left, so there is plenty for me. I don't blame her in the least and am glad that she left it and got out. When you reach that state of mind, you can't do anything anyhow.

Saturday a.m.
August 4, 1945

DEAREST BOB,

I got up here at 8:00 *a.m.*, so I could be sure to get your letter written, but things began to buzz the minute I got here. It is now

10:30, and it seems to be my first free minute. About 99% of the calls are for Elliott, and he doesn't have a 'phone at the Top Cottage, so it is messy. Then Mrs. Roosevelt called; then Fala was out of meat, and nobody knew where to get more, so I had to do research on that; then Chandler and Tony came down, and Chandler insisted that I go out and watch her take her horse over a two-foot jump; and I have been trying to get some date letters written, so you can see that I don't have much time for my own affairs!

Sometimes I wonder why in the world I am up here, working like the devil, taking care of the damn dog and Elliott's business, etc., etc., when I could be in my own home in Washington—or sitting in the office twiddling my thumbs. I guess I must be crazy or something. But I think the answer is that it is a pleasant place to be, and I like the people (Here come Elliott and the family, so I'll have to sign off).

Later:

That's over temporarily. When James was here, he went up to the Top Cottage and selected everything he wanted, so I had to give Elliott the list, and he burned up. But I had instructions from James to take the packers up there when they come and pack everything and send it, and Mrs. R. said to do it, too, so it's not my responsibility.

Little David—three years old—just came running back because he forgot to give me a "Texas hug." He is the cutest little fellow you ever saw—very affectionate but tries so hard to be tough.

Malvina certainly earns her money on this job. She gets $500 a month, she told me. That isn't bad money, but she deserves it!

Sunday, 4:30 p.m.
August 5, 1945

DEAREST BOB,

I am alone today but came up at 9:00 a.m. as usual to see if I couldn't get caught up with some of the mail. I have been working on it all day and am pretty well cleaned up—have done about 60 letters so far. About 20 letters more and I can start with a clean slate tomorrow.

Elliott and Faye have been down here all day, but they haven't bothered me much. There is also the student council from the FDR High School having a picnic and swimming here, and once in a while someone comes for something they forgot to bring. But other than that it has been very peaceful.

Of course, Fala takes his share of attention. I went down to Nelly's for dinner this noon as she was having corned beef and cabbage, and I took the little pup with me. I'll have him worn out by the time I get him down there again tonight. But I think he thoroughly enjoys going. The minute he finishes his last mouthful of supper, he comes over, sniffs, barks, and makes a great to-do to get started. He is a cute dog—as dogs go—but give me something I don't have to treat like a baby! He doesn't want to go upstairs in my room at Nelly's until bedtime, but then he settles right down, and in the morning he just waits for me to say something to him or make some movement before he disturbs me. However, sometimes I just watch him, and he lies there on edge waiting until it looks as though I'm awake. Then he comes over, stands up by the bed, "smiles," snorts, and wiggles all over and is so happy when I do get up so we can go out for our early morning walk. I'm usually not awake until about the time we get back. He gets me up earlier than usual, as by 7:00 or 7:30 I'm afraid he really has to go. Mrs. R. takes him out at 6:00 a.m.

You know, I feel so sorry for Elliott and Faye in all this turmoil they have been in. Elliott looks so harrassed and worried and down in the mouth.* I have just been talking to Faye. Elliott was out taking a walk, so she was alone, and she talked to me for almost an hour almost without stopping. That gal is a fighter, and she also has a lot of good common sense, but both of them feel that all of this is just persecution, that they hardly dare fight back, and that it will hurt Elliott terribly in trying to get a job when he is out of the Army on the 15th. They have pulled some dirty deals on him—the Army, too—and he

---

*Elliott was depressed because of the decision of the trustees of his father's estate not to rent Top Cottage to him but to sell the property at once. Since he could not afford to buy it himself, this seemed to him the end of his plans for living there and farming the adjacent land.

is just helpless. Faye is supposed to be back in California on the 20th to do a picture. She doesn't want to go and leave him while he is in such a stew and everything is so upset; yet she doesn't feel she can turn it down as they have no money and will need some sort of an income. I think she gets $500 a week. Still, Elliott doesn't want to go out there with her if he isn't working because he would feel as though she were supporting him. I really do feel terribly sorry for them both. I certainly like Faye a great deal, and she seems to be very happy with Elliott. She also knows the press and radio people and how they act, and she can really fight like a tiger with them, but Elliott is afraid to open his mouth for fear it will bring more reflections upon his father. All in all, it is a bad situation. Believe me, people in the public eye have to put up with plenty. I don't know why Faye spilled it all out to me as she did—perhaps because I was the only one here, and she was all tied up in a knot. There was nothing much I could say except to sympathize and wish them luck.

Monday, 6:00 p.m.
August 6, 1945

DEAREST BOB,

Oh, brother! Am I having a time trying to keep up with this place! My admiration for Malvina rises by the minute, although I know that she never does get caught up.

I got up here about 8:00 this morning (Fala sees to that) and spent the first 3½ hours clearing out Malvina's living room—literally shoveling it out. I have never seen such a mess! Something was sitting on everything in the room. James and Alice wanted to get in there to give it a good cleaning, and they couldn't do a thing because they didn't know what to do with things. I did a land office job, but I know it won't stay like this.

About 11:30 the packers came to pick up Col. James's things. They were mad and in a vile humor because they had to come right at their lunch time. It has been pouring rain all day, but despite everything I threw on a raincoat, took the station wagon and escorted them over to the stable, to the garage, up to the Top Cottage, and then over to the Big House. They picked up everything that had to be crated. Then I took them to the Library and turned them over to one of the men there with my blessings. Now they have to come back and go over the route again to get things like china and glass that have to be packed. I didn't get back to the cottage until 2:00 p.m., and Alice gave me some lunch. Mail was dumped all over everything, so from 2:30 until about fifteen minutes ago I just opened and sorted it. Haven't answered a letter, and they are just stacked up. Mrs. R. sent me three envelopes full from New York. I want to write her a letter to give her a report on the place, as I am sure she would like to get it. She wrote me a note in longhand, so it is the least I can do, I suppose. I am taking all the stuff she sent home with me tonight, as it is hopeless here.

Fala is having fits and spasms because he thinks it is time for us to go to Nelly's inasmuch as he has finished his supper, and James is waiting to drive me home because it is still pouring. I'm beginning to understand why Malvina works late every night—you would have to in order even to begin to keep up with all this work.

Tuesday a.m.
August 7, 1945

DEAREST BOB,

It surely has been cold and rainy up here. I am back in my uniform—my suit. I don't know why I even bother to bring anything else up here. I have one cotton and two wool blankets over me at night, and I wish I had brought my flannel pajamas. This has been a crazy summer.

I haven't done anything today but work, and I did accomplish a great deal. Just went up to the Top Cottage and had a visit with Faye. I ran out of envelopes, and Elliott said I could have some that they had up there, so Fala and I drove the station wagon up to get them. Faye was just lolling around—sans makeup; sans street clothes—and said absolutely nobody is going to get her out of the house today. I think she has her eyes wide open and has a lot of backbone. My only fear is that because she is so much smarter and more capable than

Elliott, if there is any friction, that is where it will be. He doesn't seem very astute to me, and he has a horrible inferiority complex which is quite apparent. I think Faye tries for all she is worth to build up his ego, and that is what he needs. She is supposed to be back by the 20th to start her next picture. I will certainly have to make an effort to see it when it is released. I have never seen anything she has been in, and it is hard for me to imagine her in the role of a movie actress.

Wednesday, 5:15 p.m.
August 8, 1945

DEAREST BOB,

Got rid of quite a lot of work today, but I don't seem to be able to keep up with the "general" mail. That is the stuff Malvina usually sends me in Washington. But by the time I finish what Mrs. Roosevelt sends me, then frank and mail it, open and sort all the incoming mail, and get Mrs. R.'s ready to go to her, the day is about shot.

Faye and Elliott hang around a good bit of the day, too, which is distracting. However, I do manage to keep this room in order and not let stuff accumulate all over it. Alice and James gave it a wonderful cleaning yesterday, and it is going to stay neat, at least until Malvina comes back. Then I know what it will look like in five minutes! She is supposed to get back in New York from Muriel's today and will stay there until Saturday and then come up here.

Faye surely is a nice girl; she is so friendly I almost feel as though I've known her all my life. I go up to their house once in a while when I have a free minute, and we sit and shoot the bull.

Thursday, 5:30 p.m.
August 9, 1945

DEAREST BOB,

Think I'll call it quits for tonight. I'm about a day's work behind, but as there is no fire under it, it can wait. I get so weary of the stuff that I might as well quit for all I can accomplish.

Did nothing much but work today. At noon Mr. Plog—over at the Big House—called and said he had finished fixing the President's grave the way Jimmy wanted it, and would I come over to see it? So I took the darned old station wagon, as the Ford was in the garage for service, and went over. Then I had to stop at the Library, and on my way back to the Big House, the engine stopped. I fooled with it, but nothing happened. Finally, a MP came along; he got in and tried it, but with no success. The starter just wouldn't turn over the engine. Soon two more MPs came along, and they pushed the car up and down the driveway, yelling instructions at me about letting out the clutch, stepping on the accelerator, etc., but still nothing happened. Then Mr. Plog came; he lifted the hood and said there was no spark at all. Just then it started to pour. But one of the Library pickup trucks came up the drive, and with Mr. Plog driving, Fala and I just sat comfortably in the back seat while they pushed us up to the gate. But the engine still wouldn't start. Then they got out a tow rope and hauled us to the garage in Hyde Park. The Ford was all ready to go, so I took that and left the station wagon for whatever has to be done to it. Got home about 1:30, and I was so mad! That station wagon is an awful rattletrap anyhow, and, believe me, I'll never drive it again. A car is o.k. as long as it goes, but when it stops, deliver me! I was just lucky that it didn't happen someplace in the woods on my way back where there would have been nobody to help me. Took six people as it was!

The news in the world is quite exciting these days what with the new bomb and Russia going to war with Japan. That new atomic discovery sort of gives me the horrors. It just seems too, too much to me. I suppose it is the thing to use, though, if it will make the Japs give in any sooner, but I can't help but think of the poor little Japanese kids—they are so blameless and yet must go through that hell.

Well, think I'll pick up my little dog and go on home. Must take a book, too. I have just finished a good one—*So Well Remembered* by James Hilton. Suppose I should take some work, but I don't think I could bear it.

My time is over half gone now, so it won't be long before I'll be home—for good!

Friday, 2:00 p.m.
August 10, 1945

DEAREST BOB,

Malvina called me this morning and said she and Henry will be in at 6:15, and she wants me to stay up here and have dinner with them so we can go over things tonight. They leave at 11:00 a.m. tomorrow morning for a week's vacation on the St. Lawrence, and I am so darned glad: Malvina hasn't had a vacation in twelve years and needs it. I know she wouldn't go unless I were here, because the accumulation of mail facing her when she returned would be more than anyone could stand. I'll be alone for another week to handle the work.

She was jubilant over the news about the possible surrender of Japan. She said Mrs. R. had been asked to stand by so she could broadcast if it came through officially, and that she had also written her Peace Day column. They told Mrs. R. that they expected certainty in not more than 48 hours. I hope to heaven they are right. I would hate to think of any more of those atomic bombs dropping on people, but, of course, if it did bring peace sooner, I suppose it was worth it.

Well, I must get to my work. Want to get stuff cleaned up as much as I possibly can before Malvina arrives so the place will look respectable for a few minutes at least.

Saturday
August 11, 1945

DEAREST BOB,

You lucky devil—I suppose you have the afternoon off! That is one thing I don't get up here—nor Sundays either. I have enough work cut out for me to do tomorrow to keep me going all day.

Malvina and Henry came up at 6:30 last night, and she brought a pack of work from New York with her. Gosh, what a disorderly person she is! I have kept her living room looking very nice and picked up all of the time, and she hadn't been here five minutes before stuff was strewn all over hell and gone. Her desk is a mess again, and I've been trying to collect stuff and get it into some kind of sequence ever since. She wanted me to stay for dinner and go over the work afterward, so I did. Faye and Elliott came up on the same train with them, so they ate with us. We had drinks before, and I think all of them must have had some in New York because they were surely feeling gay. I hadn't seen Henry for a long time, and he looks much older; his hair is almost white, and he has gotten heavier. About 9:00 p.m. Malvina unloaded her brief case, very hurriedly told me what to do on some things, and left the rest to my imagination.

They left at 10:00 this morning, and she seemed very happy to be going. I think she is at last in a vacation mood, and I hope she has a good time. I took them down to the train, then cashed Jimmy's check and paid his bills, went to the Post Office, and got back just in time to greet the mailman. Alice had a day off today, so I had to get my own lunch. Then I took off my shoes, settled down on a couch on the porch with all the stuff I could pick up out of the room, and proceeded to try to make some sense out of it. Have it about half done. I certainly worked in comfort if nothing else.

Sunday, 3:00 p.m.
August 12, 1945

DEAREST BOB,

Golly, I'll be glad when this day is over. I always feel so lonesome on Sundays. Today is particularly dead as nobody is here—haven't even seen Faye and Elliott. Alice has gone to the movies, and James just came in looking rather down in the mouth, so I asked him why he didn't take the afternoon off for a change. He said he would like to go to the movies, but he didn't feel he should use the gas. I told him that if he would wait until I got the mail ready—about 5:30—he could take it down to mail it, if it would ease his conscience about using the gas, and then stay down for the show. He was very pleased, and I am, too, as this letter gets mailed today, and Mrs. R.'s really should go also.

I have been working all day on the stuff Malvina left for me and will soon have it finished. However, I have a day's filing to do, so I won't be caught up before the onset of tomorrow's mail, which is always large. One is never through here.

I would like to come home August 25th instead of waiting until September 1st. I don't know what to do. It seems as though I've been away for just ages. Malvina will eventually have to get some other plan worked out for help anyhow, so she might as well start early as late. Well, no use continuing this dirge; I'd better write some more "official" letters as I suppose James will be standing on his ear waiting for them. I don't blame him—it gets pretty deadly up here at times.

Monday, 5:00 p.m.
August 13, 1945

DEAREST BOB,

I was going out to the playhouse to see if I could get some of the filing put away but have lost my ambition, so will write you and to hell with the filing! I think after I get the mail ready, I will have put in a full day's work, so I can leave what's left until tomorrow.

Mrs. Lash's baby was born last night, and I think that, in the excitement, Mrs. R. forgot to file her column, and the Syndicate was burning up the wires here about it. Alice told them to call me at Nelly's, and about six times during the evening they called, saying they couldn't get Mrs. R.'s apartment, that it was past the deadline, etc. I told them there wasn't a thing I could do about it, that I had tried to get the apartment, too, and that nobody answered. So, this morning I called Mrs. R., and she said she didn't get home until about midnight; the Syndicate reached her then, and she told them to file an extra that she had sent in, just in case of such an emergency. The baby was a boy—8 pounds 6 ounces. I guess everything went o.k.

Mrs. R. called me again this afternoon about several little chores to do. The way these people use the long distance telephone is frightening. Her bill for this last month was $205. Mostly unnecessary, too. Elliott just sits here and calls Los Angeles, San Diego, St. Louis, Washington, time after time, and it's senseless. None of it is pressing business. I think it makes him feel like a big shot; of course, mama pays the bills. That boy seems terribly irresponsible to me.

Guess I'll get the mail ready, take my little dog, go home, and unlax.

Tuesday, 5:00 p.m.
August 14, 1945

DEAREST BOB,

Have done nothing but work since 8:00 a.m. Fala got me up at 6:15 this morning. He really had to go out; he stood up by my bed and woofed and then almost wagged himself to pieces when I opened my eyes. So I got up, put on one of Nelly's coats, and took him out until he was well watered. Then came back and went to bed for another hour. I'll be glad when my responsibility for that pup is over. He is a very nice little dog, but it doesn't make for very peaceful evenings as he wants to go for a walk, has to be taken out and let in, etc. I wouldn't mind taking him for a walk except that the mosquitoes are so terrible around here. They descend in hordes all over you, and I can stand it for only a few minutes before I want to go in. There are so many pretty walks if it were bearable.

Mrs. R. called me this morning about several chores to do; also had a letter from her in the mail. These Roosevelts are funny people. The most insignificant things are important enough for a 'phone call, and everything must be done at once. Jimmy called me this afternoon from Los Angeles and wanted to know when his shipment had left. It hasn't even been all packed yet! They get into such a stew. Last night at 10:00 p.m., while I was taking Fala out for his last watering, a station wagon drew up, and here were Elliott and Faye. They were about to leave for New York and discovered they didn't have any cash—not even enough to pay their train fares. Luckily, I had $30, so Faye gave me her check for $20, which was what they wanted. They have known for two days that they were going to New York but never thought about getting any money until almost train time. Dizzy—I calls it!

The packers are coming again tomorrow to finish Jimmy's things, so I suppose I'll spend most of the morning with them. That means so much less time to get caught up on the mail. I don't know why I worry about it—Malvina is *never* caught up—but I hate to get behind too far, as it is hopeless then.

I think I'll take my little dog, get the car, and drive down to the Post Office with all the mail. There is so much of it, and I think Mrs. R. had better be getting hers at least.

Wednesday
August 15, 1945
V-J Day

DEAREST BOB,

Well, last night was quite some excitement, huh? How I wished I had been home! Everybody up here went nuts; you could hear way up at Nelly's the whistles and sirens in Poughkeepsie, and the cars, loaded with crazy people, were tearing by all night. I had no desire to get in the mobs but would have liked to have been with you. Thank God, that is over. It hardly seems real.

I didn't think about coming back to the cottage, and poor Jennings was here alone. She is old—used to be the old lady's personal maid and Mrs. R. just took her over—and calls and wires were coming in to Mrs. R. all night, and it just about floored her. President Truman was trying to get Mrs. R., and finally Jennings called me. So, I called the operator and told her to switch all calls to 21 F 4, and I also got the White House operator and gave her Mrs. R.'s number in New York, but she said nobody answered. Today telegrams have been coming in all day, but I told Western Union to keep them there, and I would come down and get them. So that is what I'll do when I finish this. I couldn't be bothered taking them over the 'phone. I suppose the mail will come in in volume again now, too. I dread to think of it.

Malvina called me this morning and said she was having a good time and would be back on Monday; then she would have to go to New York, according to Mrs. R., for a few days before they return up here for good. That is bad for me, as I hate to ask her to leave on the 25th then. I suppose I'll have to stay until September 1st. I'm trying to keep everything up to date, but I have a perfectly horrible feeling that the V-J mail is going to be pretty bad. It started even before victory was declared. It remains to be seen, though.

Well, I think I'll sign the mail, get Mrs. R.'s ready to send to her, and then go downtown and collect the telegrams. Think I'll take Fala with me. He loves to ride and behaves nicely on a leash when we get out of the car, and he gets lonesome by himself. We get no mail delivery tomorrow, so Mr. Stone informed me this morning. That will give me a day to clean up what I have on hand, and I can start fresh on Friday. The owner of the packing firm said the packers didn't show up today, but he would see that they come tomorrow. However, my bet is that they don't show up tomorrow either!

Isn't it wonderful to have no more gas rationing!

Thursday a.m.
August 16, 1945

DEAREST BOB,

Think I shall write this in the morning because I will soon have to go to town and send a half-dozen cables from Mrs. R. to the Kings, Queens, Churchill, Martha of Norway, etc., for V-J Day. I simply can't cope with giving them over the 'phone, and besides, I have to pick up messages down there which have been coming in for Mrs. R. It is the most wonderful feeling to know that gas rationing is at an end, and that it is possible to run into town without wondering whether we have gas enough.

The packers came early this morning, and I have them working at the Top Cottage now. As soon as they come back, I'll have to go over to the Big House and Library with them. I'll surely be glad when that mess is over. It is a most gorgeous day, though, clear as crystal and air that feels like October. I would just as soon be running around as sitting here pounding the typewriter.

No mail delivery today, and I am glad to have a day without it, but I dread tomorrow! Malvina won't be back until Monday, and Mrs. R. said, when she called me this morning, that she plans to be in New

York all of next week, so I suppose Malvina will have to go down there. I'm sure I'm not going to get away from this place until September 1st. Oh well, might as well stick it out as it will be the last time.

August 18, 1945

DEAREST BOB,

Yesterday the darned mail was so heavy I didn't finish opening it until 5:30. Then I had to get a letter off to Mrs. R. and get all her stuff ready to go so James could take it when he met the 6:20 to pick up Elliott and Faye.

I now have some house guests on my hands—some of Mrs. R.'s odd friends—a man who was a Major in the Air Corps and who lost one leg in the process, his wife, and their two-year-old daughter, Nancy. He wears an artificial leg. Of course, one feels sorry that such a thing should have happened, but they are poachers, if you know what I mean. Mrs. R. took them under her wing last year, and they spent practically the entire summer up here, saying they couldn't find a place to live. Now she has asked them to come up to spend their vacation, so here they are, and Mrs. R. won't be back until next Thursday. Malvina will just fly in Monday night and out again to New York on Tuesday, so I have them.

Malvina simply can't stand them and told me to do just as I pleased—to have or not to have lunch with them, and to try to keep them out of this part of the house when I am working. However, I can't be rude, so will have to put up with them. I'll have lunch with them, as I can hardly do otherwise. She said last night, "Are we going to have to eat alone? Aren't you going to stay for dinner? Why do you go down to Nelly's?" etc. But I stood firm. By the time 6:00 p.m. comes, I'm ready to clear out of this place, and I use Fala as a good excuse—he must have his walk! The little girl is cute, but when the parents are not likeable, it is even difficult to make a fuss over the child.

Well, about ten or twelve more days and I'll be on my way home. I'm going to try to leave on Wednesday, August 29th. I think I will stand a better chance of getting a reservation from New York in the middle of the week. If I can, I'm not going to work on Thursday, and I'm not going to put in leave either. I'm just going to write Mr. Magee from here that I'll be back on Friday, August 31st, and he will never have to know when I left here. I figure that I owe myself a day off after working ten hours a day, seven days a week, and losing out on the V-J celebrations.

Sunday, 2:00 p.m.
August 19, 1945

DEAREST BOB,

One more Sunday up here and before the next one I'll be on my way home. And will that ever be a happy day! No more dogs to take care of, no more Sunday work or guests to entertain—just the family!

Mrs. R. called me yesterday morning and asked if I would take her guests down to Nelly's for dinner last night, so that Alice could have the afternoon off. So, of course, I did. They really are all right when we are alone, but I can see where they might be rather pushy around Mrs. R. He was telling me how he happened to lose his leg, and it was quite a story. I rode down with them and took Fala, then rode back with them with Fala, and then Fala and I walked back to Nelly's so he could get his exercise. That dog is more darned nuisance. This morning he got me up at 6:45 and insisted that he go out. I put on Nelly's coat and just sat out on the steps while he did his stuff; then in about ten minutes I made him come back in, and I went to bed again. However, I was up here at 8:45 and have been working ever since. I want to get as nearly current as possible before Malvina comes in tomorrow. Nothing else to do anyhow, so I might as well work.

We had chicken again this noon—had chicken last night—always chicken, chicken. It's a wonder I don't cackle. They have been short on points for meat and can get chickens at the farm, so we wallow in them. I don't care if I never see another one.

Yesterday afternoon about 3:30 I was so weary that I decided I was through working for the day, so I took the car, went to town, and bought some yarn. I must have some knitting to do in the evenings or I'm not happy. Got back to the house about 4:30 and read the paper; had some drinks with the guests, and then just relaxed until time to go down for dinner. This seven-day-a-week business is the bunk. You get so saturated with the monotony of the darned mail that it is impossible to work on it.

Monday, 3:45 p.m.
August 20, 1945

DEAREST BOB,

Malvina just called me from Albany and said they would be in about 6:00 and would I please stay for dinner. So there goes my evening! She is leaving for New York first thing tomorrow, though, so I will have to go over some things with her tonight. I think I'll leave Fala with her tonight and give myself a rest from the pooch.

Talking about the pooch—late yesterday afternoon I took the car and drove down to Poughkeepsie with the mail. Took Fala along and when I got in the car to go home, a couple of sailors came up and asked if that were Fala. I said "Yes." Then three girls gathered around, and they "Oh-d" and "Ah-d" over the pup and wanted his picture, so I had to get him out and let them take it. The boys wanted to know if they could see the President's grave, and I explained that it was not yet open to the public. They were crestfallen, as they had a weekend pass and had come to Poughkeepsie with the idea of hitchhiking up to the estate just to visit the grave. So I told them I was going right back and would drive them out and take them in if they could get themselves back, and they were all excited. One of them said, "I can hardly believe this—to think I'm riding in the President's car and had a chance to pet Fala," etc. They were awfully nice fellows, kept calling me "Ma'am" all of the time, and were terribly polite. I took them out to Hyde Park and into the grounds, and as they were both Catholics, they knelt down and prayed for about ten minutes at the grave. Then, having nothing else to do, I drove them over to the cottage and showed them that and the grounds, and I have never seen two people more appreciative. I finally took them down to 9-G so they could get a ride back to town, and they both said, "Believe me, Ma'am, this is one afternoon we'll remember all of our lives. We just have no way of thanking you for what you have done." I felt quite well repaid for my effort!

If I can get a word alone with Malvina tonight, I'm going to tell her that I want to leave a week from Wednesday—August 29—so she will be prepared. I think I will have fulfilled my duty if I stay that long, and as the work here never slackens or gets caught up, there is no point in waiting until things are easier. She will just have to send things to me or hire somebody else.

Must sign the letters I wrote this morning and get them ready to mail. The less stuff sitting around when Malvina gets here the better! I imagine she must have had the best rest she has had for years—just being alone with Henry and no 'phone calls or mail or worry. I hope so, at least.

Tuesday, 3:30 p.m.
August 21, 1945

DEAREST BOB,

Gosh, it's hot today. We have had so little really hot weather that it completely exhausts me. I don't feel like doing a damned thing, but there is plenty to do!

Malvina and Henry got in last night about 6:00, and they both looked grand—tan and rested looking. They said they had had a wonderful time. Henry made some martinis, which I think were my downfall. Martinis just about lay me out, anyhow, and I know Henry gets an extra dig in them someplace. We had two each and were seeing double. As a result I couldn't get to sleep last night and then woke up a half-dozen times and feel terrible today. I surely am a sport!

Of course, our house guests were here, so we all had dinner together. The wife just hangs around like glue. I had some work to go over with Malvina, so we came back to her room after dinner, but she came right after us and sat around. Then we went upstairs to Mrs. R.'s bedroom to look at some bedspreads and to try to get a few words in private, and she tagged us up there! I can't imagine what is the matter with some people. I know Malvina was ready to blow up, but she held her peace. I went down to Nelly's about 9:30, and I surely was glad to get there. Malvina and Henry left about 9:00 this morning, driving to New York, and Henry was going right on to Washington. Malvina says she is coming back here tomorrow, which I hope is right, and that she plans to stay a couple of days, at least, but Mrs. R. will probably have other ideas.

I did manage to tell Malvina that I wanted to go home a week from tomorrow, and she said I could go whenever I felt I had to, but would I consider coming back! What she suggested was that I go down for a few days to be with you and to see Francie—a sort of vacation; they would pay my train fare both ways so the government wouldn't have to know I was down there—and then come back for two or three weeks. She asked me to please consider it, but I am going to say definitely "No." I've been up here, all told, about three months this summer, and that is long enough for anyone. I've had plenty and am anxious to get home for good. Besides, train traveling is so uncomfortable and crowded that I don't want to make the trip twice. Once is too much! This work goes on and on indefinitely, and she will have to make other arrangements sooner or later.

Mrs. R. has rented an office in New York City, and they have a girl lined up to work there when they finally go back. Up here it is hard to get anybody, and if they brought her here, they would have to pay $80 a month for room and board at Nelly's besides her salary. The government pays it for me and still would allow me time to work for Mrs. R. Lord knows, they should provide somebody for six months after the death of a President like Roosevelt. But I've had enough. Malvina was going to get in touch with the girl and see if she would be willing to come up to Hyde Park for a couple of weeks, and she wanted me here to help break her in, which, Lord knows, would be a hard job. I wanted Malvina to get her up here while they were gone, as I could have worked with her then, but she didn't bother, so now she can do it alone.

I finally got Faye and Elliott off. She was supposed to report to her studio on August 20th, and they left here at 11:00 a.m. on the 18th to *drive* to Los Angeles. She said she knew she was going to be late, and I hope to heaven they are! They'll break their fool necks one of these days. They were in New York for the V-J celebration and had such a good time they couldn't leave any earlier. She hadn't been gone a half-hour when she called long distance—she had forgotten their ration books; would I go up to get them and mail them; would I tell her maid that she had a blouse at the cleaners, etc. They surely are dizzy!

Well, this is all; I can't put off working much longer or the day will be entirely gone. Malvina picked up my glasses by mistake this morning and left hers, so my eyes get very tired. I suppose that is one reason why I feel so weary. I know that Malvina always carries an extra pair with her, so she is probably all right. But hers are so strong they make me dizzy

As I said before—the end! One week from tomorrow and I'll be on my way home! Then I wonder what will happen. Something, I'm sure, as I know life just couldn't go peacefully along for this baby.

Wednesday, 4:00 p.m.
August 22, 1945

DEAREST BOB,

My life has more complications now! They are putting poison in the pond to kill the weeds and tell me not to let Fala loose for about three days. That is all I need! It is bad enough to have to watch him every minute down at Nelly's, but if I can't let him out up here, I guess I'll do nothing but mind the dog. He might be a famous pup to some people, but he is a darned nuisance to me.

Malvina called this morning and said she wouldn't be here until tomorrow evening, and Mrs. R. wasn't coming until Sunday. So that makes another day without my glasses. I'm getting used to working without them, though, and it really doesn't bother me except that I do get more tired. She said when she took the glasses out of her purse to get to work when she reached the apartment, she had a terrible scare. She thought something terrible had happened to her eyes because she couldn't see a single thing, and it was a couple of minutes before she came to that she had picked up mine by mistake. They look exactly alike. I told her it was good enough for her.

Our guests are going Friday, which is o.k. with me. They aren't too bad, but here they are, with nobody to entertain them and, as things are buzzing in this room, they run in and out, and sit and talk when I'm trying to work. The wife always wants to help open the mail and then sits and reads letters aloud to me, and Lord knows, they are no treat for me. She doesn't know what to do with the mail, so it is no help at all. I could do much better alone. This business of being hired help and hostess, too, is a little wearing. I stick to my guns about going home for dinner at night, though; one meal with them is enough. I don't know why Mrs. R. invites people to come up here and then is never here and just leaves them to their own devices or to whoever happens to be here—such as me. Of course, I guess it is nice for them to get a week's vacation, good food, service, swimming, etc., free of charge.

I'm going to get the car now and take the mail down, just for a change. Suppose I'll have to take Fala along, too. He embarrasses me at the Post Office, as he always wants to sprinkle the marble columns. Our cat wouldn't do that!

Apartment 15-A
29 Washington Square, West
New York 11, New York

My dear Dorothy,

In leaving D-day I forgot you
would be gone before I got back
& so this is to say how grateful
I am for all you have done. Enclosed is a little gift, I couldn't
thank you except in gratitude.

I'm not saying goodbye
since surely we'll see you soon again.
Good wish. Aff-ly yours,
Eleanor Roosevelt

Letter from Eleanor Roosevelt to Dorothy Dow, August 26, 1945. Courtesy: Dorothy Dow Butturff and Franklin D. Roosevelt, Jr.

EPILOGUE

And so we come to the end of the letters, which are indeed, in the words of Horace Walpole, "extempore conversations upon paper." But Eleanor Roosevelt's activities did not end. Early in December 1945 President Truman appointed her as a member of the United States delegation to the United Nations General Assembly, and she served with distinction until the end of 1952. Termed by the *New York Times* the "most popular delegate," she became for many a symbol of all that the United Nations stood for. She had become the First Lady of the World.

In 1946 Dorothy Dow had another daughter, Barbara. For financial reasons she returned to work a few months after Barbara's birth, but instead of going back to the Social Bureau, she transferred to the correspondence section of the Executive Office of the President, soon moving on to the Office of Presidential Appointments, where she remained until her retirement in 1957. Francie's condition gradually grew worse, and in 1955 she died. In 1963 Dorothy became a research assistant to the syndicated political columnist, Doris Fleeson, with whom she remained until Miss Fleeson's death in 1970. Three years earlier Dorothy and her husband moved to Maryland, where she still lives and where he died in 1976. Her daughter, Barbara, now married, lives in San Francisco with her husband and two small boys.

Malvina Thompson died in 1953, Eleanor Roosevelt in 1962. She had once written in a "My Day" column, after visiting a friend, "You leave her presence with a sense that you have at last met an eager spirit. She is still keen to do things, has lost none of her curiosity, is kindly in her attitude toward others, and gallant and gay in her whole approach to a life which must be lonely at times." The words might well have been written about Eleanor Roosevelt herself. They might also be said of Dorothy Dow.

APPENDIX

Identifications of Persons Mentioned
in the Letters of Dorothy Dow

ADELHAIDE, PRINCESS: daughter of Karl and Zita, former emperor and empress of Austria-Hungary

ALICE: a maid at Val-Kill

ALLEN, EDWIN W.: vice president for Engineering of General Electric Company, 1926–40

ANNABELLA: née Suzanne Charpentier; movie actress

ASTOR, VINCENT: friend and Hudson Valley neighbor of President Roosevelt

ASTOR, MRS. VINCENT: née Helen Dinsmore Huntington, of Staatsburg, N. Y.; divorced Mr. Astor and subsequently married Lytle Hull, a friend of President Roosevelt

BARD, DR. SAMUEL: (1742–1821) physician; one of the founders of the medical school of Columbia University

BARUCH, BERNARD: wealthy financier; friend of Eleanor Roosevelt and would-be adviser to President Roosevelt

BELLAMY, RALPH: stage and screen actor

BIGGS, JUDGE JOHN, JR.: appointed a judge of the U. S. Circuit Court of Appeals for the Third Circuit in 1937; lifelong resident of Wilmington, Delaware

BILL: a yard boy at Val-Kill

BLACK, MR. AND MRS. EUGENE R.: He was chairman of the Federal Reserve Board.

BLANCHE, MADAME: pâtissière in New York City

BOETTIGER, ANNA ROOSEVELT: only daughter of President and Mrs. Roosevelt; married Curtis Dall in 1926, whom she divorced in 1934; married John Boettiger in 1935

BOETTIGER, JOHN: White House correspondent for the *Chicago Tribune;* later, publisher of the *Seattle Post Intelligencer;* second husband of Anna Roosevelt; President and Mrs. Roosevelt's son-in-law

BOSWELL, CONNIE (CONNEE): singer regularly appearing on the Kraft Music Hall and Bing Crosby Show radio programs

BUTTURFF, BARBARA: daughter of Robert and Dorothy Dow Butturff

BUTURFF, FRANCES ELIZABETH: oldest daughter of Robert and Dorothy Dow Butturff

BUTURFF, ROBERT R.: husband of Dorothy Dow; civil service employee in Washington, D. C.

BUZZIE. *See* DALL, CURTIS, JR.

BYE, MR. AND MRS. GEORGE. He was Eleanor Roosevelt's literary agent for many years.

CABOT, BRUCE: movie actor

CARLIN, MR. AND MRS. GEORGE. He was manager of the United Feature Syndicate for which Eleanor Roosevelt wrote her column, "My Day."

CARTER: an employee in the White House flower room

CATHERINE. *See* HEFFRON, CATHERINE

CHARLIE. *See* THOMPSON, CHARLES

CHARLTON, HARRY: a messenger in the White House Social Bureau

CHENEY, ROY: a friend of Henry Osthagen

CHIANG KAI-SHEK, MADAME: née Soong Mei-ling; wife of Generalissimo Chiang Kai-shek, president of the Chinese republic and commander in chief of the Chinese army

CHURCHILL, WINSTON: prime minister of Great Britain during World War II

COLLINS, MISS. *See* SHIELDS-COLLINS, ELIZABETH

CONN, IRVING: (né Cohn); composer, with Frank Silver, of "Yes, We

Have No Bananas"; conductor of an orchestra playing in New York City hotels

CONNOR, DR. ROBERT DIGGES WIMBERLY: appointed first Archivist of the United States in 1934

COOK, NANCY: friend of Eleanor Roosevelt who lived in the stone cottage adjacent to Mrs. Roosevelt's residence at Val-Kill; co-owner with Mrs. Roosevelt and Marion Dickerman of Val-Kill Industries

COOLIDGE, MRS. CALVIN: née Grace Goodhue; wife of President Coolidge

COOPER, DR. ROBERT L.: director of the Wiltwyck School for Boys at Esopus, Ulster County, New York

COWAN, RUTH: Associated Press war correspondent, of Washington, D. C.

CRAWFORD, WILLIAM WALLACE, 3RD: usually called Scoop; son of Faye Emerson by her first marriage; stepson of Elliott Roosevelt

CRIM, HOWELL G.: a White House usher who succeeded Raymond D. Muir as Chief Usher in 1942

CUMMINGS, MRS. HOMER: wife of the attorney general

DALL, ANNA ELEANOR: usually called Sistie; daughter of Anna Roosevelt and her first husband, Curtis Dall; granddaughter of President and Mrs. Roosevelt

DALL, ANNA ROOSEVELT. See Boettiger, Anna Roosevelt

DALL, CURTIS: first husband of Anna Roosevelt

DALL, CURTIS, JR.: usually called Buzzie; son of Curtis and Anna Roosevelt Dall; grandson of President and Mrs. Roosevelt

DAMITA, LILI: movie actress

DANIELS, JONATHAN: son of Josephus Daniels; journalist; administrative assistant in the Executive Office of the White House; later assistant press secretary

DANIELS, JOSEPHUS: secretary of the navy under President Wilson

DEANS, the: guests of Mrs. Roosevelt at a Val-Kill party

DELANO, FREDERIC A.: President Roosevelt's uncle

DELANO, LAURA: President Roosevelt's cousin

DERN, GEORGE: secretary of war, 1933–36

DERN, MRS. GEORGE H.: wife of the secretary of war

DICKERMAN, MARION: friend of Eleanor Roosevelt who lived in the stone cottage adjacent to Mrs. Roosevelt's residence at Val-Kill; co-owner with Mrs. Roosevelt and Nancy Cook of Val-Kill Industries; principal of the Todhunter School in New York City

"DOC". *See* THOMAS, A. M.

DONOVAN, COL. (later Major General) WILLIAM J.: millionaire lawyer; organizer and director of the Office of Strategic Services, 1942–45

DOW, AMIE TAPPAN: Dorothy Dow's mother

DOW, EDWARD EVERETT: Dorothy Dow's father

DRESSLER, MARIE: movie actress, best known for her *Tugboat Annie* films; died July 28, 1934

EARLY, STEVE: President Roosevelt's press secretary, 1933–45

EISENHOWER, DWIGHT D.: Supreme Commander of the Allied forces in Europe; president of the United States, 1953–61

EMERSON, FAYE: movie and television actress; Elliott Roosevelt's third wife

FARLEY, JAMES A.: postmaster general, 1933–40

FAYERWEATHER, MARGARET DOANE: friend of Eleanor Roosevelt

FELIX, PRINCE: son of Karl and Zita, former emperor and empress of Austria-Hungary

FERDINAND, PRINCE: son of Karl and Zita, former emperor and empress of Austria-Hungary

FERRIS, HELEN JOSEPHINE: editor in chief of the·Junior Literary Guild since 1929; author; married Albert B. Tibbets in 1924

FITZGERALD, MR.: chairman of the New York Democratic Committee

FLANIGAN, COMMANDER HOWARD A.: Naval Reserve officer; vice-president for Operations of the New York World's Fair

FLEESON, DORIS: first syndicated woman political columnist; her column, written for United Feature Syndicate, appeared in over one hundred newspapers

FLYNN, ERROL: movie actor

FOX, DR. GEORGE A.: physician at the White House; assistant to Dr. Ross T. McIntire, President Roosevelt's personal physician

FRAN. *See* SPENCER, FRANCES DOW

FRANCIE. *See* BUTTURFF, FRANCES ELIZABETH

FRECE, PRUDENCE: employee in the White House Social Bureau

GENNERICH, GUS: President Roosevelt's bodyguard

GEORGIA. *See* THOMAS, GEORGIA

GEORGIE: a maid at Val-Kill; possibly Georgiana Turner

GIEGENGACK, AUGUSTUS E.: Public Printer of the United States

GILLIS, ANN: employee of the National Broadcasting Corporation

GREEN, MITZI: movie actress

GRIFFIN: a yard man at Val-Kill

GUS. *See* GENNERICH, GUS

HANNEGAN, MR. AND MRS. ROBERT E. He was postmaster general, 1945–47.

HARALD, PRINCE: son of Crown Princess Martha of Norway

HATCH, CARL: senator from New Mexico, 1933–41

HEFFRON, CATHERINE: employee in the White House Social Bureau

HELM, EDITH BENHAM: social secretary for Mrs. Wilson, Mrs. Roosevelt, and Mrs. Truman; widow of Admiral James Helm

HERSHOLT, JEAN: movie actor

HICKOK, LORENA: journalist; friend of Eleanor Roosevelt

HINES, BRIGADIER GENERAL FRANK THOMAS: administrator of the Veterans Administration since 1930; director of the U. S. Veterans Bureau, 1923–30

HOOKER, MAJOR HENRY (HARRY): former law partner of President Roosevelt; family lawyer and friend of the Roosevelt family

HOOVER, MRS. HERBERT: née Lou Henry; wife of President Hoover

HOOVER, IRWIN H. (IKE): chief usher at the White House. His service began in 1891 when he became the White House electrician after installing its first electric lights; he was soon promoted to usher and became chief usher during the Taft administration; he died September 14, 1933.

HOPKINS, DIANA: daughter of Harry Hopkins

HOPKINS, HARRY L.: secretary of commerce, 1938–40

HOWE, LOUIS MCHENRY: journalist; secretary and political adviser to President Roosevelt

HULL, MRS. LYTLE. *See* ASTOR, MRS. VINCENT

HURST, FANNIE: novelist and short story writer

ICKES, MR. AND MRS. HAROLD. He was secretary of the interior, 1933–46.

INSULL, SAMUEL: a public utilities magnate

JAMES (1): a chauffeur and handyman at Val-Kill who stole Mrs. Roosevelt's automobile and wrecked it

JAMES (2): a chauffeur at Val-Kill

JENNINGS, KATE: personal maid of Sara Delano Roosevelt, President Roosevelt's mother

JOHANNESSEN, KARL: son of Nelly Johannessen

JOHANNESSEN, NELLY: a Norwegian widow who did catering for Mrs. Roosevelt and weaving for Val-Kill Industries; proprietor of the Val-Kill Tea Room

JOHNSON, BRIGADIER GENERAL HUGH S.: administrator of the National Recovery Administration, 1933–34

KARL, KING (CHARLES I): last emperor of Austria and, as Charles IV, King of Hungary, 1916–18; abdicated in 1918; died in exile, 1922

KEYES, FRANCES PARKINSON: novelist and magazine writer

KING AND QUEEN OF ENGLAND: George VI and Elizabeth (née Lady Elizabeth Bowes-Lyon); parents of Queen Elizabeth II

KNOX, FRANK: secretary of the navy, 1940–44

LA GUARDIA, FIORELLO H.: mayor of New York City, 1934–45; appointed director of Civilian Defense, 1941; nicknamed "the Little Flower"

LASH, JOSEPH P.: friend and biographer of Eleanor Roosevelt

LASH, MRS. JOSEPH P.: formerly Trude Pratt, wife of Elliott Pratt, whom she divorced; friend of Eleanor Roosevelt

LAWRENCE, DAVID: newspaper columnist and author; president and editor of *United States News* since 1933

LEEDS, ANDREA: movie actress

LEHAND, MARGUERITE ("MISSY"): private secretary to President Roosevelt

LEWIS, FRANK J.: wealthy business executive; president of F. J. Lewis Manufacturing Company of Chicago; acquaintance of Mrs. Roosevelt through their mutual interest in the Wiltwyck School for Boys

LINAKA, SHEILA: daughter of Russell Linaka, a groundskeeper on the Roosevelt estate at Hyde Park; she assisted with the mail at Val-Kill in 1945

LINDSAY, LADY: née Elizabeth Sherman Hoyt, of New York City; wife of the Right Honorable Sir Ronald Lindsay, British ambassador to the United States

LINDSAY, RIGHT HONORABLE SIR RONALD: British ambassador to the United States since 1930; dean of the diplomatic corps in Washington; son of the 26th Earl of Crawford

LONGWORTH, ALICE ROOSEVELT: cousin of Eleanor Roosevelt; daughter of President Theodore Roosevelt and widow of Speaker of the House of Representatives Nicholas Longworth

LUCY: a cook at Val-Kill

LUND, CHARLES: brother-in-law of Malvina Thompson

LUND, ELEANOR: niece of Malvina Thompson; daughter of Charles and Muriel Lund

LUND, MURIEL: sister of Malvina Thompson; employee in the White House Social Bureau

MABEL: *See* WEBSTER, MABEL

MACLEISH, MR. AND MRS. ARCHIBALD. A poet, he was Librarian of Congress, 1939–44, and during World War II, was for a time director of the Office of Facts and Figures; he was an editor of *Fortune* and won a Pulitzer Prize in 1932.

MCMILLIN, MRS. BENTON: née Lucille Foster; a civil service commissioner since 1933; wife of Congressman McMillin of Carthage, Tennessee

MAGEE, RALPH L.: a longtime employee of the White House Social Bureau, supervising the handling of correspondence

MARTHA, CROWN PRINCESS: wife of Crown Prince Olav, the only son of Haakon VII of Norway, who succeeded his father as King Olav V in 1957

MILLER, EARL: a friend of Eleanor Roosevelt who, as a New York State trooper, had been her bodyguard while Franklin D. Roosevelt was governor of New York State

MINGO, JAMES: a White House butler

MOLLY (MOLLIE). *See* SOMERVILLE, MOLLY

MORGAN, MARIE: (née Newsom), wife of William Forbes Morgan, III, who was a cousin of Eleanor Roosevelt

MORGENTHAU, HENRY, JR.: secretary of the treasury, 1934–45; friend and Hudson Valley neighbor of President Roosevelt

MORGENTHAU, MRS. HENRY, JR.: née Elinor Fatman; wife of the secretary of the treasury; close friend of Eleanor Roosevelt

MORISON, SAMUEL ELIOT: historian; professor at Harvard University; winner of Pultizer Prizes in 1943 and 1960; appointed official U.S. Navy historian for World War II in 1942

MUIR, RAYMOND D.: succeeded "Ike" Hoover as chief usher at the White House in 1933

MULCHAHY, MR.: a publicity man for the Twentieth Century-Fox Film Corporation

MURIEL. *See* LUND, MURIEL

NANCY. *See* ROBINSON, NANCY

NANCY: a cook at Val-Kill

NIXON, DR. EDGAR: senior archivist and editor at the Franklin D. Roosevelt Library at Hyde Park

OBENCHAIN, CHARLES A.: assistant to the commissioner of the General Land Office, Department of the Interior

ODUM, REATHEL: private secretary to Mrs. Harry S. Truman

ORNDORFF, IRENE ("TUNIE"): a correspondence clerk in the White House Social Bureau

OSTGAARD, COUNTESS RAGIN: lady-in-waiting to Crown Princess Martha of Norway

OSTHAGEN, HENRY: friend of Malvina Thompson; employee of the Treasury Department

OTTO, ARCHDUKE: oldest son of Karl and Zita, former emperor and empress of Austria-Hungary

PARISH, MRS. HENRY, JR.: Eleanor Roosevelt's cousin Susie

PEARL: a maid at Val-Kill

PERKINS, FRANCES: secretary of labor, 1933–45

PIXIE: not identified

PLOG (pronounced Plow), WILLIAM: head gardener at the Hyde Park home of President Roosevelt

POWELL, ELEANOR: movie actress

PRATT, ELLIOTT: first husband of Trude Pratt Lash

PRATT, TRUDE. *See* LASH, MRS. JOSEPH P.

PRUDENCE. *See* FRECE, PRUDENCE

RASET, ZENA: companion of Hall Roosevelt, Eleanor Roosevelt's brother

REEVES, WILLIAM: chief florist at the White House

RITTER, MR.: a furrier; member of the New York City firm of Ritter Bros., Inc.

ROBINSON, MONROE DOUGLAS: cousin of Eleanor Roosevelt

ROBINSON, NANCY: a child guest at Val-Kill

ROCKWELL, WILLIAM E.: a longtime employee of the White House Social Bureau, supervising invitations and other matters relating to entertainments

ROGERS, WILL: actor and humorist; nicknamed the "cowboy philosopher," he also wrote a syndicated newspaper column

ROMMIE. *See* ROOSEVELT, MRS. JAMES

ROOSEVELT, BILL. *See* ROOSEVELT, WILLIAM DONNER

ROOSEVELT, CHANDLER: daughter of Elliott Roosevelt and his second wife, Ruth Chandler Googins; President and Mrs. Roosevelt's granddaughter

ROOSEVELT, DAVID: son of Elliott Roosevelt and his second wife, Ruth Chandler Googins; President and Mrs. Roosevelt's grandson

ROOSEVELT, ELEANOR: wife of President Franklin D. Roosevelt; author, lecturer, syndicated newspaper columnist ("My Day"); later delegate to the United Nations General Assembly, 1945–52; often called First Lady of the World

ROOSEVELT, ELLIOTT: son of President and Mrs. Roosevelt

ROOSEVELT, ELLIOTT, JR.: usually called Tony; son of Elliott Roosevelt and his second wife, Ruth Chandler Googins; President and Mrs. Roosevelt's grandson

ROOSEVELT, FRANKLIN DELANO: president of the United States, 1933–45

ROOSEVELT, FRANKLIN DELANO, JR.: son of President and Mrs. Roosevelt

ROOSEVELT, HALL: Eleanor Roosevelt's brother; son of Elliott and Anna Hall Roosevelt

ROOSEVELT, JAMES: President and Mrs. Roosevelt's oldest son

ROOSEVELT, JOHN: President and Mrs. Roosevelt's youngest son

ROOSEVELT, MRS. ELLIOTT: née Ruth Chandler Googins; Elliott Roosevelt's second wife

ROOSEVELT, MRS. FRANKLIN D., JR.: née Ethel du Pont; daughter of Pierre du Pont and first wife of Franklin D. Roosevelt, Jr.

ROOSEVELT, MRS. JAMES: née Sara Delano, President Roosevelt's mother

ROOSEVELT, MRS. JAMES: née Romelle Schneider, second wife of James Roosevelt, son of President and Mrs. Roosevelt

ROOSEVELT, MRS. JOHN: née Anne Sturges, first wife of John Roosevelt, son of President and Mrs. Roosevelt

ROOSEVELT, MRS. J. R.: née Elizabeth Riley, usually called Betty; widow of President Roosevelt's older half-brother, James Roosevelt ("Rosy") Roosevelt

ROOSEVELT, MRS. KERMIT: née Belle Willard; widow of Kermit Roosevelt, son of President Theodore Roosevelt and cousin of Eleanor Roosevelt

ROOSEVELT, MRS. ROOSEVELT. *See* ROOSEVELT, MRS. J R.

ROOSEVELT, SARA DELANO: oldest child of James Roosevelt and his first wife, Betsey Cushing; granddaughter of President and Mrs. Roosevelt

ROOSEVELT, TONY. *See* ROOSEVELT, ELLIOTT, JR.

ROOSEVELT, WILLIAM DONNER: son of Elliott Roosevelt and his first wife, Betty Donner; President and Mrs. Roosevelt's grandson

ROPER, MRS. DANIEL C.: wife of the secretary of commerce, 1933–38

SCHAFFER: a White House chauffeur; he usually drove for Mrs. Roosevelt

SCHEIDER, MRS. *See* THOMPSON, MALVINA

SCOOP. *See* CRAWFORD, WILLIAM WALLACE, 3RD

SHIELDS-COLLINS, ELIZABETH: secretary of the World Youth Congress, with offices in Geneva, Switzerland

SHIPMAN, FRED: first director of the Franklin D. Roosevelt Library at Hyde Park

SISTIE. *See* DALL, ANNA ELEANOR

SMITH, ANN: daughter of Mr. and Mrs. Clifford Smith of Hyde Park

SMITH, C. RAYMOND: a file clerk in the White House Social Bureau

SNYDER, MONTE: a White House chauffeur; he usually drove for President Roosevelt

SOMERVILLE, MOLLY (MOLLIE): secretary for Anna Roosevelt Dall and also, occasionally, for Eleanor Roosevelt

SPENCER, FRANCES: née Dow; Dorothy Dow's sister; married William L. Spencer

STARLING, COL. EDMUND W.: member of the White House Detail of the Secret Service, 1914–35; chief of the detail, 1935–44

STASSEN, HAROLD E.: governor of Minnesota, 1939–43

STEPHENS, DONALD: a guest at Val-Kill

STONE, CLARENCE: mail carrier at Hyde Park

STRAUS, MRS. NATHAN, JR.: née Helen E. Sachs; wife of the administrator of the U. S. Housing Authority, 1937–42

TABOUIS, MME GENEVIEVE: French refugee; journalist; foreign news editor of *L'Oeuvre*, 1932–40; author; wife of Robert Tabouis, administrator of radio for France

TEMPLE, MR. AND MRS. GEORGE F.: parents of Shirley Temple

TEMPLE, SHIRLEY: child movie actress

THOMAS, A. M. ("DOC"): chief electrician at the White House

THOMAS, GEORGIA: employee in the White House Social Bureau

THOMPSON, CHARLES: a White House messenger

THOMPSON, DOROTHY: journalist; political columnist; writer; formerly a foreign correspondent

THOMPSON, MALVINA: private secretary to Eleanor Roosevelt; nicknamed "Tommy"; married Frank J. Scheider, 1921; divorced him and resumed use of her maiden name, 1938

TRUMAN, HARRY S.: president of the United States, 1945–53

TRUMAN, MARGARET: only child of President and Mrs. Truman

TRUMAN, MRS. HARRY S.: née Elizabeth Virginia Wallace ("Bess"); wife of President Truman

TULLY, GRACE: assistant to "Missy" LeHand, President Roosevelt's private secretary, and her successor, 1941–45

TUNIE. *See* ORNDORFF, IRENE

TUNNEY, MRS. GENE: née Mary Josephine Lauder; wife of James Joseph (Gene) Tunney, heavyweight boxing champion, 1926–28

WALDO, MRS.: a guest at Val-Kill

WALKER, MR. AND MRS. FRANK C.: He was postmaster general, 1940–45.

WALLACE, HENRY A.: secretary of agriculture, 1933–40; President Roosevelt's running mate in the 1940 presidential campaign; vice president, 1941–45

WARREN, MISS: head nurse at the Children's Rehabilitation Institute, Baltimore, Maryland

WEBSTER, MABEL: Mrs. Roosevelt's personal maid

WEBSTER, N. P.: accountant and general staff assistant at the White House

WILLIAMS, AUBREY: director of the National Youth Administration

WILLKIE, WENDELL L.: industrialist and politician; Republican candidate for President in 1940; president of Commonwealth and Southern Corporation, 1933–40

WILSON, MARGUERITE: an authority on the cotton industry

WINCHELL, WALTER: gossip columnist for the New York *Mirror;* radio commentator

WINSOR, BETTY: née Elizabeth Donnor; Elliott Roosevelt's first wife

WOODWARD, ELLEN S.: director of Women's Work in the Works Progress Administration until December, 1938; thereafter, until 1946, a member of the Social Security Board

WOOLLCOTT, ALEXANDER H.: literary and dramatic critic; columnist for *The New Yorker;* stage and screen actor; writer

ZITA, EMPRESS: widow of Karl (Charles I), last emperor of Austria and king of Hungary; daughter of Duke Robert of Bourbon-Parma; lived in the United States and Canada, 1940–49